#08 Echo Park Branch Library
1410 W. Temple Street
Los Angeles, CA 90026

W9-BRA-961

I'M PERFECT, YOU'RE DOOMED

Tales from a Jehovah's Witness Upbringing

KYRIA ABRAHAMS

A Touchstone Book
Published by Simon & Schuster
New York London Toronto Sydney

Touchstone
A Division of Simon & Schuster, Inc.
1230 Avenue of the Americas
New York, NY 10020

This book is a memoir. It contains the author's present recollections of her
experiences since childhood. Certain names and identifying characteristics
have been changed and certain incidents have been compressed or reordered.

Copyright © 2009 by Kyria Abrahams

All rights reserved, including the right to reproduce this book or portions
thereof in any form whatsoever. For information address Touchstone Subsidiary
Rights Department, 1230 Avenue of the Americas, New York, NY 10020.

First Touchstone hardcover edition March 2009

TOUCHSTONE and colophon are registered trademarks of Simon & Schuster, Inc.

For information about special discounts for bulk purchases,
please contact Simon & Schuster Special Sales at
1-800-456-6798 or business@simonandschuster.com.

Designed by Carla Jayne Little

Manufactured in the United States of America

10   9   8   7   6   5   4   3   2   1

Library of Congress Cataloging-in-Publication Data
Abrahams, Kyria.
    I'm perfect, you're doomed : tales from a Jehovah's witness upbringing / Kyria
Abrahams.
            p.   cm.
    1. Abrahams, Kyria. 2. Jehovah's Witnesses—United States—Biography.
I. Title.
  BX8527.A27A3   2009
  289.9'2092—dc22   2008041136
  [B]

ISBN-13: 978-1-4165-5684-8
ISBN-10:   1-4165-5684-2

For my mother and father, and for my brother

Many factors come together to create
this specific unique person which is *I*.
—Frederick S. Perls, *Gestalt Therapy Verbatim*

Contents

Contents

CONTENTS

CHAPTER 1

Hark! God's Awesome Promise Is at Hand!

As usual, my little brother had to one-up me. It was the night of my debut performance at the Pawtucket, Rhode Island, Kingdom Hall of Jehovah's Witnesses and I needed to choose the perfect dress for giving a presentation about freedom from demon possession. I was eight years old, but I knew that with the right outfit, I could pass for double digits.

This was my special night and I needed privacy—mature, demon-free wardrobes don't choose themselves, after all. Yet here was my annoying brother, standing in my bedroom doorway, breathing both in *and* out. Ever since my father had (on the sly) told him he was smarter than I was, this is how he had behaved. Omnipresent. Gloating.

"Dad said not to tell you, but I'm smarter than you are," he'd told me one afternoon as I dumped Kix cereal into a glass Ball jar.

"You are not!" I screamed. "I'm older than you, anyway, so it's not even possible that you could be smarter than me."

"No, it's true! Dad showed me the test. I got a higher score than you. I'm smarter than you are."

"You're a liar. You're not smart, you're a *doof*."

That was the end of it. I never found out what this mysterious test was, exactly how much higher his score was, or why my father had betrayed me with this information. In his mind, Aaron was, and always will be, smarter than I am. And now he was soiling my canopy bed by looking at it with his dorky face.

"Get out of my room, *Nippy*!" I yelled. I'd given him this nickname in honor of the stash of Caramel Nips that our diabetic grandmother, Mom-Mom, secretly kept in a covered dish on the bookcase next to her Herb Alpert records. Aaron was apathetic toward the candy, but he *hated* the nickname, and that was what counted.

Mom-Mom was the reason we were Jehovah's Witnesses. Born Rose Rubin and, for all intents and purposes, a nice Jewish girl, she left her Brooklyn home to become the wife of a media man named Nathan Abrahams, have three children, and spend the rest of her living days lamenting the fact that Chinese food was never as good as it was in New York.

After a short time, the family moved to Coral Gables, Florida. Here, my pre-dad dressed in khaki shorts and posed for photos in coconut trees. Birthdays were celebrated, avocados were consumed. Years later, I would note that he was always happy when he was warm.

One day, Rose Rubin Abrahams, non-practicing Jew, maker of salmon croquettes, wearer of housecoats, found a *Watchtower* lying atop a trash can. She then began a weekly Bible study with her local Kingdom Hall, during which she learned that God has a plan for this world and it did not involve owning a separate refrigerator for dairy products. Her children stopped celebrating their birthdays and began reading the New Testament. Shortly afterward, my grandfather died of a heart attack.

I only knew two of my grandmother's siblings, Ruth and Margaret—spinster sisters who never married, although Ruth supposedly once had "a steady beau." Instead, they moved to New

England, became roommates, and began their official career as our great-aunts.

The first thing you saw upon entering the apartment of Ruth and Margaret was a painting of a rabbi holding a Kiddush cup. Below it, on a black-lacquered credenza, was a gray-speckled ashtray filled with lemon drops and a book we were not allowed to play "library" with.

The book wasn't in English. It was in Hebrew, like the first books of the Bible were. The cover was mother-of-pearl, inlaid with a silver-and-turquoise crown and a likeness of the Torah. Once, I was allowed to remove it from its clear plastic case and look inside. The metal hinges creaked like Dracula's coffin. The pages were so thin it felt like running my fingers across the scalp of a newborn baby. When I asked them what it said, they told me they didn't know—it was in Hebrew.

The aunts were never Jewish in the sense of visiting Israel or eschewing light switches after sundown on Friday, but they were Jewish enough for us—awesomely Jewish, in fact. When they muttered insults in Yiddish or called Bill Cosby "an annoying *schvartze*," I felt that I belonged to something special. My brother, Aaron, and I read a joke book called *How to Be a Jewish Mother*, then ran around the house accusing each other of being *zaftig schmucks* and insisting the other close the window and put on a sweater.

"Dad says not to be mean to me, *schmuck*, because someday I'm gonna be bigger than you are and then you're gonna regret it when I beat you up," Aaron reminded me.

Sentiments like these were often echoed by Ruth and Margaret.

"Someday, Kyria, when your brother is dead, you'll regret having treated him so cruelly," one great-aunt would croak, putting out a cigarette in the ashtray of their '75 Dodge Dart. This was the way elderly Jewish spinsters responded to squabbling children— by evoking mortality and regret, then taking us on a Sunday drive to purchase rye bread and macaroons.

The fact that I was an obedient Jehovah's Witness child who thought I was Jewish because I snacked on egg and onion matzo and owned a coffee mug with Yiddish curse words on it was the least of my problems. Right now, I had a performance to give. I needed to choose an outfit. I needed Aaron to leave.

"Come on and get *out*, Aaron! I'm getting ready for the Kingdom Hall."

"I invented a new color," he announced, repeatedly turning my glass doorknob so it would spring back into place with a door-shaking *thud*.

"So what, dork?"

"It's called mephamonium."

"I don't care. Plus you can't invent a new color, liar."

He was coming into my room now. Running his sticky hands along my rainbow wallpaper.

"Yes, I can," he insisted. "It's called mephamonium. I invented it!"

"Oh, yeah?" I challenged. "Then what's it look like?"

"It's like white, but kinda orange and purple. Like rainbow sherbet."

Rainbow sherbet? Please. Only our mother ate that. Now I knew for certain he was lying. I yelled loudly for Mom, who was downstairs in the kitchen, microwaving broccoflower and listening to Julio Iglesias and Willie Nelson sing "To All the Girls I've Loved Before" on her boom box.

"I have to pee!" Aaron shouted down the stairs in his defense.

My bedroom was directly next to the bathroom. This close proximity to our chipped, claw-foot tub gave me the distinct advantage in case of hide-and-seek, earthquake, or Armageddon. It also gave Aaron the perfect excuse to stand in my doorway. He was, after all, just on his way to pee.

"Go ahead and pee, then! See if I care!"

"Remember," he warned, "I'm smarter than you are."

"You are not! You aren't!"

"Children!" my mother screamed. "Enough is enough!"

My mother did not have the time for this. Or the inclination.

"I have neither the time *nor* the inclination to come upstairs and separate you two," she yelled. "Don't make me get the yard-stick!"

At this, my father was summoned. What Mom merely threatened, Dad usually carried out. Dad stood in the doorway, freshly bathed, with a towel around his neck and a Q-tip hanging from one ear, breathing like a bull. Usually, this was all it took. There was a yardstick balanced above each of our bedroom doors for easy-access discipline. If we continued fighting, he'd reach his hand up to the wood molding, grab the long ruler, and officially end the quarrel.

He glared at my brother. "Find your Bible and your notepad. Lay your suit out on the bed. Get ready for the meeting. Dinner is almost on the table."

This time, Aaron did exactly as he'd been told. He zipped underneath Dad's legs and out of the room.

"And you," Dad said, holding up a frayed bath towel and pointing his finger at my face. "Don't *you* encourage him."

To help us get to the meetings on time, Mom came home from work and prepared dinner for a family of four. She was retro-gourmet, rocking the Crock-Pot and the Le Creuset Dutch oven in order to present meals plucked straight from the cover of a *Better Homes and Gardens* from 1965. We owned porcelain eggcups, Tupperware cake carriers, and enamel chopsticks with mother-of-pearl inlays. For breakfast, Mom drew a smiling face and hair on our soft-boiled eggs with Magic Markers. My brother's face was always drawn in baby blue, mine in pink. Then she'd slice the top off the egg and we'd lap the egg person's brains up with a small spoon. This was my mother's idea of what a real family should look like.

"You're not those kids down the block, you know," Mom would counter whenever we'd complain about the upsetting nature of our meals. "I'm not just going to fill you full of sugar and be done with you, like some ignorant mother who doesn't know any better!"

Although many of our "meeting night" meals were reheated frozen leftovers, there was always the knowledge that the prior week, they'd been better than what the neighbors were eating.

In addition to being Betty Crocker, Mom also took the bus downtown every day, where she worked full-time as a legal secretary. It was hard to bring any subject up with Mom without hearing how she did everything while the rest of us sat on our behinds and watched "the boob tube." So sometimes, like tonight, it was all she could do to crank up the Micro-Go-Round, pour a drink, and boil water.

"More raw spaghetti tonight?" Dad asked.

Mom was half-undressed from work and half-dressed for the Kingdom Hall, wearing a bathrobe, knee-highs, a girdle, and bootie slippers she knit herself 15 years ago. She slammed an enamel lid onto a pot of sauce. "It's not raw, Gerald. It's *al-dent-ey*."

"Raw spaghetti," Dad mumbled. "You're trying to kill me."

There were many ways in which my mother was trying to kill my father. Leaving half-empty glasses on tables and cooking pasta *like a damn European* were simply two of her more popular efforts. It would be many years before I realized that raw spaghetti was not an effective murder weapon.

Wiping away a grape-juice mustache, my brother repeated his recent discovery. "I invented a new color. It's called mephamonium."

My father stopped spreading margarine on his microwaved broccoflower and turned a concerned eye toward his son.

"Been getting at your mother's liquor cabinet lately?"

This was my father's sense of humor. He was also fond of referring to my mom's family as "a bunch of illiterate white-trash alcoholics."

Mom lifted a glass of rum and 7-Up and sneered, "Say the prayer, Gerald. Your children's dinner is getting cold."

"Sure. God forbid my *heartburn* gets cold."

"Well, I'm sorry I don't have time to make the sauce from scratch, Gerald. You know, I work all day, and *all I ask—*"

My father interrupted this rant by giving thanks to our Lord.

"Jehovah, God, our heavenly father. Thank you, Jehovah, for this day of life and for the food we are about to receive, Jehovah."

Dad called out God's name so many times during a single prayer that one might wonder if, in addition to being the creator of the universe, God wasn't also suffering from ADD.

"Jehovah, we ask that you bless Kyria while she gives her first talk tonight. We pray, Jehovah, for the arrival of your promised New System of Things in your own due time. Thank you, Lord, Jehovah. In Jesus' name, amen."

"Amen," I agreed.

"Amen," my mother repeated.

"Mephamonium," said Aaron.

I had picked out the perfect white eyelet dress because that night I was officially becoming a member of the Theocratic Ministry School. The "school" took place every Thursday night and was designed to help true Christians excel in the arena of public speaking. It was for both adults and children alike, and was not considered a replacement for our actual elementary schools, which we attended in order to perfect our arithmetic skills and learn how to be hated for being different.

This particular night was to be my grand debut. (Technically, my grand debut was at age five, when Mom-Mom coerced me into doing my impression of Carol Channing singing "Diamonds Are a Girl's Best Friend" in the community room of her retirement complex. But there was no raised stage in Douglas Manor, only flat linoleum, an American flag, and a handful of tight-lipped elderly women sitting at folding tables. I ran away in tears before I ever got to belt out, "A kiss on the hand may be quite Continental," and my grandmother never forgave me.)

My presentation was going to take place in our church, or rather, the building that we adamantly refused to refer to as a church. Churches were pagan seats of false religion, the Great Harlot—part of This System of Things Which Is Soon to Pass Away. As members of the only true religion, we were neither part of This System, nor were we ever going to Pass Away.

Instead, our church was unequivocally referred to as the Kingdom Hall (or, for any of the Spanish-speakers who we graciously allowed to hold their own separate service, the Salón del Reino). This admittedly sounds more majestic than it actually was, but the roots of the name were simple. Our main goal as Witnesses of Jehovah was to proclaim his coming Kingdom, and "Kingdom Vinyl-Sided Ranch House" sounded stupid.

Our hall was a modest, one-story building with a handful of parking spaces and one nice bush. There were no spires, gargoyles, or stained-glass windows depicting lepers lounging atop virgins. The interior design scheme boasted burnt-umber motor-home curtains and bland gray rugs. There were no pagan crosses, but we did have hand-painted murals of children hugging lions and eating ripe tomatoes in paradise. The seating was an ergonomic nightmare—ripped cushions that felt like they were manufactured from concrete and shards of glass.

An outside observer might have noted that our congregation was very punctual, unaware that we were merely vying for the prime, duct tape–free seating.

"These seats are going to kill me!" my father would moan, squirming as we read scriptures evoking the unbearable punishment God would soon rain down upon all evildoers. If we were lucky enough to snag one of the plush yellow vinyl-seated stackable chairs, my father still had something to discuss—the chair's projected life expectancy while under the care of the Spanish congregation.

"Those Spanish brothers! Look at this—the screws are loose, half the rubber stoppers are lost," Dad would say, rocking back diagonally and placing a folded piece of notebook paper under a too-short metal leg. "They're well-meaning, but someone really needs to show them how to stack these chairs!"

My mother helped me to understand why the Spanish brothers acted this way.

"They're not used to having nice things, sweetie. They don't know what to do with them," she said. Adding sympathetically, "Some people feel more comfortable when things are broken."

It seemed that no matter what you had, Spanish people would eventually ruin it. I was embarrassed that I knew how to count to *diez* and ask for a glass of *agua* in this inferior, chair-destroying language.

The English-speaking congregation attended the Kingdom Hall on Tuesdays, Thursdays, and Sundays, sitting with scrubbed ears and shined shoes to learn about the end of the world for a few hours. Here was a congregation at attention—shiny, obedient, 1950s-sitcom perfection.

Joining the Theocratic Ministry School was a mandatory privilege, something we were supposed to do before being allowed to knock on doors and ask people if they knew they'd accidentally chosen the wrong religion. Students would be assigned a simple topic, such as "Is This Life All There Is?" or "Why Does God Allow Suffering?" The performances had a strict five-minute limit, more than enough time to clear up any lingering misconceptions about the ontological questions that have plagued mankind since its inception.

We called these performances "talks." Some people gave the kind of rousing, inspirational talks you made sure not to be in the bathroom during. And some people accidentally shut off the microphone, then rambled on about how Michael Jackson turned his back on the Jehovah's Witnesses after filming the demon-fueled *Thriller* video.

Talent was a toss-up. The Ministry School was a Jehovah's Witness open-mike night, only without the hairy veteran who always takes his pants off.

It would have all descended into chaos if not for the genteel hand and wide neckties of our school overseer. This position was filled by a prominent brother in the congregation, someone who perhaps had not yet been appointed as an elder, but still owned a variety of powder-blue suits. During our talks, he sat ominously in one corner of the stage, holding a stopwatch, with a facial expression that said, Don't mind me, I'm just timing you! Really. It's fine. You have two minutes left. Don't mind me. Hurry!

After the stopwatch beeped and the spiritual conundrum had been comprehensively answered, the overseer would publicly critique our performance. We would be counseled on points like vocal inflection, diction, and the effective use of gestures (with fear of being critiqued on the latter point often causing a speaker to launch into a series of regal, sweeping arm motions, as if he were on a parade float with the Miss America theme being piped through loudspeakers).

That's five minutes with the eyes of an entire congregation trained on you, followed by a brief session while Brother Pendel-haus discussed your facial twitch and your lisp. Somehow, at the age of eight, this sounded like a fabulous idea.

Most children of Jehovah's Witnesses began to give talks around the age of 12 or so, and were jealous of any prodigies who started earlier. When you're a fundamentalist kid, it's cool to be a zealot. If you can't be bad, you might as well be very, very good. So me and my JW homies had our own crew. After the meetings, we'd hang out in the Kingdom Hall parking lot, not smoking, and brag about how totally unrebellious we were. Then we'd put down a square of cardboard and not break-dance.

But no friends my age had actually given any talks yet, although we often played "Kingdom Hall" in the backyard while dressed in muddy bathing suits. So it couldn't have been peer pressure that drove me to don my most mature velvet dress (midnight blue) and approach one of our elders after a Sunday meeting to ask if I could be allowed to join the Ministry School. With a timid curtsy, I informed Brother Wentz that I was meant for the stage.

"Joining the Ministry School, are we?" he chuckled, bending over to squint at me like I was a shiny toy lying in a puddle.

Brother Wentz was a round-faced man with a pastel-green polyester suit. His wife shook like a Chihuahua and had a chronic facial tic. When I asked my mother why, she told me it was because of "nerves." And, she added, because Brother Wentz used to beat her up. I was eight, so apparently it was time to start me on the road to vicious slander and inappropriate gossip.

My mother took her upturned hand and jammed a diamond ring into my shoulder, giving me a *go on* nudge toward the kindly face of spousal abuse.

"Well," Brother Wentz said, grabbing onto his thighs. "Can you read?"

I was "a precocious child," with crisp blue eyes that could have been made of glass and set into a Kewpie doll; the kid who tugged on your jacket and asked if you wanted to hear her spell a hard word like "antidisestablishmentarianism." Now this insolent adult was asking if I could *read*? The audacity!

Not only could I read, but I had recently perfected the art of carrying around the largest book from the school library, which at that point was *Roots*. I brought *Roots* with me everywhere, placing it in prominent "So, I see you're reading *Roots*" positions. I sneered at the other eight-year-olds in my class as they debased themselves with reading material such as *Where the Wild Things Are*. No book of mine would bear a Caldecott Medal!

To this day, I have never read *Roots*. But I checked it out of the Nathanael Greene Elementary School library 179 times.

I rolled my child-star eyes at Brother Wentz. "Yes, I can read!" I snorted. Then I spelled "supercalifragilisticexpialidocious."

Brother Wentz tried to think of a second, less confrontational question. "Do you love Jehovah?" he asked.

"I love Jehovah with my whole heart, my whole soul, and my whole mind," I told the elder who held my performing future in the palm of his formerly violent hand.

"You're very young, you know," he said, harrumphing and raising one disconcerting white eyebrow.

Young? That was the whole idea! I would get onstage and the entire congregation would *ooh* and *ahh* and *young* at me. It would be no great accomplishment if I waited until I was a teenager. I had to strike while the iron was eight.

The elder considered me for a moment. His wispy white hair was so baby-fine that it moved on its own, as if by a nonexistent breeze in our ever-stuffy Kingdom Hall. "Young Sister Abrahams, welcome to the Theocratic Ministry School!"

A few weeks later, Brother Wentz approached me with a slip of paper bearing the topic of my talk: "Resisting Wicked Spirits." I would be doing research from the book *You Can Live Forever in Paradise on Earth*, and I was officially assigned a partner.

The men did not need partners. They spoke to us from behind a lectern like budding high school presidents. The women, however, being of the "weaker sex," were not allowed to teach anything to men. The succession of power was this: Jesus was the head over man; man was the head over woman; and woman was the head over cooking peach cobbler and shutting up.

In order to participate in the Theocratic Ministry School, women performed together in two-person scenes. In this way, the men would not actually be instructed by us, but merely observe while we instructed each other. As long as we gave our talks facing another sister instead of the congregation, we were not usurping man's authority. It was as if two friends had unwittingly found themselves on the stage and began having a private chat about the prophecies of Daniel in front of 80 people who were kind enough to stop their service and listen to them chat for a spell.

Facing the congregation = uppity and sinful.

Ninety degrees clockwise = making Jehovah's heart smile.

Depending on the enthusiasm of the budding actresses, we would either spend five minutes shifting around uncomfortably or be whisked away into a *My Dinner with Andre*–esque fantasy world of two people sitting together at a table.

So, I was assigned my very own elderly woman. My partner's name was Sister Douglas. Like me, she loved Jehovah, and unlike me, she owned a large collection of vintage flowery hats.

"I'm very pleased to be your partner," she told me. *"You're making Jehovah's heart smile."*

Why, with my spunk and her silver-haired maturity, we were a heartwarming buddy flick just waiting to happen! *This summer, get ready to talk. Paramount Pictures presents "Sister Douglas and the Kid!"*

The main dilemma I faced was how to ease into a conversation about the spirit realm with a 60-year-old woman. She could be a neighbor, but who cranes their head over the fence to ask, "Excuse me, little girl, but how can I get rid of a possessed doll when it simply won't burn?" I could make her my teacher, but that was hacky.

Most of the other talks took on the same plot—pretending to have a home Bible study, or helping to encourage a sister after the meeting. Bor-ing! I always yearned for two sisters to meet in Snow White's cottage and discuss the danger of speaking to witches. Instead I got:

"Oh, hello, Sister Easily Stumbled. I notice you've been missing some of the Tuesday night Book Study meetings lately. Is this because you feel overwhelmed by the weight of Satan's world?"

"I do feel overwhelmed, Sister Spiritual. To tell you the truth, lately I am just not sure that the Jehovah's Witnesses are really the one true religion."

"Oh, Sister Easily Stumbled. Of course Jehovah's Witnesses are the one true religion and all other wicked religions will be destroyed at Armageddon. Now let's turn to page forty-seven in the book *Happiness—How to Find It* to see why . . ."

Somehow, sitting in a Kingdom Hall and watching a short play about two women sitting in a Kingdom Hall was underwhelming to me. I wanted to up the ante, and dare I say, I instinctively knew how. This old woman and I would not simply be Theocratic Ministry ships passing in the night. We would be family friends going out for ice cream!

"Hello, Sister Inquisitive. Are you ready to get that ice cream we've been talking about?"

"Oh, hello there, Kyria. I sure am. But first, I wanted to ask you how a true Christian should deal with voices from the spirit realm."

The introduction of ice cream gave me a setting, a raison d'être, an arc. And who knew, maybe after the meeting was over, my parents would celebrate by taking me to Newport Creamery, where I could continue giving glory to God by partaking of a junior butterscotch sundae!

I camped out at the dining room table with a stack of Jehovah's Witness literature, a set of index cards, a No. 2 pencil, an art gum eraser, a calligraphy pen, a set of Hi-Liters, and a sharpener jammed with crayons. First, I invented a family of roller-skating cartoon creatures I called the Pigwees. Once the final antennae had been colored in, I began intently cross-referencing demons. I immersed myself in Watchtower Society publications with names like *The Truth That Leads to Eternal Life*. I found I was especially proficient at numbering my index cards. I excelled in drawing a circle around each number, as well as perfect corner placement. My mother helped with the more involved tasks, such as having the talk make sense.

Sister Douglas even stopped by our house to practice with me and nibble on vanilla ladyfingers with my mother. The air around us crackled as I drew circles around numbers like *9* and *12*. Unless it was the white frosting talking, I could tell that Sister Douglas and the Kid were going places.

When the big day came, I could barely sit still in school. As a Jehovah's Witness child who had never celebrated a single sinful holiday, this coming night was the equivalent of an acceptable, non-pagan Christmas Eve. I was wriggly all over. I would, of course, be giving my talk in the main auditorium of the Kingdom Hall. I just had to! I was an attraction, a third grader vocalizing her love of the Bible. P. T. Barnum would have scooped me up and put me in a cage next to his syphilitic Pygmy.

That night, after dinner, we all finished scrubbing behind our ears and stuffed our book bags with reference books, Bibles, and notepads. Then we took a stroll around the corner to the Kingdom Hall. It was less than a five-minute walk, but our family made it into a huge ordeal, packing Kleenex, cough drops, and extra sweaters as if we wouldn't be home for days. In my mother's mind, it seemed, the worst possible thing that could happen to a person was to be caught in an air-conditioned building while wearing only short sleeves.

"Can we walk up Power Road instead?" I asked my father. I was nervous already, and I didn't want to walk past Crazy Louie the Apostate. Apostates were the worst kind of people in the world, even worse than people who had never been Jehovah's Witnesses to begin with, because they once had the Truth and they let it go.

Crazy Louie sat on a fence across from the Kingdom Hall and glared at all the members of the congregation as they walked by. He'd been disfellowshipped a few years ago, and was now to be shunned by all us true Christians. I heard he'd been cast out for smoking, but my father told me that Louie had never really had a full set of stairs leading to the attic, and smoking was just a small part of his whole attitude problem.

Louie could repent if he wanted to. He could go sit quietly in the back of the Kingdom Hall, then leave just before the service ended so as not to attract attention or "stumble" anyone. There were different ways to stumble someone. If a person was weak in the Truth, you could stumble them by sinning, because they might be tempted to copy your behavior. Or you could stumble someone who was very spiritual by being known as a sinner and simply being near them; they could be so offended and upset by your presence that they actually suffer emotional harm. Louie was not allowed to speak to anyone or be spoken to. If he did this for a year or two, the elders might see signs of repentance and consider allowing him to come back. Instead, he sat on a fence across the street from the building, three times a week, and glared at the congregation members as they passed in and out. My father said this was because Crazy Louie knew in his heart that Jehovah's Witnesses were the true religion, but Satan was in his head and wouldn't allow him to make the final step across the threshold to come inside. Louie the Apostate was like a real-life monster with Satan right inside him, and he scared the living Hades out of me. In my mind, being disfellowshipped was right up there with getting bitten by Dracula. You may have been a nice person once, but now you needed a stake through the heart.

Fence-sitting apostates aside, my main concern was which outfit to wear for my debut. I'd eventually chosen a white lace dress and a white wicker hat adorned with a pink bow and other fineries that stopped just short of a cigarette holder and a monocle. I felt stunning. But I was eight, and my current idea of haute couture was a tiara, a hula hoop, and a ball gown made of emeralds.

When we arrived at the Kingdom Hall, I discovered I had been relegated to the basement auditorium, located next to the cloakroom and storage closet. Downstairs, there were no microphones, no windows, and no people. Since most people preferred to stay seated in the non-damp, non-dark main auditorium, I would be performing for a mere handful of our congregation members.

I wanted to jump directly onto the stage and launch into my soon-to-be-legendary performance, but I first had to sit through someone else's talk, one that would almost definitely not mention dessert. I distracted myself by faking tuberculosis until Dad offered me a Smith Brothers licorice drop. My mother handed me a steno pad on which she had written, "Jehovah, Jesus, Angels, Armageddon, Paradise, and New System of Things." I was to make a checkmark next to each word when it was said from the stage. But I was too excited for checkmarking, so I shuffled my index cards and crunched my licorice drop until it was time for Sister Douglas and the Kid to take the stage.

When they called my name, I seated myself onstage in a plush, yellow seat and spread my index cards out next to my Bible on the faux-wood mini–conference table. Sister Douglas and I sat with our hands folded in our laps while the brother whose responsibility it was to adjust the height of the microphones did his job.

"Are you ready to get that ice cream we've been talking about?" Sister Inquisitive began. I answered immediately, because people were *watching* this time.

"Yes, I certainly do enjoy ice cream. But first, I wanted to ask you if you've ever thought about what we should do if we are contacted by a demon spirit."

My feet dangled off the seat. I emoted, I gestured. I loudly read each scripture, which my mother had helped me bookmark with paper clips. But none of it meant anything to me—it was all filler, just the rambling verse leading up to my toe-tapping, catchy chorus. Four minutes and 52 seconds later, when it was time for my big finale, I lifted my head high and crowed, "Now let's go get that ice cream!" I couldn't have been more proud if

Jehovah himself had come down from heaven, grabbed my steno pad, and made a checkmark next to his own name.

It was then that something rather unexpected happened. Everyone in the audience laughed.

Had I mispronounced "cream"? Had I accidentally said "ice milk" and not realized it? What had I done to deserve this?

I climbed off the stage, confounded by the applause and laughter. People were smiling at the young sister with the love of Jehovah and the cute hat. My mother reached over to grab my shaky little hand in hers. "Great job, kiddo," she said, chuckling. I spun around in my seat. Chuckles! The entire audience was suffused with them. Those people. They were laughing at my *art*!

I felt a ticklish, allergic sensation in my nose and my eyes, not unlike rolling around in a field of dusty cats coated in pollen. I choked on gobs of wet air. I did not want to be crying, not immediately after accomplishing something so *grown-up*. I pulled my wicker hat down over my eyes so no one could see the tears. Sister Douglas sat next to me, her hands folded in her lap, focused intently on the next speaker. When my galumphing sobs became something she couldn't ignore, she grabbed my shoulders and asked if she had done something to make me cry.

If she didn't know, I certainly wasn't going to tell her. Ice cream was not humorous! This was high-concept. The talk *began* with ice cream and it *ended* with ice cream. At eight years old, I had done what even the adults failed to do. I'd had *plot resolution*.

"I don't know why I'm crying," I told Sister Douglas.

"She's just excited, Elaine," my mother whispered to Sister Douglas, adding far too loudly, "She *gets* like this."

It was true, I did get like this. I was excited. Excited to take the stage. Excited by didactic five-minute lectures, swooping gestures, and perfect diction. So excited, in fact, that I never, ever wanted to do it again.

CHAPTER 2

Rejoice! For the Dead Are Rising!

"Would you like to see a picture of my dead baby?" Sister Bailey asked me, already opening her wallet. "This is Jason. He died."

Sister Bailey did not look well. For one thing, surgical gauze was flapping off the side of her face. She had recently lost one of her eyes to cancer and didn't seem all too interested in getting it replaced. In lieu of a glass eye, she regularly covered her ocular cavity with a flesh-colored vinyl patch. She held this in place with surgical tape, wrapped her whole head in gauze, then accessorized the entire dressing with a lunch-lady hairnet.

"I'm sorry your baby died," I said. At ten years old, I didn't know how to respond to an unrequested dead-baby picture. I'd merely been walking down the aisle of our Kingdom Hall, looking for my friend Michelle Jordan so we could play hide-and-seek under the coatrack. Now I was confronted with Sister Bailey's dead son.

"Don't be sorry, sweetie! He's only sleeping," she chided. "We'll see him again in the New System!"

One of my favorite Kingdom Melodies was called "Keep Your Eyes on the Prize." It told the story of how, after Armageddon, Jehovah was going to bring us all back to perfect health and resurrect our loved ones into paradise. Sister Bailey always punched it when we got to the line about how the eyes of the blind will see again.

Someday, Sister Bailey would be able to see again. Jason would be reunited with his mother, and she would greet him with two wholly beautiful blue eyes. Still, I got the feeling that Sister Bailey might continue to wrap her head in gauze, even after paradise. It was her signature style, her single white glove.

Then, too, you'll see the dead arise. If you keep your eyes on the prize.

Jason was gray. He had white streaks through his face from having been folded and unfolded so many times. I asked what he died from.

"He just died," she answered. "It was a long time ago."

If I'd thought Sister Bailey was crazy before, this was definitive proof. I couldn't wait to tell my friends that Sister Bailey had shown me a picture of her dead baby, then wouldn't even tell me how he died.

"Sista Bailey smells like cat pees," was Michelle's only reply when I finally found her. "Wanna play hide 'n' seeks?"

My mother had no patience for people like Sister Bailey. Most of our congregation had already had it up to here with her antics.

"She just wants attention," my mother said. "Well, guess what? Don't give it to her." Mom stamped her feet and cackled a purposefully fake, slapstick laugh. This was her signature note of sarcasm and schadenfreude.

Sister Bailey was self-involved. Naturally. What other reason could someone have for refusing to get a glass eye?

It was hard to garner pity in our congregation, especially when Ida Wachohowitz had already been in a concentration camp. Michelle told me that Ida always drank her coffee scalding hot and in one single gulp. She'd gotten used to doing it that way under the Nazis and never quite dropped the habit.

"She had it rough," my mother sighed. "Real, *real* rough."

Unfortunately, she hadn't been locked up for being a Jehovah's Witness, which could have made her a congregation celebrity. She was just Polish or something. Still, it was impressive. The point was, she'd been persecuted by Nazis and you didn't hear *her* complaining. Our congregation had a low tolerance for whining, but a high demand for a good story. And, frankly, Sister Bailey's missing eye had long ago grown boring.

Sister Bailey was just one of the large group of insane, elderly sisters for which our Kingdom Hall was slowly becoming infamous throughout New England. While every Kingdom Hall had at least one "eccentric" member, we boasted an entire coffee klatch of mumbling, mothball-scented, silk flower–behatted widows with spotty memories for taking their antipsychotics.

Sister Blanche was our very own Minnie Pearl, with price tags dangling from her clothes like a septuagenarian shoplifter. She believed the secret to longevity lay in the consumption of raw garlic. She swallowed her ambrosia in whole cloves, with a spoonful of honey, immediately before clutching a Bible to her chest and shuffling off to the Kingdom Hall.

It became a game to my father to presuppose where "the garlic factory" would settle during any given meeting. Then, with all the drama of a high school cafeteria, he would make a big show of seating our family on the opposite side of the room.

Like all factories, Sister Blanche belched. She became increasingly huffy with each passing eruption. "Ex-*cuse* me!" she'd exclaim indignantly, as if she'd had just about enough of these shenanigans and demanded to know exactly where this disruption was coming from.

"Jeez Louise!" my father would not quite whisper to whoever was sitting nearby. "Maybe if our sisters didn't eat an entire

Italian restaurant before every meeting, we wouldn't have this problem."

Sister Dubin was our resident schizophrenic. She was only occasionally aware of what year it was and held the deep-seated belief that house cats were actually demons in disguise. While Sister Blanche fell into the "old bat" category, Sister Dubin was crazy for *real*. One Sunday, our congregation received a phone call from an irate neighbor claiming that someone from our Kingdom Hall had verbally accosted her kitty. Sister Dubin had been "in service" that day, knocking on doors and reading from the *Watchtower*, and apparently calling down the wrath of Jehovah on local house pets. Soon after this incident, Sister Dubin was privately taken aside and asked if she might not prefer to praise Jehovah in a more personal, silent way. For example, by staying home.

My father told me this was because Sister Dubin was "making us look bad," but I didn't understand how Jehovah could allow himself to look bad. Wouldn't his Holy Spirit stop that from happening?

"It did," Dad explained. "The Holy Spirit moved the elders to tell her to stop preaching."

Despite our member's fluctuating serotonin levels, we were all expected to attend the Kingdom Hall three times a week for a different "spiritual meal."

Each meeting was slightly different, but they all had the same mise-en-scène. The Sunday *Watchtower* Study was the meeting we usually presented to outsiders. It began with an hour-long talk and ended with an hour-long Q&A of the latest *Watchtower* article. The Theocratic Ministry School, which took place every Thursday at 7:00 PM, was more Jehovah's Witness–centric. This was the night when congregation members gave their five-minute talks, death and disfellowshipping announcements were made, and congregation budgets were read aloud in the interest of full disclosure (unlike all false Christians, who, we noted, were just in it to make money). Meanwhile, for the Tuesday night Book Study, the congregation separated into small groups and met in private homes. Only those who were in good standing with the congregation could be chosen to host—people like ministerial servants and their Pioneering wives. (Pioneers spent 90 hours each month proselytizing door-to-door, and were generally married to someone with a well-paying blue-collar construction job.) It also appeared to be mandatory that the family own a rocking chair, a braided rug, and a grandfather clock, but this was solely my own interpretation.

When I excused myself halfway through the Book Study and wiped my hands on the velvety matching bathroom towels, I felt that Tuesday, rather than Sunday, would be the best way to introduce a new Bible study to the Truth—depending on what that Bible study was looking for out of religion.

In the same way you didn't skip breakfast, you didn't skip a single meeting. It may have been 7:30 PM on a weeknight, but there was nowhere else you needed to be. There was nothing else that would save your life. Mothers rushed through their dinners, fathers ran home from their jobs, children missed their favorite television shows. The Kingdom Hall filled with the exhaled calm of people who'd collectively *made it.*

Sister Bailey very rarely missed a meeting. Every time a question was asked of the audience, her hand shot straight into the air, teacher's-pet style. Sometimes she would even grunt or "ooh" like a member of the Sweathogs trying to get the attention of Mr. Kotter. Eventually the brother conducting the meeting had no choice but to call on her.

"Here we go," my father would say. "Here it comes."

"Jehovah is good and kind!" Sister Bailey would screech into the microphone, completely ignoring the original question. "When I had my operation, my eye operation, you see, I lost my eye to cancer! Well, I prayed to Jehovah to bless me with his Holy Spirit. And the Jehovah's Witnesses are the *only* true religion. The

Kingdom Hall is the *only* place to be free of the demons in this world. Satan lives in the churches and Jehovah's power is awesome!"

Sister Bailey didn't say anything we didn't believe. It's not like she'd up and announce that the Lord had been speaking to her through chicken soup or that it was perfectly acceptable to be Jewish. It was more about her *style*. Proper Jehovah's Witnesses didn't answer questions by talking about their missing eyes and how "awesome" God was. That was for Baptist churches, places where people got carried away with emotion, babbled demonically in tongues, and praised the Lord without permission. We all knew what was in our thoughts (intense love for Jehovah, possibly coupled with a need to pee) and there was no need to cause problems by talking about actual *feelings*.

The correct way to comment during a meeting was by reading an underlined passage directly from your book or *Watchtower*. This showed that you had read and understood the literature and also helped to avoid stumbling others by spouting off unchecked opinions about God's will. In this way, there were no "wrong" answers given during the meetings. Everyone was always right and Jehovah was always praised.

Brother Rickman, for example, was a man who knew how to comment. He was concise and funny and managed to adapt the society's answers into his own words so as to sound exceptionally knowledgeable. On top of that, he almost always threw in a zinger or a punch line at the end. People perked up when he commented.

Because he dressed impeccably, never had a girlfriend, and spoke with a slightly effeminate lisp, it became a running joke in the congregation that he was gay. Not that he was actually sleeping with men, but we bet he would if he could. Because of this, all of his jokes seemed funnier. Eventually, he got in on the act and began to make self-deprecating comments about his penchant for nice clothing. We all know I'm sublimating my true sexuality, he seemed to be saying, so let's at least have a laugh about it. Also, I am dying inside.

Say we were studying *You Can Live Forever in Paradise on Earth*. If the question was "Why have Jehovah's Witnesses established many large printing factories?" and the paragraph read "To help the more than 3,500,000 Jehovah's Witnesses, large factories have been established in many countries," Brother Rickman might have answered, "The society has blessed us with large factories all over the world so that the more than 3,500,000 Witnesses can easily get the literature they need. And, if you've ever gone alone with the congregation on the annual bus trip to the factory in New York, we also know what it's like to be blessed together in New York traffic." At this, the congregation would explode with laughter.

This was how we had all learned to comment. Stay on-topic, keep it short, and unless you are as witty as a closeted homosexual, don't ever talk about your actual *life*. You had to *earn* the right to go off-script, and having cancer just didn't cut the mustard. In short, Sister Bailey was horrendously inappropriate. But sometimes when she was done, I wished everyone would be that interesting.

Perhaps in exchange for our excess insanity, our congregation was blessed to have a real, live member of the anointed class among us.

Sister Griffin was one of only 144,000 Jehovah's Witnesses who were "anointed" by the Holy Spirit to go to heaven. The rest of us were going to live forever, or, if we died before Armageddon, were going to be resurrected into paradise.

Our anointed sister didn't radiate any godly light or seem to be in possession of any secret knowledge of the universe. In fact, she had very few pearls of wisdom for someone who'd be sitting at the right hand of God in heaven as soon as she had her fatal stroke. It felt a lot like going to the zoo for an afternoon of animal antics only to find that the polar bear walks with a limp and the toucan suffers from malaise.

Sister Griffin was a stocky, elderly woman of few words. Perhaps due to her advanced age, she didn't spend much time in the preaching work. She didn't give talks or belong to the Theocratic Ministry School. She rarely raised her hand or commented at meetings. She was anointed, and she was coasting.

Most perplexing of all, she never even mentioned the fact that she was going to heaven. She was so secretive about her status, I sometimes wondered if I was talking to the wrong elderly sister. With their 1960s costume brooches and strappy sandals, they did all look a little similar. One might expect a conversation with a heaven-bound elderly woman to occasionally center on her next home, or be peppered with passive-aggressive references to her angelic status such as, "Why don't I finish that pie for you, sweetie? At least one of us won't gain weight in *heaven*."

The anointed had one night each year in which to earn their keep—the Lord's Evening Meal, also known as the Memorial. On this night, they partook of the "emblems," which means they drank a glass of wine, ate some matzo, and spent two hours listening to a sermon about their imminent death.

As the one and only holiday Jehovah's Witnesses celebrate, we held the Memorial to be intensely sacred. It took place after sundown on Nisan 14, better known to the rest of the hat-wearing world as Easter Sunday. Some people went out for dinner after the Memorial, but this sort of merriment was frowned upon. The son of God died for our sins and we damn well weren't supposed to enjoy it.

Even families who didn't attend the Kingdom Hall on any other night would be at the Memorial. This was half the fun. If we didn't see you at the Memorial, we could self-righteously shake our heads and *tsk*, for you were clearly lost.

We opened the Memorial with the same song every year, "The Lord's Evening Meal," with lines like " 'Twas Nisan 14, when your glory was seen." We listened to an impossibly boring sermon, most of which was spent calling the Catholics idiots for thinking the wine actually turned into blood. I mean, *please*, what we served was clearly plain old wine coming out of a plain old bottle which just needed to be ingested by the 144,000 human bodies that God had personally chosen to sit at his right hand in heaven. Let's not get silly about it.

The highlight of the event was when every member of the congregation passed the bread and the wine. You held the dish for a moment, felt the lightness of what was in your hand, then passed it to the person sitting next to you. If a congregation was lucky enough to have an anointed member like ours was, everything culminated in this plate and glass reaching them unharmed. Otherwise, you put it back on the table, uneaten, and later, disposed of it like medical waste.

Being a member of the 144,000 was not something to take lightly. You couldn't just run around all willy-nilly announcing that you were going to heaven and getting T-shirts made. There were few sins more intense than partaking of the matzo and the wine if you weren't actually going to use it. If you were lying, or even just mistaken, Jehovah would be *totally* pissed at you. Surely, there was a special, torturous Armageddon reserved specifically for Ye Anointed Who Are Totally Faking It.

How did the anointed know for certain that they were anointed? They were aware that they were going to heaven in the same way a mechanic named Barney might know, beyond a shadow of a doubt, that he is a mechanic named Barney. There was no questioning of who you were. The anointed, like mechanics, just *knew*.

However, you still had to take the elders aside and inform them of your situation before it was made public, like the heaven semifinals. The pre-anointed went through a prayer-filled interrogation, during which God's Holy Spirit would clearly reveal if they were lying.

I imagine the questioning was along these lines:

"Are you sure you're anointed?"

"Yup."

"Really sure? Like, really super-sure?"

"Yeah, I mean, I said I'm anointed, so I'm anointed."

"Well, the reason I ask, is because maybe you just *think* you hear voices in your head telling you that you're anointed. Maybe you're not actually hearing the voices."

"No. God definitely speaks to me."

"Well, that argument sounds airtight. I can't think of anything to add, really. Welcome to the anointed!"

The first time I was allowed to pass the plate on my own, I was ten years old and had more people directing me than a NASA shuttle launch. The intense anxiety that I might accidentally fall mouth-first into the matzo and incur the never-ending wrath of Jehovah was almost too much to bear. If even a single crumb accidentally made its way into my mouth, my face would melt like the Nazis in *Raiders of the Lost Ark*.

When Sister Griffin received her plate, I craned my neck to catch a glimpse of her before my mother smacked me back into place. Our anointed sister was going to drink this wine and eat this unleavened bread and thus prove to us that Jehovah was real—he actually *spoke* to people. I wanted Sister Griffin to shoot straight into the sky, beams of light emanating from her ears, mouth, and eyes, as proof of this most holy snacking experience. For even though the box may have said "Kosher for Passover," this matzo sent you directly to Jesus.

Many of the fair-weather, Memorial-only Witnesses also flocked to our special conventions, of which there were two kinds: the Circuit Assembly and the District Assembly.

The Circuit Assembly was held at the local mega–Kingdom Hall known somewhat un-mega-like as the Assembly Hall. Located in Natick, Massachusetts, this building had been constructed *by* Jehovah's Witnesses *for* Jehovah's Witnesses and held as many Jehovah's Witnesses as five Kingdom Halls.

Located on an unimposing residential street, the Assembly Hall was a sleek white ranch-style building surrounded by a suburban metal fence—enthusiastic postwar kitsch. This architecture, when it first appeared, must have virtually screamed "Religious tolerance. Get used to it!"

Twice yearly, my family made the grueling 90-minute 35 m.p.h. trek to the Natick Assembly Hall for the Circuit Assembly. For a family of Rhode Islanders who could get anywhere in the state within 14 seconds, this was a trip worthy of an Airstream motor home and mail forwarding. We brought blankets, magnetic board games, and a ziplock bag filled with dried fruit, in case we were stranded so long that we ceased being regular.

I preferred taking these drives in the winter, when the affluent Middlesex County homes sparkled with Christmas cheer and good credit. I wasn't used to what you'd call "classy" decorations. My Pawtucket neighbors decked out their front lawns with cheap plastic Nativity scenes and particle-board stop signs telling Santa where to land. So the first time I saw a home illuminated by only a series of tasteful turquoise bulbs in two perfectly sculpted topiaries, I felt doubly confused. I shouldn't even have been *looking* at Christmas lights, let alone enjoying and admiring them (which, due to the complete lack of decorating talent in the city of Pawtucket, hadn't really been an issue up to that point).

As we approached the Assembly Hall, my father would immediately begin to survey our parking options. Here, the question became, Had our family left on time today, or had we, once again, dawdled like the heathens we were and therefore forfeited a space close to the main entrance? The answer, more often than not, involved heathen-dawdling.

You could tell how spiritual a family was by noting how close to the Assembly Hall they had parked. The Pendleburys, for example, were a tight ship of an elder's family, always on time. Their recently waxed Cadillac was never any farther back than the fifth or sixth space.

"Looks like the brothers are out in full force today!" my father would say as we drove past the cool, silent cars of elders and ministerial servants.

We drove until we were no longer in the realm of the God-fearing early-risers. Past the Crawleys' pickup truck and the VW Bug of a sister who was once publicly reprimanded for smoking. My father drove past all of them, until we reached the very back of the lot and could go no farther. Then Dad would park sideways, taking up two spaces.

"It's better to park back here," Dad reasoned as he handed us our Bibles and made an obligatory dig at women drivers. "Safe from all the sisters trying to back out of their *blind spots*, if you know what I mean."

If we happened to be running especially late, we might have the misfortune of seeing another family who had arrived at the assembly so early they were actually returning to their car for a forgotten pen. This was the most embarrassing of all possible entrances, caught red-handed moseying in ten minutes late. For some reason, it seemed to happen to us most often with the radiant and enviable Gonsalves family. Like the day their daughter Carolina was getting baptized.

"Just getting extra pencil so Jasmine can take her notes," Sister Gonsalves said, waving to us as we lugged our heavy book bags from parking-lot Siberia. "Jou know my oldest, Carolina, is getting *baptize* today?"

"Congratu-laaaaay-tions, Rosalind!" my mother said in an overly enunciated singsong tone. The Gonsalves family were Portuguese but still attended our English congregation, something that caused no end of confusion for my mother.

"They don't want to go to the Spanish meetings, I guess," Mom conjectured. "But such a hardworking couple. And her husband? Such a smart man!"

The interior-design scheme of the Assembly Hall could be described as "1960s Funeral Home," with lots of vertical stonework and just-vacuumed rows constantly visible in the shag carpeting. The auditorium featured bright purple seating with matching bright purple carpet runners. Wide swaths of each wall were painted in a brash pink more often seen in the penthouse of an interior decorator with a pet leopard than in the house of the Lord. Two blue bowl-shaped swiveling side chairs sat on either side of the stage, as if waiting for Dick Cavett to interview Janis Joplin. Behind the podium, a bright pink wooden sign proclaimed "I Will Say to Jehovah, You Are My Refuge and My Stronghold."

The centerpiece of the hall was an impressive baptismal pool in the foyer, with white brick siding and a pastel mural of paradise on the wall above it. Two brothers were placed on duty here at all times, standing on the brick stairs behind purple velvet–roped steps like presidential bodyguards, ensuring that no one would drown or soil the decorative plastic ferns. The fresh-faced Gonsalves girls milled about here, staring into the water as ripples of salvation flickered across their idyllic faces and onto the mural of paradise.

The pool, in addition to being an easy place to meet for lunch, was a symbol of why we were attending the assembly. Those who lay down in this pool made a public declaration that they believed the Witnesses were the only true religion. It was here that true lovers of truth and righteousness donned modest swimsuits and then screwed up their hair for Jehovah. All vanity disappeared as your sins and makeup floated away. Although, once, a girl named Marlene wore bright pink circles of waterproof makeup she'd bought especially for the occasion. Several years later, I heard that she married a professional surfer at Walt Disney World, after pulling up to her wedding in Cinderella's carriage. I wondered what sort of cartoon character–proof cosmetics she'd chosen for the ride.

Since the hall was Jehovah's Witness–owned and operated, there were several perks which wouldn't have been available to us in a worldly convention center. Having complete control of the sound system, for example, allowed us to pipe the sermons directly into the bathrooms so that we would not have to miss a moment of the Lord's spiritual blessings, even while dealing with a bad fish sandwich. Anyone unfortunate enough to be trapped in the bathroom while the prayer was being said would immediately stop what he was doing and put his head down, as if playing urination freeze tag. Sinks ran, water dripped off fingers, urethras snapped shut while we psychically gabbed with God. The Lord may have invented pee, but that didn't mean he had to put up with it. In contrast with the modest Circuit Assemblies, our District Assemblies were JW rock concerts that could draw audiences of thousands. We filled the Providence, Rhode Island, Civic Center and performed mass baptisms in chlorinated hotel pools. Over the course of three days, Jehovah's Witnesses invaded parking lots, demanded bulk hotel discounts, and overran fast-food joints, with name-tagged families publicly praying over their Egg McMuffins.

Both Circuit and District Assemblies were multiple-day events composed of demonstrations, presentations, baptisms, and highly anticipated biblical theater known as the Drama. These were free, motivational seminars on living through the apocalypse. Jehovah's Witnesses came from all over to worship together peacefully and feast on God's love. This, we said, was Jehovah's "spiritual banquet." It was a taste of what life would be like after Armageddon, only with more cafeteria sandwiches wrapped in plastic.

Information at the assemblies was rarely mind-blowing. It consisted of the same boring sermons we'd heard a million times before—only, now they were excitedly punctuated by the thunderous applause of 3,000 people. There were the costume dramas and book releases and real, live Jehovah's Witnesses getting up onstage to be interviewed. These were the shining examples of Jehovah's Witness–dom, carted before us to describe the sacrifices they'd made in order to be among the holiest people in the building.

Women told us how they'd given up their jobs in order to serve Jehovah full-time. Men spoke of supporting their wives' decisions to leave the workplace, even though it meant not being able to afford season baseball tickets. The smallest child was generally saved for last, as it was simply impossible to follow the intense applause generated by a four-year-old saying, "Betwuz I wuv Jehovers!"

During the more conspicuous District Assemblies, the six-o'clock news usually broadcast a brief local-interest piece, remarking on the well-dressed Christian families that had recently infiltrated the city.

And in other news, you may have noticed a bit of a buzz around the downtown Civic Center this weekend. If you're wondering exactly what all the fanfare is about, well, you've been looking at a convention of none other than . . . Jehovah's Witnesses. That's right, Providence, they'll be in town until Monday. And now, Larry Schwartz with sports.

Any television spot or news clipping that even mentioned the convention in passing would inevitably be read from the stage as proof of the prophecy in Ezekiel that says, "And the nations will have to know that I am Jehovah."

"Even the Nyantic *Registry*'s weekend regional page recognizes the glory of God at work in *all* his Witnesses!" a voice would boom over the loudspeakers as a tiny brother waved a tinier swatch of newspaper in front of 2,640 people. Thunderous applause would ensue.

Part of our duty during the convention was to put forth a

good public face. To let the nations of Providence know that we were well behaved, stylish, and way holier than all those *other* Christians.

Like most Witness kids, my brother and I went on fancy shopping trips before every assembly. Unfortunately, unlike me, nine-year-old Aaron didn't have much say in how he was attired. To my mother, he was a male Dressy Bessy. Mom razor-buzzed his hair, scrubbed his cheeks rosy, and all but took him out into the sun with a magnifying glass to see if his plastic feet would singe. Aaron, to his credit, took all of this in stride. As young children with little concept of peer pressure, we enjoyed playing dress-up and pleasing our mother. Without her, we'd have left the house in Underoos and dish-towel capes.

Nothing pleased my mother more than the two small and shiny humans who hung on her every word and depended on her for socks and underwear. But once we began to get a little older and voice our actual opinions on fashion, we weren't so much fun anymore. Dress-up dolls were not supposed to have favorite colors.

This is the crossroad at which we stood during the 1985 District Assembly, the year my mother attempted to dress my brother like Dick Van Dyke in *Mary Poppins*.

Mom called it "a spring outfit," but its style transcended that of any particular season. The Candy Man, as we affectionately called it, was a red-and-white-striped three-piece suit that would make an 1890s barbershop quartet think twice about leaving the house. Lacking only a straw hat, the suit had little red buttons, snazzy long lapels, and was topped with a complementary bright red tie of the "bow" variety.

At first, Aaron patently refused to wear the suit. My father stepped in briefly to defend his son, but quickly decided that "there's no reasoning with that crazy woman." So Aaron wore the suit, giving Dad an opportunity to bond with his son over their combined hatred of controlling women.

"Do you know how much I paid for this suit? It's a beautiful suit," my mother said. I smiled and nodded my head.

It was Aaron and Dad against my mother. It was my mother against all men. It was me against nobody, neither agreeing with my mother nor being allowed to penetrate the secret pact between father and son. We made our way to the Civic Center to get a taste of life in Jehovah's peaceful promised kingdom.

The human spirit, as it turns out, is not so easily dominated, even by a domineering mother. For, while the body may be in chains, the spirit remains free to complain loudly to anyone who will listen. Mom, therefore, spent most of the assembly working overtime on damage control.

Aaron spent the entire lunch break wandering the aisles of the Civic Center—*busking*. "Popcoooan. Peanuuuts," he'd yell. "Get yer fresh hot buttahd popcoan he-ah!"

My father could not have been more proud.

"He's too young to appreciate it, but it's a beautiful suit," my mother would tell horrified strangers as Aaron did a soft-shoe and fell to one knee, singing, "Chim chiminey, chim chiminey, chim chim cheroo!"

My mother would laugh it off as if to say, Men! They're such animals, but it was tinged with the nervousness of knowing she was outnumbered.

When Mom wasn't looking, Aaron would take off the bow tie and hide it in his pocket. When my mother spotted him walking around tieless, she'd demand its immediate return. The tie clipped off, the tie clipped back on. More energy was expended playing hide-the-tie than driving to Filene's and purchasing a new suit.

"That tie!" she'd say. "The tie *makes* the suit!"

"I hate this suit," Aaron would say matter-of-factly. "I hate this tie. I hate this assembly. And I hate you."

My mother's exasperated "His father eggs him on! It's a beautiful suit" eventually morphed into an angry "Well, if this is the thanks I get, you can get your own suits from now on! You're not doing me any favors, you know! And here among Jehovah's people, of all things!"

By the end of the assembly, the bow tie was unclipped for good. Perhaps later, someone found a red piece of clip-on fabric floating at the edge of the baptismal pool. Dad put his arm around his son's shoulder and together they walked to the food distribution tables to snag some chocolate pudding for the drive home, making certain to spill copious amounts all over the suit.

CHAPTER 3

The Light of Truth Shines Like a Beacon

through Satan's Tempting Playthings

Since 1914, when Satan the devil lost the Great War of Armageddon and was cast out of heaven, he has spent his days walking among us here on earth, tricking humans into turning away from the one true God. Satan lurks everywhere. In churches, chairs, and cans of soup. I learned this information like the alphabet. It was something we memorized because we'd use it every day. We could not form a single sentence without it.

At bedtime, I'd lie on my canopy bed and thumb through Jehovah's Witness literature, reading aloud stories of the coming paradise interspersed with pictures of the wicked being swallowed by pits of lava. My children's books alternated between Dr. Seuss rhymes and tales of how sinners would scream and gnash their teeth at Armageddon. It was no more unusual for God to vanquish his enemies than it was for the Cat in the Hat to clean pink cake out of the bathtub.

When Great-Aunt Ruth babysat us, she would read any book

we brought to her, except a yellow hardcover book called *My Book of Bible Stories.* It contained colorful illustrations of Samson and Jesus, designed to help children better understand Jehovah's plan for this world.

"Anything but that," Ruth would say. "Absolutely any other book you want, but not that one."

I didn't understand why she disliked this book so much, but eventually I stopped asking and stuck to *The Story About Ping.*

Having child-friendly Jehovah's Witness literature was vital. As a conscientious parent, there is much information with which you must arm your child—what not to eat, what not to touch. For hardworking Jehovah's Witness parents, a proper education does not stop there. In addition to physical health, there is also your child's spiritual health to be concerned with.

Mostly, our literature and sermons stressed that true Christians must keep free from the lure of spiritism. Youngsters needed to learn that a game of Dungeons & Dragons will possess you within 14 seconds of the first dice roll and send you running off a cliff. Traditional folk-art hex signs from Pennsylvania Dutch country were made by witches and would bring demons into your home. Used books purchased at yard sales were once owned by devil worshippers. Also, children should never wish someone "good luck," which was deemed pagan, or read horoscopes, because astrologers were demon-possessed. These things would have your head spinning around faster than you could say "Linda Blair."

Then there were the Smurfs.

The '80s were a time of many battles. Coke versus Pepsi. DeLoreans versus the Lamborghini Countach. And in the great war of the Snorks against the Smurfs, I sided squarely as a Snork gal. It's not because I preferred the cheap, underwater rip-offs to the real deal. The problem was that Smurfs were little blue demons, and any Jehovah's Witness who owned Smurf paraphernalia would bring Satan's malevolence to her toy box.

I don't know why Snorks were deemed acceptable while the

Smurfs were thought to make your walls drip blood. Perhaps the reasoning was if the Snorks were truly possessed by Satan, the show would have had better ratings.

As such, I needed an alibi when my classmates brought their Smurf figurines and coloring books to school. I'd nonchalantly say, "Yeah, I'm more into the Snorks, actually," thereby seeming erudite and superior while avoiding laying hands upon cuddly black-arts toys. I feared the dark power of the Smurf, and had no problem resisting Satan's licensed merchandise. If I was going to get possessed by the devil, it certainly wasn't going to be through a Gargamel pencil-topper.

The moratorium on Smurfs began after a young boy (and Michelle Jordan assured me that this was true) brought a plush Smurf to his Kingdom Hall. The doll immediately began to shake and moan and otherwise cause a bit of a ruckus.

"Shit, fuck, shit!" said the Smurf. "I have had enough of this shit!"

"Jehovah! Jehovah," cried the little boy, evoking the name that causes even the knees of Satan himself to tremble.

Upon hearing Jehovah's name made audible, the evil azure demon jumped right out of the boy's lap and ran down the aisle of the Kingdom Hall screaming the word "shit" repeatedly until he reached the heavy doors of the main exit.

At this point, one would surmise that the Smurf either stood on a crate or asked an unassuming elder to let him out. Then he ran down the sidewalk and burst into flames.

As possessed dolls are wont to do, Beelze-Smurf trembled—nay, crumbled—before the powerful name of Jehovah. The tale of the plushy demon spread through Jehovah's Witness culture with memelike voracity. Soon, similar urban legends were popping up in Kingdom Halls from London to Los Angeles.

There were stories of how a child with Smurf bedsheets awoke one night to find silk-screened characters jumping off his comforter and running around the bedroom. Smurf dolls followed children around stores, giggled demoniacally, trying to trip them down the stairs, or drown them in swimming pools. One story involved a plush doll attempting to smother a toddler while she slept, a Satanic ritual now more commonly referred to as sudden infant death syndrome.

This was a cross-cultural, pervasive meme with no known origin. Smurf lore had spread across the ocean like the Spanish influenza.

Who knows, maybe Michelle and I started it all.

The exact type of Smurf, sadly, was never revealed. It's only right to believe that a Brainy Smurf would cause less damage than, say, a Papa Smurf, while the wake of destruction left by a Smurfette or a Hefty could be an irreversible bloodbath. Instead, our demon Smurf was a nameless Smurf, lacking any special skill such as doctoring or bringing plagues upon all mankind.

Across the board, Smurfs were a well-known portal to the demon realm. Parents knew it; elders knew it. It was mentioned from the stage and in public comments during the *Watchtower* Study, often in the same breath as Michael Jackson's "Thriller" video. It proved the point that Satan was treacherous and vile, like a serpent. He would stop at nothing to turn us away from Jehovah, even targeting unsuspecting children.

Smurfs, it seemed, were decidedly un-Smurfy. Never once did I dare to Smurf a Smurf or Smurf a ride to Smurftown. I made it through the entire '80s without *once* owning a single item with a Smurf on it. And for my self-sacrifice in this matter, Jehovah found me totally Smurftastic.

There were other objects that, while they wouldn't necessarily jump off your lap and yell "Oh, shit," could still never be brought into the house. Christian crosses, holiday-themed school projects, and anything that reeked of patriotism, such as American flags set atop an ice cream sundae, were all disallowed. Jehovah's Witnesses are politically neutral, as we were told that the only government worth advancing was the Kingdom of God. Our frozen desserts would play no part in any political coup.

Godliness was not limited to desserts; it also permeated the most important meal of the day, breakfast. None of the families I knew would purchase any cereals from the Count Chocula slash Boo Berry or Lucky Charms product line. Once, my mother even made a dubious decision to avoid any likeness of the Cookie Crisp "Cookie Crook," which to this day I still maintain was a doctrinal error in judgment. After all, didn't Jesus eat with sinners and tax collectors? What about cartoon mascots?

Still, it was better to be safe than sorry. Once demons infested your house like termites, all bets were off. At the Kingdom Hall, we learned how demons would turn your clocks back to make you miss all the meetings. They'd hide your *Watchtowers*, push you into walls, give you laryngitis before your Bible study. Or they'd paralyze you in your bed and rape you. Because there's nothing like a cheerful "raped by a demon" story with which to put a young girl to bed with at night.

Soon Jehovah would win his Great War and we would no longer have to worry about demons hurting us. But until that day, like The Warriors trying to get to Coney Island, we had to dodge gangs of demons on roller skates and make it home unscathed.

When it rained, I prayed. In addition to flooding our basement, every storm brought the possibility of Armageddon. I sat at my window and waited for the ground to fissure. Was the end of all time brewin' up or was it just a sun shower? Would I need a raincoat or a bomb shelter?

"Mom, is this Armageddon?" I'd ask.

"I don't know," Mom would answer diplomatically. "It's probably just a storm. But you never know."

The best way to get possessed by Satan was to pull your car off to the side of the road, walk up a stranger's driveway, and buy something at his yard sale. The devil was lurking in every creepy antique book and every doll with broken glass eyes. It seemed all evil spirits did in their spare time was hang out in people's cedar chests finding old photos and backward-masked tapes to jump into. You just didn't know what kind of hobbies worldly people were into.

For example, after my grandfather's funeral, my mother's side of the family sat down to dinner at a quaint inn outside Westerly, Rhode Island. Upon paying the bill, we were horrified to read a sign noting that they had a weekly tarot card reading in the attic. My mother said it was such a shame, because the food had been excellent, but of course, we could never go back. She shredded their business card and we threw out our leftovers.

So when my mother's friend gave me a fabulous leather box filled with grown-up antique junk jewelry, it's not surprising that it ended up in the trash before the week was out.

The demons started in the basement. Strange tapping noises, whispered canticles, black shadowy entities moving across the canned goods. Finally, they entered our kitchen, where my parents fought as heavy and nonstop as a 1950s dance contest. For a week, I was completely oblivious.

While I excitedly played dress-up with my gaudy new rings, Satan misplaced my father's keys. When Michelle and I innocently traded flowery clip-on earrings, the demons shook the basement, shut off the heat, made the clocks run slower. I played; my parents fought.

"Something is in this house," Dad told me. "Something is making your mother and I fight. It's that witch jewelry from that possessed friend of hers."

The possessed friend was Lynne, who owned an antique jewelry store called Busy Bee Antiques. I liked the store, quite simply, because there was a cartoon bee on her sign. However, evil lurked in the heart of that bee. Lynne had acquired and resold antique costume jewelry in the shape of strange, possibly pagan, crosses. Some of her gemstones shimmered so strangely that my father knew the only explanation was that they had once been owned by a witch.

"Go away, Satan," I said to the box of jewelry, because this is what we were told to do when something in our house was possessed—tell the devil to check hisself before he wrecks hisself.

According to Dad, the majority of antique jewelry in this world was previously owned by witches. Witches who were also, most likely, lesbians.

For example, it was well known that witches had turned two young Pioneer sisters into lesbians. We heard about this during a Sunday sermon, so this was serious stuff. They shared an attic apartment together and furnished it with a rocking chair they'd purchased at a local yard sale. Immediately, they began a torrid love affair.

Naturally, the Pioneer sisters didn't feel comfortable going in service after servicing each other. A group of concerned elders paid them a visit of encouragement and what they found upon arrival were two women locked in a sinful, lesbianic embrace.

The fallen Pioneers tearfully confessed their horrible mistake, then cried and prayed with the elders until one of them noticed a strange rocking chair.

"Where did you get that chair?" an elder asked, as it no doubt creaked and rolled on its own across the apartment floor.

The sisters explained that they'd bought it at a yard sale down the street. Why, they had been merely trying to decorate their apartment, and the chair had seemed very attractive.

"Down the street? At 666 Ravenswood Lane?"

"Why yes, that's the home where we purchased our chair. But—"

"But nothing!" gasped the elders. "That is the home of a well-known local witch!"

Immediately, the group set to cutting the rocking chair into pieces and burning it. After many prayers and false starts, the wood finally began to burn. In the flames could be heard the screaming of demons. And once the screaming stopped, the women, by the glory of Jehovah God and his Holy Spirit, had become heterosexual once more.

So my father hated yard sales.

I didn't cry when Dad took my box of possessed jewelry away. I wanted to do the right thing but wished it didn't have to be like this. We had to "get those witch trinkets out of the house," Dad said. Couldn't the beautiful baubles be brand-new? Why couldn't Lynne have given me something that wasn't possessed? Satan had to ruin all my fun.

I was glad that Satan was banished, because it meant my parents would stop fighting. I could always get new jewelry.

If someone asked, I told them *Fantasia* was my favorite movie. Since it was about magic, I'd never actually seen it, but I knew it was a classic. For one thing, it was beloved by my spinster great-aunts. The aunts were very particular, educated ladies, so I constantly sought to impress them with my knowledge of old-fashioned entertainment like Shirley Temple and the Dionne Quintuplets. We discussed only wholesome, quality films. Anything indecent (Benny Hill) or violent (Godzilla movies) or black (Bill Cosby) was better left unmentioned where Ruth and Margaret were concerned.

The aunts and I spent many an hour discussing how the cartooning in *Fantasia* was "so ahead of its time" and the music was "really very classical. For the longhair set." The movie was groundbreaking, and this is why my mother purchased a recording of Mussorgsky's *Night on Bald Mountain*. It quickly became one of our favorite albums, right up there with this record about flying kites that we bought with proofs of purchase from a box of Dixie cups. Mom even made a tape of *Night on Bald Mountain* so we could "save the record" and play the song on the boom box instead. It follows, then, that when I found her breaking it with a hammer, I was perplexed.

Mom was crouched on the kitchen floor. The album sleeve sat next to her on the floor, ripped in two. The paper bag she was hitting with a hammer was making a disturbingly loud crunch and creating small dents in the soft linoleum. With each blow, she repeated the word "Jehovah" like a mantra under her breath.

"Mom?" I asked. "Whatchya doin'?"

"Jehovah. Jehovah God. Jehovah our God," she repeated, and with one final pound, she stood and shook her head.

"I found out from Betty that this song is demonic, okay? It has to do with a fight between demons. It's night on Bald Mountain, okay? *Night*. Demons love the darkness."

"Oh, no!" I cried. "Do you think . . . Mommy, do you think our house is possessed by demons?"

"I sure hope not, sweetie," Mom said, as if to console both of us simultaneously. "Hopefully, this has taken care of it. We'll just have to pray and wait and see."

For the rest of the week, I walked around on a constant internal prayer-loop, begging Jehovah to save me from classical music. I lay in bed, wiggling my toes, making sure I hadn't been paralyzed by a demon. Whenever the steam-fed radiator clanked, I'd dive under a table and assume the "duck and cover" position.

"We had a demonic record," I bragged to the other kids at the Kingdom Hall.

"Was there backward masking on it? Like 'Stairway to Heaven'?" my friend Caesar asked.

"Probably," I said. That would be more impressive.

" 'Stairway to Heaven,' " Caesar said, "is a really bad song."

"Yeah," I agreed. "It's totally got Satanic words on it if you play it backward."

"It's not as bad as 'Eye of the Tiger,' though."

I pretended I knew the song he was referring to so I could seem cool.

"Oh, yeah. 'Eye of the Tiger' is a really bad song. . . . What's it about again?"

"It's the worst one," he said. "Trust me. Don't ever listen to it."

If I had to quote one scripture that was drilled into our brains from childbirth, it would be 1 Corinthians 15:33, which reads "Do not be misled. Bad associations spoil useful habits." It didn't matter what *kind* of person you were. People who were Jehovah's Witnesses were considered good associations, and that is where the criteria for friendship ended. The concept of "bad associations" did not discriminate on the basis of markers such as personal spirituality or morality. It discriminated solely on the basis of religion.

Sure, some people might *appear* to be nice on the outside. They might do community work, or even *claim* to be Christian. But Satan used them as an opportunity to lead Jehovah's Witnesses astray. Eventually, worldly people might ask you to attend their church or go to a bisexual disco. Sin lurked in their hearts.

Mother Teresa, the Dalai Lama, and Elie Wiesel were all considered bad associations. Not only did they not worship Jehovah, but they were *activists*, which meant they didn't trust in God to make changes on this earth and felt the need to take matters into their own hands. They were turning people away from Jehovah.

My father said this is probably why John Lennon was shot, because God knew he was too close to bringing peace to the whole world.

The point was, if someone wasn't a Jehovah's Witnesses, he was going to die at Armageddon, and there was no point in befriending the condemned.

Thankfully, my parents weren't the best Jehovah's Witnesses. Not that we were lapsed Christians by any stretch. We attended the Kingdom Hall and hated the things it was most important to hate: holidays, patriotism, blood transfusions, and Catholics. But being disciplined is not necessarily a prerequisite for being a fundamentalist, and it's not easy being perfect when you have two preteens and hold down a full-time job. The best you can do is aim for an immaculate and unparalleled existence, and then berate both yourself and your children when you fall short of this goal.

So we watched the *Charlie Brown Christmas* special, but changed the channel when they sang "O Christmas Tree" at the end. We ate the turkey my father got free from his job, but never once uttered the word "Thanksgiving." And my Jehovah's Witness friends didn't know about Samantha, the worldly girl I befriended at school. Hanging out with worldly kids was just not done. "Bad associations spoil useful habits," we were told—end of story. But I couldn't see Samantha as a bad association. She wasn't a harlot or a Satanist or a heroin-smoking junkie—just a girl in my class who liked Tears for Fears, button candy, and making crank calls.

It takes a lot of malicious energy to stop your children from having friends, to look them in the eye and tell them you'd rather they sit in their bedroom alone instead of going to a pool party. My parents wanted to live forever in paradise, but they weren't sociopaths. Instead, I got a nudge, a wink, and the knowledge that my friendship with Samantha was wrong.

"Do you think Brother Pendlebury would let his children have worldly friends?" my mother would chide each time she dropped me off at Samantha's white ranch house.

"No," I said.

"You're right, he wouldn't. So be grateful that you're not Brother Pendlebury's daughter. If you were the daughter of an elder, you wouldn't even be seeing Samantha at all."

It wasn't like I was hanging out with a *lot* of worldly kids. Samantha was the sanctioned friend, but the others were still off-limits. Samantha was like a free HBO trial that the cable company forgot to shut off after a week. My parents reserved the right to terminate service without warning, so I had to enjoy her while she lasted.

Later, my brother would also make a worldly friend at school, a tall, shy boy named Dave. Aaron quickly became scarce around the house, sticking to Dave like a voluntarily conjoined twin. The younger brother who used to be my friend and playmate now existed only in theory. I found out about Dave when toys I knew my parents hadn't bought began appearing in his bedroom, like Transformers and video game cartridges that weren't benign like Super Mario/Duck Hunt. On the rare occasions when Aaron actually *was* home, he locked himself in his bedroom and sat in front of the Nintendo for hours. My mother ineffectually yelled about her lazy son while the theme from The Legend of Zelda emanated from beneath his door like toxic gas.

Mom found out about Dave while rifling through her absentee son's bedroom. In the underwear drawer, she found twelve-sided dice and a guidebook for the most insidious scheme ever perpetrated by the world's nerds.

"*Advanced* Dungeons and Dragons?" my mother screamed when my unsuspecting brother wandered up the stairs with a backpack full of borrowed Optimus Prime. "When did you get to *Advanced*?"

My mother then proceeded to shred a pile of character sheets into confetti while Aaron stood in the doorway to his bedroom, so in shock that someone should have offered him a foil blanket. After that, he pretty much disappeared from our home entirely.

I was more discreet with my own worldly friend. Samantha was not into live-action role-playing, and her Nintendo games were far more interesting than just running through a maze collecting bags of gold coins. If Samantha and I were feeling especially cheeky, we'd play Math Dragon, a single-screen game in which you stopped a fire-breathing dragon from destroying a pixelated city by solving basic multiplication problems. The message herein was clear. When you suck at math, innocent people die.

But this was all before the Ouija board.

I did not attend sinful birthday parties, so I had no idea that one of Samantha's sister's presents had been a Parker Brothers Ouija board. I first learned of it when her little sister yelled from the other room: "Wanna come play Ouijas?" and all time stopped for just one moment.

The Ouija, or "yes-yes," board is *the* foremost implement for allowing demons into your home. Now I was standing 20 feet from one. This was what I got for not listening to Jehovah, for trusting a *bad association*. It had only been a matter of time. This seemingly innocent girl who taught me how to save Math City from the Math Dragon had just brought the portal of hell onto her sunporch.

When I learned of the witch board on the dining room table, I immediately excused myself to use the bathroom.

"It's just a toy," Samantha said.

"I have to pee," I cried.

I locked the bathroom door so no demons could get in. In the other room, wallpaper was surely streaked with blood and tasteful oak end tables were caught in a swirling vortex above a pentagram made of wailing black cats. "Go away, Satan!" I prayed. I opened the door and ran home with wicked things at my heels.

At home, I immediately confided the incident to my mother, and she prayed with me right where we stood.

"You can't go back there," she told me. I was simultaneously devastated and relieved.

The fact that this was a cardboard game put out by Parker Brothers and purchased at Toys R Us was of no consequence. That's what made it so diabolical. Naturally, Satan wanted to make this conduit to Hades *seem* like a toy. In that way, he could trick people into thinking it was safe. Thankfully, Jehovah's Witnesses knew better.

There was only one solution. My mother told me that I had to write a letter (with the appropriate Bible verses and *Watchtowers* included) and inform Samantha and her family that I could no longer enter her home or be friends with her.

> Dear Samantha,
>
> As Jehovah's Witnesses, we are taught to resist unseen voices from the spirit realm. In Matthew 4:10, Jesus hears the voice of Satan and rejects it by saying, "Go away, Satan!" and this is what we should do when confronted with voices. We should not be curious! Christians have been instructed to condemn "anyone who employs divination or anyone who consults a spirit medium or a professional foreteller of events or anyone who inquires of the dead." While we are not condemning you and I will still see you at school, as Witnesses of Jehovah we cannot visit your house anymore. We have enclosed articles about resisting the spirit realm, which will teach you that "Satan himself keeps transforming himself into an angel of light."
>
> Love, Kyria

Several months later, Samantha's mother, Grace, ran into my mother at school. She said Samantha missed me. Their whole family, in fact, missed me. They would even throw the board away if it meant that much.

In a vacuum, my mother could forbid me from seeing Samantha. But with Grace pleading for the sake of both girls, she caved. Pretty soon, I was back at Samantha's, crank-calling strangers and asking if their refrigerator was running. Math City was safe from the Math Dragon once more.

CHAPTER 4

BFFs Are Never Enemies of God

Emily Fein had been my best Jehovah's Witness friend since the day I was born; she actually met me as a newborn while I was still in the hospital. Her mother, Betty, was best friends with my mother. The two women did everything together, bonding over the loveless marriages in which they were both trapped because the Jehovah's Witnesses do not approve of divorce. As much as they hated their husbands, neither woman wanted to risk losing it all by getting disfellowshipped.

Emily was everything I wanted to be. Even then, she had an air of quiet rebellion around her. She held her teething rattle to her mouth like a lit cigarette at recess. Meanwhile, I was swaddled in hospital-label fashion and had barely opened my eyes.

Emily owned dogs and petted them without screaming. She poured her own milk. I saw her as fearless. During weekends at the beach, she forced me to go into the ocean even after I had seen commercials for *Jaws* on television, even after I had watched a nature documentary about poisonous rocks in Australia that will kill you within 60 seconds of stepping on them. I pretended to be absolutely thrilled at the idea of bodysurfing in the freezing North Atlantic, until I was caught by an undertow and ended up facedown in two inches of sandy water, flapping my arms like Curly from the Three Stooges.

"Yayyy!" I yelled.

"Hooray!" Emily yelled.

Somewhere on the sand, inside our intricate ecosystem of straw mats and giant umbrellas, Emily's mother, Betty, watched us run down the sand and shook with terror. My mother took a photo of a sandwich.

"My mom gets scared when I go in. You know, because of *Michael*," Emily said.

People rarely mentioned Michael, the family secret. Before Emily and her sister were born, their mother had been barren. Betty adopted Michael, but the babysitter was just a teenager, some Jehovah's Witness girl from their congregation. She didn't understand how a boy might run off looking for something. While the babysitter was reading a book, Michael drowned in the reservoir across the street. The babysitter was a Jehovah's Witness, and I wondered how anyone in the Truth could be involved in the death of someone else's child.

At the Kingdom Hall, we were told stories about angels showing up and saving people's lives all the time. Once, a sister who was out in service called upon the home of a murderer and rapist. He stood and listened, even accepting a *Watchtower.* When later questioned by the police as to why he did not harm the woman, he answered, "Because of those two large men she had standing behind her, of course!" The woman had been alone. The men had been angels.

Why hadn't two angels stood behind Michael, each taking an arm, and stopped him from falling in?

When I told Emily that her mother looked upset, she dismissed the whole thing. "My mom totally overreacts," she said.

This was Emily, not caring about her mother's dead adopted

son, going ahead and diving into any ocean she damn well pleased. I pretended to be the same kind of diver.

My mother and Betty would drink coffee and discuss their loveless marriages while Emily and I picked buckets of sticky red berries off a backyard bush and took part in what we called a "poison fight." When Mom drove past the reservoir, I thought of adopted Michael, floating facedown, and the babysitter, with her feet up and a pulp novel in her hands.

"Michael died, but Jehovah blessed Betty by giving her Maya and Emily," my mother told me. "So now you have a best friend. And Michael will be back in the New System of Things."

"If Betty ever saw the babysitter again, would she scream at her and say, 'You killed my son!'?"

"No, Kyria. She sees her now and then," my mother explained, as if I really should know that people keep in touch with babysitters that let their children die. "Betty has forgiven her, because the girl was just a teenager when it happened."

This was the most horrible thing I'd ever heard in my entire life. More horrible, even, than the night I stayed up until 11:00 PM to watch *Of Mice and Men* even though my father told me not to. When I couldn't sleep and had to ask Dad why George would kill his best friend, my father's only response was, "I told you not to stay up and watch that movie."

This story was even worse than that, because Michael was real once, and "tell me about the rabbits," was only the eight-o'clock movie on Channel 38's *The Movie Loft with Dana Hersey*.

I promised myself that when I became a teenager and got an after-school job, I would never kill anyone's child, even if he was adopted.

Despite the fact that Emily and I had been best friends since the day I was born, I was never sure if she actually liked me. When I slept over at the Feins, I felt like a constant source of irritation.

I also felt constantly irritated, as I was severely allergic to their entire home. If I wasn't covered in hives from my severe mold, dust, and dander allergies, I was asking for an extra blanket or accidentally getting scratched by their Siamese cat.

"Mommm, get the peroxide! Come on, Kyria, can't you just leave that stupid cat alone?"

No, I could not leave that cat alone. It was a Siamese cat, the meanest of all the cats in the world! Therefore, I was inexplicably drawn to it. Like an inept Grizzly Adams, I wanted to tame it and win its heart. I did this by poking it and singing excerpts from *Lady and the Tramp*: "We are Siamese if you ple-ease/We are Siamese if you don't please."

Time and again, my singing failed to impress the coldhearted, velvet-haired, blue-eyed bitch they call Siamese.

Then my allergies kicked in. After a few hours in the Fein household, my entire face would inevitably swell and my eyelids would get so puffy that Emily, in one of our less PC childhood moments, took to calling me "Chinese Eyes." Swollen eyes, an angry cat who hates Disney, and my friend yelling racial epithets at me—now, this was a sleepover!

Still, when I heard Mom's leather-roofed Gran Torino crunching up the stone driveway, I fled outside without my shoes on and hid in the crab apple tree. I was only hiding so my mother would see how much I wanted to live here. I liked Emily's house better than mine, even if I needed an oxygen mask to sit in the living room, because I liked her mother better than mine. I craved the perceived leniency of the Fein family and wanted more of Emily's fearlessness.

At dusk, Emily's mom let us stand in the driveway to light sparklers. My mother wouldn't let me light matches on my own, let alone have fun immediately after doing so. Fire plus fun simply set a bad precedent. Even our stove had electric burners.

When we played with sparklers, I stood on the other side of

the driveway and Emily yelled to me, "Oh, come on! What's to be scared of? They're just sparklers!"

Just sparklers? That's like saying "Just a disastrous brush fire," or "Just a facial skin graft."

Emily and Maya chided me, until finally, with one sparkler left, I came forth. I closed my eyes and stretched my arm out so far it almost came out of the socket, while someone else struck a match. There was a sizzle, a pop, and only then did I discover what they had been telling me for half an hour: It was no big deal. I wouldn't get hurt. In fact, this was fun, and I should have tried it before all the sparklers were gone.

The only problem with visiting the Feins was that I didn't care for Emily's father, Terry. He was distant and uncomfortable, had rusty tin cans in his car, and he wasn't even a baptized Jehovah's Witness although he attended the Kingdom Hall. He slept in a separate bedroom that was cold and had screwdrivers on the dresser. Years later, he'd move into some family-owned property, but for now, Betty was setting a good example as a proper Jehovah's Witness wife. Instead of dishonoring the godly bonds of matrimony by divorcing him, she followed the congregation's instruction to practice humility and patience.

God, we said, *hates a divorcing.*

Those who divorced their mates just because they didn't love them anymore risked being disfellowshipped and shunned by their families and congregations. The only reason to divorce someone was if they had cheated on you.

Most of the sins that were actually sinful enough to get you cast out of your congregation involved drugs or unclean sexual behavior such as fornication, adultery, homosexuality, or owning a VHS tape called *Jo-Jo's Anal Vacation.* Disagreeing with official doctrine or printing your own Bible-based literature was also grounds for disfellowshipping, so printing my Armageddonthemed zine *Apoetry-geddon* was not a creative option for me.

Ultimately, *anything* could be a disfellowshipping offense if the sinner refused to repent. Sometimes, the elders were guided by the Holy Spirit to realize that the sinner wasn't even actually sorry, but was just lying to avoid being killed at Armageddon.

People weren't really disfellowshipped for what they *did* as much as for their *attitude* about what they'd done, which, in turn, could infect the congregation. Someone could be disfellowshipped for celebrating their birthday (which isn't a disfellowshipping offense in itself) if they decided to look the elders in the eye and say they thought the organization was wrong about birthdays.

Punishment was not only up to a committee of elders from your congregation. It was made a matter of prayer and guided by Jehovah, the one who can see what is truly in your heart. This meant that there was always a chance that the sinner could be forgiven. If repentant, you might receive only a "public reprimand," which was an embarrassing, vague announcement made at the Kingdom Hall such as, "Brother We-All-Know-Likes-Whiskey-Too-Much has been publicly reprimanded in accordance with God's laws on proper conduct. And now, let us turn to song 306, *Have Intense Love for One Another*." It was then a matter of conscience within the congregation to decide if you were a good association or not. If your aunt suddenly stopped bringing you fresh tomatoes from her garden on Sunday, you knew why.

I personally only knew of one case in which something like this had happened. It was with an engaged couple in my congregation who had both been recently baptized. As their wedding date drew closer, the couple made the mistake of being alone together and were tempted into committing fornication. However, they were smart enough to call the elders and confess what had happened. The elders told them to cancel their upcoming wedding, go to City Hall, and elope immediately. At the next meeting, the couple appeared as man and wife, and then they were both publicly reprimanded in front of the congregation.

My father said he figured they got off easy because they hadn't been raised as Jehovah's Witnesses, but converted as adults. Since they'd both had sex in the past, they were unfortunate enough to know what they were missing. And now that they were married, they were safe from temptation.

"Sometimes, a couple gets to a point where it's unsafe to do anything but go and get married already," my dad said. "Just get it out of the way and get down to business!"

We believed that God's laws for marriage were solid. In the Kingdom Hall, we heard encouraging experiences of true Christians who respected the marriage bonds even in the face of abuse from an unbelieving spouse. Their actions eventually caused the unbeliever to wonder what gave Jehovah's Witnesses such inner strength. These stories usually ended with the abusive unbeliever getting baptized.

If Betty stayed, eventually Terry would be filled with the Holy Spirit. He would throw away his rusty tin cans and smile. Until that day, Betty could always kvetch about him to my mother.

I didn't dislike Terry just because Betty wanted him to clean the garage. He had always made me uncomfortable.

Back when I was four years old, Terry had offered to take Emily and me to the circus. But my mother answered our front door to find that our chaperone was standing there alone. Emily might have been sick—Terry was a bit vague about it. My mother said only, "Oh."

I heard my mother saying, "Oh," over and over again, as I tried to be a big girl and hide my disappointment that Emily was sick.

"Do you still want to go to the circus?" Mom asked me, holding the screen door open so I could peer out.

"Yeah!" I tried to act excited, so as not to embarrass my mother by bursting into tears and being rude.

Besides, Terry was a Jehovah's Witness, so he was like family. My mother waved goodbye from the porch as Terry belted me into his chemical-smelling green car.

We drove in silence, save for the sound of a plastic-handled screwdriver rolling out from under the seat and hitting a tin can at every stoplight. I wasn't used to silence. Usually I got compliments, like "What a pretty dress," or "What do you want to be when you grow up?" I guessed that Terry was shy.

"This is really great," I said. "Are you shy? Do you like the circus? I'm so excited because I love animals and also I've never been to the circus before."

Having never been to a circus, I wasn't sure what to expect. For example, I didn't know that once we sat down, I would break out in full-body hives as if I'd just had a pollen facial. Between the lions, the ponies, and the air thick with hay, it took about 14 seconds before I couldn't breathe and my eyes swelled like a prizefighter's. I pulled out a ziplock bag filled with tissues and began systematically filling them with snot. Despite my body's rocketing histamine levels and the fact that Terry had not spoken more than four words to me since we'd left my house, I was having a good time. There was, after all, a real clown.

I was never the kind of kid that was frightened by clowns. I was more pragmatic—I was frightened by volcanoes. As I saw it, clowns were attempting to entertain, while volcanoes sought only to mortally wound.

"Ah'm sowwy, buh Ah tink . . ." I paused to blow a giant ball of mucus into sandpapery store-brand tissue. "Ah tink Ah haffa weave. Is mah awwergies."

Terry wordlessly got up from his seat. I thought he might be angry because he couldn't finish watching the circus now, and it was all my fault. I had ruined the circus for Terry. I apologized, but he didn't respond. I apologized again.

We made our way to the parking lot. The lion-free air cleared my nose, and my eyes slowly began to deflate. We got into the car and Terry started the engine, but we didn't go anywhere. He was clearly upset with me. I needed to explain. I was the kid with allergies.

"My mom always says I'll grow out of my allergies and I hope so because also I'm allergic to cats a lot but I can't have oranges or tomatoes or I break out in hives because of the acid but spaghetti sauce is my favorite sauce so I hate getting hives but sometimes I eat it anyway because it's my favorite, you know, what is your favorite animal or kind of spaghetti?"

Terry put the car in reverse but only drove across the lot and parked again. I was certain I was going to get a spanking.

Terry looked straight ahead, while his hand landed on my thigh—a position I immediately decided I did not like. I felt that I was in trouble. I looked out the window at the reflection in the rearview mirror. I liked mirrors, I thought. Then I started to cry.

Although I was not a "brat," I had a hard time keeping my discomfort inside. I didn't want to be a bad kid, and knew that my mother would not allow temper tantrums in public. Still, I let loose a loud, very loud, wail.

Terry told me to stop crying. He took his hand away and told me to stop crying again. I was really going at it now, really puking up the tears, making a scene. Terry was mad at me, yelling. *Stop crying!* He finally started the car and slammed into reverse so fast that I had to hang on to the door handle or I would have rolled around just like the loose screwdriver.

I stopped crying when he began to drive away, but it hadn't been soon enough. The damage was done. My nose was running and Terry wouldn't even speak to me. He was driving away fast. I had been unable to stop crying just like I had been unable to stop sneezing. I had ruined *everything*.

Finally, Terry spoke. He told me not to say anything to anyone. I was so relieved that he finally talked to me. Now I could redeem myself for crying and being allergic to lions' manes.

We drove home in silence, and when Terry dropped me off,

I gave him a big hug and apologized for my allergies. He was distant and I got the feeling he didn't really like me. He'd been looking straight ahead the whole time.

Over the next few years, I began to realize that it wasn't only me who felt uncomfortable around Terry. Emily, Betty, and my mother all seemed to agree. He completely stopped going to the Kingdom Hall. Still, the elders felt this was not adequate grounds for divorce.

Unfortunately for Betty, until God's Holy Spirit moved the elders to change their minds, there was nothing that could be done.

CHAPTER 5

Cross Your Legs, for the Son of Man

Is Approaching!

Annabelle Gonsalves was in love with the Karate Kid, Ralph Macchio, and I was in love with blond heartthrob Ricky Schroder. We had detailed plans for our marriages. I was certain that Anna and Ralph would consummate their relationship first. She had curly hair, which was certain to attract more *Tiger Beat* centerfolds. In addition to her perfectly round ringlets, she had also been allowed to get her ears pierced before me. Surely, no man could ever love a woman whose mom wouldn't let her have pierced ears.

"I'm going to marry Ricky Schroder," I announced at the kitchen table one night, earlobes fully intact.

"He doesn't seem like a very nice boy," my mother said.

"Yeah, well. You just watch yourself now," Dad added.

My parents took my announcement so seriously that I began to wonder if perhaps Ricky Schroder had been calling the house. Was this real? Could the *Silver Spoons* mansion actually become my future summer home?

"Well, I think he's cute and I'm in love with him!" I said defensively.

"He's worldly, Kyria," my father said. "Do you want to end up with a worldly boy?"

"Maybe I could study with him and make him a Witness," I offered.

"Then you can think about marrying him *after* he gets baptized," Mom said, and scraped my dinner plate into the trash.

This is how it worked. Jehovah's Witnesses fell in love with other Jehovah's Witnesses and dated only as preparation for marriage. Eleven-year-olds couldn't get married and therefore didn't need to have crushes. Especially not on worldly boys with a roomful of violent arcade games.

I wasn't allowed to have any pop culture pictures or posters, so I couldn't secretly swoon over Ricky. Movie stars were considered false idols and hanging a poster of one would be idol worship. To profess our adoration for Kirk Cameron of *Growing Pains* was like the Israelites worshipping Ba'al and melting their jewelry to make golden calves. In their stead, my bedroom was covered in posters I'd gotten free from school book clubs—that is, a lot of rainbow-colored hot-air balloon races that said *Scholastic Reader* in the corner. These hung atop my nursery wallpaper, a series of crude rainbows and primary-colored block-shaped houses, along with a single wall of green and yellow vertical stripes. All I needed was a pit of plastic balls and my room would have been indistinguishable from a Gymboree.

I'd never owned a *Tiger Beat*, a *Teen Beat*, a *Bop*, or even a *Seventeen*. Portraits of 13-year-old boys with mullets were sinful and pagan, not to mention pornographic. My wallpaper was devoid of push-pinned Scott Baios and instead crammed with taped-up kittens. I would not allow myself to be a worshipper of Ba'al, even if Ba'al were wearing colorful suspenders and parachute pants.

Some Jehovah's Witness kids I knew weren't allowed to hang

any posters at all, which seemed extreme even for us. Surely, God couldn't think we were worshipping cats dangling from branches or horses nuzzling each other. I would have loved a unicorn or two, but those were magical demons. Just in case God was peevish, I tried not to overdo it with the decorating.

My walls were filled with idyllic mountain scenes that were more suited to the ceiling of a dentist's office than the walls of a preteen girl. I sublimated my nearly sexual desires under a few tasteful posters of dogs in bonnets taped strategically to the closet door. My secret crush on oh-so-blond Ricky Schroder remained hidden away in an unowned copy of *Bop* magazine, and my blooming sexuality was replaced by a rosy-cheeked urchin who proclaimed, "I know I'm somebody cuz God don't make no junk!"

Unfortunately for my parents, one of my favorite hobbies has always been masturbating. I was sharing intimate moments with my yellow beanbag as early as age seven, even before I knew that kissing isn't actually sex.

The first time I partook of carnal beanbagging, I was in the living room watching *Spider-Man*. I don't remember if it was the short-lived live-action series or the "catches thieves just like flies" cartoon series. All I know is one minute I was sitting on my beanbag and the next I felt like a woman. And *Spider-Man* suddenly became my favorite show.

Since I was an early bloomer, my parents hadn't sat me down to discuss the birds and the beanbags yet. I had not learned that sexual urges are evil and should be repressed, not fulfilled. As such, I left the door wide open at all times. My mother found me masturbating on my Raggedy Ann and Andy pillow as breezily as if I were having a teddy bear tea party. Mom immediately took action, driving a pressurized rush of shame into my lungs like CPR.

"What are you doing? What are you doing?" she screamed, grabbing my shoulders and pulling me off Raggedy Ann.

"I don't know," I said, because I had no idea what I was doing. Actually, I was hoping that maybe she could tell me, because it was kind of awesome.

"Kyria, this is dirty and not something Jehovah approves of."

I was doing something wrong? Jehovah disapproves of pillows?

"This is masturbating, Kyria," Mom explained. "This is a sin. It's filthy. Let's pray to Jehovah God for forgiveness."

Filthy. I was filthy. I thought I was just playing, and it turns out I'd been shitting on the kitchen table.

Mom grabbed both my hands in both of hers. We bowed our heads and she told Jehovah what I'd done. She told him I was sorry. She asked him to forgive me. I said, "Amen." I was crying.

"Don't cry, sweetie," Mom said. "We've prayed for forgiveness now and what's done is done."

I was forgiven. I would not die at Armageddon and God still loved me. The next time I masturbated on Raggedy Ann, I closed the door and ended with a prayer.

It took about two weeks for my mother to once again catch me in the throes of beanbaggery. Not that I hadn't been trying to hide it from her, but a seven-year-old can lie about as effectively as a seven-year-old can comprehend realpolitik. I was hardly a savvy con artist—when I was three years old, I was caught stealing a piece of licorice candy from Vic's Fruit Stand. I hid in the bathroom in order to consume my bounty and, several minutes later, approached my mother with a sticky black circle of guilt around my mouth.

This time, Mom caught me by noticing it was quiet in my bedroom and opening the door. I was splayed across my canopy bed, fully clothed, humping a gold satin comforter that had once belonged to my grandmother. My mother let out a Chihuahua-like yelp.

"Kyria, this is wrong. People don't do this. Do you think Jennifer across the street does this?" Mom asked me, sitting on the edge of my bed.

"I don't know. I bet she does."

"I bet she doesn't, Kyria. Why don't you ask her? She'll say that she doesn't. People don't do this dirty, filthy thing."

I saw Jennifer the next day. She had freckles and red hair and lived across the street. Was this the face of filth?

"Do you ever rub your vagina on a pillow?" I asked.

"What?" Jennifer looked upset and decidedly non-carnal.

"You know, so it feels funny," I said, surprised that I had to explain.

"No. Why would I do that?"

"I don't know. My mom told me to ask you."

Jennifer looked at me in a way that said I'm never sleeping over again, and I knew that my mother had been right. I was the only one in the world who masturbated.

At least Mom would be happy when I told her that I had done as she asked, and she'd been right. But when I reported my findings, her eyes got huge and angry.

"You actually asked her that? You actually said that?"

"But you told me to ask!"

"I didn't tell you to ask!" my mother said, backtracking. "I asked if you *think* she rubs herself on a pillow. Then I said Jennifer *doesn't* rub herself on a pillow like you do!"

Mom took me into the kitchen. Apparently, we had to have a "talk" about something, like I had to apologize to Jennifer. Mom pulled out a Bible and explained to me that when a man and a woman want to have a baby, the man gets *effected*. His penis comes out. Or, it comes up. Wait. The man's penis, I heard her say, comes *off* inside the woman.

"So it stays inside the woman?"

"Yes, it stays inside the woman."

"For how long?"

"Until the woman is pregnant."

"But it *stays inside*?"

"Yes. The man puts it in the vagina and it stays inside the vagina."

"But how?"

"It just does."

"But *how*?"

"Kyria! It stays inside the woman's vagina!"

So the man's penis falls off inside the woman and stays there forever. I had to admit, I was surprised. It was decidedly un-beanbag-like.

"So, you can only have sex once?" I asked, searching for clarity.

"What? You can have sex as many times as you want, Kyria!"

Now I was "exacerbating the situation." This is what Mom called it when I got like this.

"And sometimes"—Mom opened her Bible—"a man tries to have sex with another man. He puts his penis in the other man's anus."

What? *What?*

"These are called homosexuals. Now, Jehovah does not approve of these men. These are sodomites, just like the men in Sodom and Gomorrah. God destroyed that city, and he is going to destroy these homosexuals at Armageddon.

I had begun to cry. Weep, even. A penis was something that my dad peed with and hid under a towel after he took a bath. Now I was finding out that it came off inside your vagina and even went inside another man's bum. Mom got up from the table and went into the cabinet where we kept the vitamins. She came back with half a tablet of Actifed Cold Remedy and a glass of grape juice. How could the man's penis come off inside the woman? How could he pee? And besides, my dad still had one! I swallowed the tablet and within 15 minutes, was fast asleep.

CHAPTER 6

Educating Ourselves to Graduate from Jehovah!

About a week before the start of each elementary school year, my mother would schedule a one-on-one introductory meeting with my new teachers, for which we'd go to JCPenney to purchase gifts. For example, in the sixth grade, Mrs. Cheverie received a pink faux-snakeskin snap-front lipstick case, while Mr. McGibbons, the wacky math and history teacher who wore red bow ties and green plaid pants, got a set of multicolored handkerchiefs.

With our gift-wrapped altruism in tow, we made our way through the empty hallways of Nathanael Greene Elementary to find the only classroom with lights on. We sat in small pastel chairs in front of a desk filled with various paperweights proclaiming this teacher to be the "World's Best." While I stared down a smiling, myopic worm extruding from a wooden apple, Mom informed Mrs. Cheverie that she was blessed to have an eager and intelligent Jehovah's Witness in her class this year.

On cue, I held up a handful of magazines with pictures of reverent Jehovah's Witness kids on the cover. They had headlines like "Should True Christians Salute the Flag?" or "Halloween: Is It for True Christians?" or "How Should True Christians Feel About Christmas?"

Ms. Cheverie smiled and blinked. She was clearly not responding well to my exceedingly special needs.

"I'm Christian too," she said. "I would never have the children do something that is inappropriate."

My mother explained that we were not *just* Christian, we were Jehovah's Witnesses. So I would not celebrate birthdays, create any holiday-themed art projects, salute the flag, or participate in extracurricular activities such as cheerleading. Unlike all the other students in the school, I was special.

In short, the rest of my class was going to die at Armageddon. I was going to live forever, as long as I refrained from singing the national anthem or drawing a turkey from the outline of my hand. As such, the teachers would need to create a separate curriculum entirely for me. It was very nice to meet them and would they please accept this faux-snakeskin lipstick case in exchange for their trouble?

We thanked our teachers sincerely for their time, pretended they weren't scowling at us, bowed our heads in prayer, and left a stack of *Watchtowers* on their table.

Although the teachers complied with our request, no one said my replacement assignments had to be very interesting. When a teacher handed out red paper and cotton balls to create a festive Santa display, I was given a pencil and told to draw a "winter scene." During the Thanksgiving play, I stayed in the classroom and read a large-print book meant for adult ESL students. It was about contaminated water that dissolved everything it touched, turning that thing into contaminated water, and creating an unstoppable, rolling apocalypse. I wouldn't use a faucet for months.

Students hated me. Teachers hated me. Student-teachers hated me. Even the janitor averted his eyes and looked at a bucket of sawdust whenever I walked by.

The final holdout was Mr. Panzini, the ████████████
vored my sweet clarinet-playing skills, unti███████████
play "Hot Cross Buns" because it was abo███████████
that, I was on my own.

During the Pledge of Allegiance, I sat with my ██
I ignored all sneeze-inspired *God-bless-you*'s and never wisheu
anyone a happy birthday. I *begged* to clean the chalkboard. I said
things like, "This book is too easy. Can I have a harder one?"

I was, as is the vernacular, a stuck-up little bitch. After all, you
can't get much more stuck-up than thinking everyone else in a
room is going to die except for you, unless you hold a private
meeting with your teacher to inform her of this.

In the fourth grade, I became a genius on Tuesdays. The decree came down in the form of a mysterious envelope my teacher
told me to give to my parents. The fact that my teacher entrusted
me to deliver the envelope unharmed should have been a bright,
flashing neon sign that read "Loser—Open 24 Hours." On my
own, I would never have thought, even for a moment, of opening this letter. But my hyper after-school companion Michelle
did not take kindly to such directions. Her mother, Sister Jordan,
babysat me after school so there would be another child to dis-
tract her whirligig of a daughter running backward into walls.

"Kyriaaaa! Just open it, puhhhleeeeease!" Michelle screamed,
crawling on her belly across her mother's Pledge-slick dining
room table.

"I can't! I'm not supposed to!"

"You got into the *gifteds*. I just know you did!"

"What's gifted?" I asked. The faint sound of motherly foot-
steps approached from the kitchen and I hadn't much time.
"What does gifteds mean?"

With *Mission: Impossible*–type grace, Michelle slid across the
slippery table and snatched the envelope right out of my hand.
"It's gifteds!" she screamed, tearing the envelope open, and running in circles around the table while reading it.

The letter announced that I had been accepted into the Paw-tucket, Rhode Island, Gifted Program, and would henceforth be bussed to another school every Tuesday so I could learn about harder things with smarter kids.

"I knew it! It's not fair!" Michelle yelled, and began jumping up and down and sobbing hysterically.

Mrs. Jordon ran from the kitchen and pulled her daughter's head into her apron.

"Your parents are not going to be very pleased with you when I tell them what you did today," she sneered, waving the ripped letter at me. "Rubbing your *gifted-class* letter in Michelle's face like this."

Then she leaned down and whispered to Michelle, "You'd better stop crying this instant or you're gonna get a beatin'."

The following Tuesday, I was bussed to a different school on the other side of town. We "gifteds" were relegated to a basement classroom with concrete walls and exposed pipes, hidden away from the rest of the students.

For my very first assignment, I sat in front of a green-screen monitor with a blinking cursor called a "turtle" in the center. I was told that if I typed in LEFT the turtle would move to the left. If I typed FORWARD the turtle would move forward. This was called Logo, and it was just a small taste of what it meant to be a total genius.

I was then given a mimeographed sheet of paper so smudged with purple ink that it looked like it had been illustrated by Ralph Steadman. The page contained a series of inexplicable dots and scribbles called "Bips" and "Bops," which were supposed to be placed in the correct "corral" or something. I had no idea what was going on. On the other side of the room, a boy was making a turtle turn right. I drew cat faces on all the scribbles and cried a little.

For several weeks after I became a genius, Michelle refused to speak to me. Eventually her entire family moved to New Hampshire, and I'm pretty sure the move was partially incited by my intimidating knowledge of Logo.

Halloween was the one holiday all fundamentalists, not just Jehovah's Witnesses, could agree to despise. This was a pagan Oscar Night, Satan and his wicked spirits parading up and down the red carpet sidewalk. It was *disgusting*.

"Right out in the open," Mom would say. "Just flaunting his demonic Hell Night in our faces!"

On Halloween, you could look out your window and see a long line of "little devil worshippers," with their open invitation for Satan to take control of their minds.

Since we didn't answer the door or give out candy, there was the distinct possibility of getting our windows soaped or the porch toilet-papered. After a group of kids egged our Kingdom Hall one year, an overnight watch team was formed. My father was among those brothers who were privileged enough to bring a thermos of black coffee and sit on the steps in front of a space heater hooked to an extension cord until the sun rose.

Normally, we turned off all our downstairs lights and closed the drapes. The television stayed off, so the trick-or-treaters wouldn't see any blue flashes.

One year, however, the porch light was left on.

Aaron and I went upstairs and stood on the radiator, as usual. We hoisted the window screen open and hung ourselves halfway out the window.

Craning our necks to see over the gutters, we watched the neighbor kids systematically working their way from home to home, swinging flashlights and plastic pumpkins.

"Look! Batman!" Aaron would squeal.

"That's bad Mike from down the block," I'd say. "I bet he'll throw eggs."

"Who's he supposed to be?"

"He's Jason."

"Who's that?"

"From *Friday the 13th,* duh!" I was switching from foot to foot because the radiator was hot.

"Oh, that's demonic!"

"So what, dork?"

"I'm no dork. You're a dork!"

Then something completely unexpected happened. The doorbell rang and our mother called us downstairs.

"Kyria and Aaron! We have trick-or-treaters!"

My heart raced. Were we actually handing out candy this year? Maybe Jehovah had changed his mind and his Witnesses were going to celebrate Halloween from now on! I imagined all the costumes I could wear if this were so. In order to make up for lost time, I'd have to create some kind of uber-costume, like a Strawberry Shortcake princess singing the theme to *Jem and the Holograms* on *The Muppet Show*.

Aaron and I flew down the steps to the living room. Mom handed each of us a *Watchtower* with the perfect tube of an *Awake!* magazine rolled inside it. She opened the front door, revealing our front porch filled with masks and sheets and wrinkled paper bags.

Mom opened the door and put her hands on her hips.

"Well, kids, I am sorry to say that you will not find any sugary candy here tonight!" she said, "However, you will find something much more valuable, and that's *spiritual* food!"

ET took a small step back. Darth Vader cocked his helmet to the side. My fantasy of becoming Jem-Shortcake-Cinderella dissipated. I still wanted to be in costume, but now only because it would allow me to hide my face.

"Here is an *Awake!* and a *Watchtower* magazine, which will tell you the origins of Halloween," Mom said. "Even though we like dressing up and eating candy just like you do, we do not do it on All Saints' Day, which is a pagan ritual."

My brother and I handed them their tubes of salvation. These were neighborhood kids. We knew them when they put "Kick Me," signs on our backs and pushed us at recess. Some of them were juvenile delinquents, kids that got into fights. But in the presence of this adult, and the baffling lack of candy, they were subdued.

The following morning we found the *Watchtowers*, ripped to shreds and scattered all over the front lawn like the lining of a gerbil cage. Some of them hadn't even been unrolled—the tubes had just been jammed through the diamond links of our silver metal fence. The house had a few eggs on it too. Mom came out with the garden hose and they washed off easily.

My worldly friend Samantha moved to a private school, where she wore a blue uniform with a crest that said "Bay Bridge Academy." The few relationships that I managed to keep during school hours were now tenuous at best. At recess, I'd stand underneath the bleachers with a Mormon girl I knew only as BJ and play with my shoelaces while she made fun of me. Sometimes we were joined by Hannah, a silent, anorexically thin girl with blond eyebrows and a shock of white hair whose mother and father eerily looked like twins, and whose three identical brothers all seemed a little retarded. Years earlier, Hannah and I had bonded over having the same Stride Rite–brand shoes with a lion stamped into the rubber sole. For the most part, though, I kept my distance. I was wary of more Ouija boards, more breakup letters.

The day the class returned from Christmas vacation, BJ and Hannah joined forces to confront me about my distinct lack of holiday cheer. The school seemed pregnant with new toys, weighted down by the bounty of recently unwrapped Teddy Ruxpins, Rubik's Snakes, and red leather Michael Jackson jackets.

"Don't you mind not having Christmas?" BJ asked, kicking up her legs to reveal a pair of brand-new Velcro high-tops.

"Christmas is a pagan holiday based on sun worship, not the birth of Jesus," I answered.

"But you don't get any gifts," Hannah challenged. Other kids were gathering around now. Specifically, José Ramon who once inexplicably called me "Sheila E.," for an entire day until I kicked him in the crotch, and James Barbados, who at least taunted me with the more appropriate "Abraham Sandwich."

What Hannah didn't know is that I had heard her "no gifts suck" argument before, and I was prepared for it. My parents had prepared me for it. My congregation had prepared me for it. Twelve years of life had been leading up to this perfectly rehearsed answer.

"Unlike you, I get gifts all through the year," I said, holding court now, emoting. "My parents buy me presents just because they love me, and not because some holiday commands it. You have to wait until Christmas to get the things you need. Besides, after Christmas is over, we go shopping and hit all the post-Christmas sales!"

The group was silent. Like young Jesus reprimanding the Pharisees, I had silenced them!

"Um, I don't have to wait until Christmas to get gifts," José said.

"Yes, you do," I countered. What? No one had ever disagreed with me when I made this argument in my *mind*. "You do have to wait until Christmas!" I wasn't going to let this Ramon kid knock down all that I knew to be true. Worldly kids went through the entire year with broken teeth and hole-filled socks, desperately waiting for December 25.

"Okay, but I don't," he said.

"I don't know what I'd do without Christmas," BJ mumbled, clearly unable to counter my bulletproof argument that Christmas was based on a pagan ritual and Jesus wasn't even born in December.

"Go eat an Abraham Sandwich, Abra-*Hams*," said James.

Whatever. At least Jehovah's Witnesses didn't have to wait until Christmas to get pajamas. We were the lucky ones.

In lieu of Christmas, some Jehovah's Witness parents allowed their kids to have a fake holiday with an innocuous name like Gift Giving Day or Totally Not Pagan Toy Party for Jehovah. My parents did not indulge in such faux debauchery.

"It implies, Kyria, that we are missing something by not celebrating a materialistic, pagan holiday," Mom said. "Do you think it needs to be replaced? Well, I'll tell you. You do not want to become materialistic."

There was another advantage to not celebrating non-Christmas: saving money. Ever since Dad had lost his bookkeeping position at the Gersch Elevator company, he'd had difficulty finding "something full-time." In other words, he'd been unemployed for two years.

My mother considered this to be bad timing. She wanted to buy a house and move out of our creaky, rented duplex with no shower and move somewhere with a dishwasher and carpeting you wouldn't trip on. She also wanted a completely different husband, but I don't think my father would have bought one for her.

Dad was in between jobs, and the jobs he was in between didn't offer the kind of paycheck you buy a house on. We rarely ate in restaurants. Neither of my parents went to college, but my mother had been employed as a legal secretary for years. As far as I was concerned, she was a career woman. I considered her front desk in the swanky law office to be the top of the corporate ladder.

Meanwhile, Dad got a job with a brother in our congregation

who had a business polishing supermarket floors at three in the morning. Dad kept a set of earplugs on his dresser, which we were not allowed to touch. With a blue ballpoint pen, he marked an X on one side of each earplug. After a week, he'd flip them over and use the other side. He was making things last.

Eventually he stopped polishing floors because his back hurt too much. I felt bad for him and tried to be on my best behavior.

I also felt bad for my mother. Her father had been a fisherman, and no one else in her family ever worked in an office like she did. But she'd bought beautiful sweaters from the second-hand store, dyed her hair blond, and gone out of her way to look classy. I guessed that working around lawyers and rich mahogany executive desks didn't make her feel comfortable with what we had. I didn't really feel comfortable with what we had either.

"Your mother wants a *house*," Dad would scoff. "Well, not in this system of things, I'll tell you. The New System is almost here. What would be the point?"

For the most part, Mom worked on the weekends while we stayed home and watched cartoons with Dad. In this way, Mom explained that our father tried to "turn her kids against her." Here I'd thought Saturdays were for Roger Williams Park and monster movies, but apparently they were also about Shakespearean familial backstabbing.

"Your mother certainly puts on a lot of makeup and perfume to go to an empty office on a Sunday afternoon," Dad would say, adding under his breath, "Harlot."

After Mom left, we did everything harlots don't let you do when they're home. We watched Godzilla movies during the *Creature Double Feature*. We wrestled next to the coffee table. We bought 99-cent pizzas and covered them in cold cuts while singing "That's Amore!"

The more fun we had with Dad, the more our mother hated him. She'd bring me to the Feins, where I'd play with Emily, then be fed Entenmann's crumb cake and listen to a discussion of "the situation at home."

"One day, Betty, they'll understand. No one appreciates how hard I work. All the kids see is how much *fun* their unemployed father is. Well, he's having fun while I support the family!"

"They're too young to understand the situation," Betty would agree.

"I'm not too young! I love Dad," I'd say, spewing raspberry jelly–coated crumbs from my protesting lips.

"Kyria, sweetie, I know you love your dad, but he's not being very nice to me right now. Someday, believe me, you'll look back on this differently."

It's not like Dad wasn't looking for a job. He'd already tried to get hired at the post office. He studied for weeks, slamming doors and asking for "a little peace and quiet."

With a job at the post office, we'd be set for life. Dad would only need to walk around for a few hours with a sack of mail, taking in the sunshine. "I get any government job and we're set for life. Bennies, vacations, pension, you name it. Set for life, I'm telling you."

We'd be in the money. We'd get a diamond-studded above-ground swimming pool and drink orange juice from a carton instead of concentrate.

I had no doubt that Dad would pass the test. He'd taught himself to play the guitar and could count in Spanish. He could open any coconut at any time and not lose a drop of milk. We didn't have to buy new appliances because Dad could fix anything. He had a tool bench in the basement, impeccably organized with every kind of lug nut or alligator clip you could possibly need. As long as I didn't mess anything up, I could stand next to him and pointlessly sand rounded edges onto a block of wood while he oiled up our turquoise Hoover from 1958.

He could also fix any car at any time. This came in handy, considering we owned an ever-changing series of used, late- '80s economy vehicles with the stamina of soapbox racers. Unfortunately, our car didn't usually inform us that it would rather remain parked until *after* we'd packed our picnic lunch and loaded a bag full of Frisbees into the trunk.

"Pump the gas, Daddy! But don't flood it," I'd yell, certain that he would not be able to drive a car without my advice. The majority of our trips to the zoo ended with us unwrapping our peanut butter sandwiches and eating them on the front steps of our house.

Dad failed the post office exam. I didn't believe it at first, being that he had that whole Spanish coconut-opening thing down cold. I'd heard that there was some math he didn't quite get, which I didn't believe, because he always helped me with my homework.

I knew it was a big deal when even my mother was sympathetic.

"Your father is very disappointed in himself," she said. "Let's just leave him alone for a while."

After that, Dad worked a lot of part-time jobs, like selling hypoallergenic vacuum cleaners door-to-door. After all, if anyone knew about vacuums, it was Dad.

One morning, Dad came home with his hands behind his back. He walked toward me with an odd grin and silently put a knit hat on my head. It was purple with a white pom-pom. In the center was an iron-on patch of a Snork that said, succinctly, "The Snorks."

Despite my professed love for the Snorks at school, I knew that actually wearing a Snork-related hat was terribly uncool. My reputation at school couldn't handle this kind of target—this giant Hanna-Barbera bull's-eye in the center of my forehead.

"How did you afford this?" I asked.

"I afforded it," Dad said.

"But we don't have any money."

"Sure we do. I thought you might like it. Do you like it?"

The Snork was prominent, that was for certain. I could already hear James's voice: *Nice skippy Snork hat, Abraham Sandwich.*

"I was afraid you wouldn't like it," Dad said with a smile.

With the hat still on my head, I hugged him. I wore it every day, showing Emily and BJ that I got gifts whenever I wanted them, and never had to wait for Christmas.

CHAPTER 7

Listen! Jehovah Is Spelling His

Kingdom Promise Aloud!

The second time I was onstage, I misspelled the word "caterpillar" and soaked a perfectly good purple skirt with my own urine. I'd beaten my entire fourth-grade class to get to the Citywide Spelling Bee, so maybe it can be forgiven that a naive part of me thought I could win the whole shebang. I was in "the gifteds," and not only that, I was the youngest kid in my congregation to be in the Theocratic Ministry School. My parents repeatedly told me how smart I was, and I knew that really meant smarter than everyone else in the whole world.

Someone else's teacher was slouched over an oak lectern in the Tolman High School auditorium.

"The correct spelling of caterpillar is *c-a-t* . . ." she said into a short, bendable microphone.

Wasn't that what I'd said? I'd said that, right? I'd definitely *meant* to say that.

When they'd first called my name, an uncontrollable turkey-baster spurt of pee asserted itself from my bladder, just enough to leave a dark wet heart on the back of my brand-new purple skirt, but not enough to alleviate the need to *go*. Then I misspelled "caterpillar."

I looked to my father, staring at me from the third row. He had a Botox-tight mouth that said both I am trying really, really hard not to have any facial expressions right now and My God, I raised an amazingly stupid daughter.

I waited for my second chance, my *do-over*, just like in kickball.

Unceremoniously, I was led back to my seat.

Fucking caterpillars. Those no-faced, back-haired, white-trash butterfly wannabes disqualified me on my first turn. I was stunned. No child could possibly be allowed to lose so quickly. Where was my gold star for trying real hard?

I was used to getting all the answers right. I usually had them all in front of me, underlined in a copy of the *Watchtower*, and all I had to do was raise my hand and read the sentence out loud. My parents, my grandmother, and my great-aunts agreed on one thing: I was a *very bright child*.

But here, I had no underlined passage to read from, no index cards like on the Kingdom Hall stage. Instead, I sat on the stage of another school's auditorium, crossing my legs and bouncing like I was sitting on a Hoppity Hop. And I didn't bother to tell a single adult that I needed to pee.

"Oh, so you *peed* on yourself! Well, that explains it," my father said afterward, finally enlightened. "I wondered why you were walking funny and had both your hands spread flat across your butt like that."

I taught myself to play "Song of the Volga Boatmen" on my best friend's piano, I thought. I know all the books of the Old Testament by heart.

"Why didn't you just ask one of the teachers to go to the bathroom?" Dad asked.

Genesis, Exodus, Leviticus, Numbers . . .

"I don't know," I said.

But I did know that one thing I abjectly did not do was assert myself with strange adults. My parents had gotten me wise to the fact that this world was controlled by adults who were controlled by Satan.

I was warned that kidnappers were dressed as clowns and driving black vans around our neighborhood, abducting children in broad daylight before they'd even gotten to the other side of the school crosswalk.

In Cape Cod, I got "*Kyria Lydia*" embroidered in yellow thread on a red sun visor, but I wasn't allowed to wear it in public lest I be abducted. I was led to believe predators were lined up outside the school, waiting to approach children and call to them via their personalized clothing.

"Hello, little girl . . . er . . . *Kee-ree-uh*," the child-nabber would say, cocking his head to the side and phonetically pronouncing the name sewn into the collar of my puffy ski jacket. "Your mother told me to come pick you up after school today. She said she won't be able to make it, but I am her very, very, very good friend. Now let's get into my black van. It's the one with the boarded-up windows and the bloody Little League uniforms hanging from the back."

Not only were kidnappers afoot, but I heard that enterprising drug dealers were trolling the grounds of Nathanael Greene Elementary School, forcing children to lick LSD-laced Mickey Mouse stickers. The goal, I was told, was to trick young kids into getting hooked on acid.

I am not certain how fourth graders had become the economic base of a booming drug empire. Perhaps the dealers worked on a volume-based business model and functioned by accumulating a steady $1.25 in lunch money per customer over an extended fiscal period. I never questioned it.

Because of this, my sticker album, once filled with scratch-and-sniff cherries, now began to stagnate. I feared to trade anything, even with my best-sticker-friend Michelle Jordan. When would Armageddon come and destroy all these sticker-hating druggies so I could have my childhood back?

Such was the wicked world we lived in. Since the prophetic date of 1914, the world had become *increasingly lawless*. There were more rapes and more wars and more violence and more death than ever before in history. Of course, there were probably fewer wars and less death since the advent of the Geneva Convention and penicillin. But Reagan was president, so it was easy to imagine the world was quickly descending into chaos.

Satan was wreaking havoc on the earth and all of God's people. He knew his time was running out and he had to turn as many people as possible away from Jehovah before the Great War of Armageddon began. Anyone who wasn't a Jehovah's Witness would just as soon kill us as shake our hand. The devil worked through wicked unbelievers to deceive us into turning away from the truth. These were the kidnappers, the LSD dealers, the birthday cake decorators. The wicked were like the invisible dust mites that live on your skin and look like alien dinosaurs—they were *everywhere*.

So how, after all this, could I have asked a strange adult to show me where the bathroom was?

I was also deathly afraid of pudding. I was never sure how to tell if it was *blood* pudding and eating blood was a sin. Blood pudding, blood sausage, and blood transfusions were all mentioned at the Kingdom Hall as things to avoid, so that we might, as it says in Acts 15, "keep abstaining from blood." I didn't know what blood pudding was, but I knew that if I accidentally put the wrong type of pudding in my mouth, I wouldn't make it into paradise.

So, sitting in Lum's restaurant, I refused the free dish of pudding included with my kids' hot dog meal. At picnics I'd eat extra potato salad and pass on the Pudding Pops. In school, I visibly disturbed our lunch lady by asking if the pudding "had any blood in it." (Answer: "Why would you ask such a thing? What on earth would make you ask such a horrible thing?")

My father stayed away from ethnic food because "You never know what those people could put in their recipes." The last thing you wanted to end up eating was some sacrificial goat head stuffed with virgin blood, so we never had Thai.

Since a hospital will feed you intravenously when you are too weak to eat, Jehovah's Witnesses reasoned that receiving a blood transfusion was the same as eating blood. Additionally, by refusing transfusions, we would be safe from the tainted bathhouse blood donated by homosexuals and druggies. For even though AIDS hadn't yet existed when the Bible was written, Jehovah's laws were so wise and pragmatic that they transcended all time and space. We marveled at how lucky we were to have God as a safety net in these last days.

To ensure that we would not forcibly be given a transfusion by some godless doctor with no regard for our spiritual life, baptized Witnesses were issued a "No Blood" card. This was a signed and legally binding wallet-size card. If we were ever in an accident that required a blood transfusion, this card was all that stood between us and some gay blood in our body. It was the type O-negative version of "Do Not Resuscitate."

For while you *might* die if you didn't accept a blood transfusion, you would *definitely* die at Armageddon if you did. Death was not to be feared; it was merely like falling asleep. By standing your ground and refusing a transfusion, you could be assured that Jehovah would rouse you in paradise.

At the Kingdom Hall, we read *Watchtowers* that featured the faces of children who had died for their faith, youngsters who had professed their love of God and would be rewarded with eternal life. Children even younger than me had convinced doctors and judges that blood transfusions were sinful. These children weren't just saying this because their parents told them to—they truly had faith.

Now, what if a doctor insisted on "saving" your child's life by giving him a blood transfusion anyway? Good parenting skills came into play here. The issue would go to court and elders might be stationed in the hospital in case a vigilante surgeon suddenly decided to inject you with a tainted infusion. A parent would have to be strong.

In most cases, Jehovah would save the child's life and then all would see his power and glory at work. The doctors would often apologize and announce a newfound respect for the family and the religion. Sometimes, doctors might even renounce blood transfusions altogether or actually become Jehovah's Witnesses. That is what I hoped would happen if I ever got hit by a train.

I knew I'd choose death over having time-release sin pumping through my veins. Even if I survived the operation, there would be no point in living. I trusted that my parents would let me die so I could be resurrected in paradise.

"Mom, if the doctors ever say I have to get a blood transfusion because I'm in a coma, will you make sure that I don't get it?" I asked.

"We'll deal with that when it comes up," she said.

I felt safer knowing my mother would let me die. She always looked after my health. She made me take vitamins and dressed me in a one-piece snowsuit after a frozen winter rain. Meanwhile, Emily's mother let her run outside in nothing more than a puffy jacket.

I knew the snowsuit was embarrassing and almost always unnecessary, but it was like wearing a warm mug of cocoa over my entire body. Even when Mom wasn't looking, I couldn't bring myself to throw my insulated mittens on the ground and brave the cold.

The less I felt of the cold, the more my tolerance for it

dropped. I became nearly powerless against Old Man Winter—and Old Man Fall, for that matter. I couldn't withstand the temperature change after a bath without leaping directly in front of our radiator and crouching there until my thighs looked sunburned. Eventually my parents broke down and bought me a heated electric mattress pad, which I would splay my body across, flat on my stomach, soaking up heat like an iguana on a heated toy rock. Electric blankets had wires that got twisted while you slept and caused a fire, my parents said. Mattress pads were safer.

Meanwhile, Dad dubbed our home "The Fire Hazard" and bought a First Alert safety ladder to keep under the bed. This was because Mom hoarded her entire past in our basement—deflated inner tubes, hand-knit shawls, and stacks of Butterick Quick 'n Easy patterns from 1965. Coupled with the close proximity to the oil burner, we were certain the whole place would go up in flames any day now.

Every night before bed, I arranged a "go bag" with my most precious childhood items—for when I had to escape down the metal chain in my footie pajamas like the child in the picture on the front of the box. It was also good to have my best doll within reach, in case of Armageddon. Whether it was a man-made fire, or fire shot down to earth from the fingertips of God, I fell asleep knowing where my favorite necklace was.

Despite knowing, as my parents told me, that I was "safe in the arms of Jehovah," I never managed to reach childhood satori.

Too many things in this world were dangerous, especially when they involved worldly children. When my class went on a school field trip to see *Sesame Street on Ice*, my mother decided that I should be allowed to go—I just shouldn't be allowed to take the bus with the other children. She picked me up from school, and we drove in tandem with the school bus that carried my wicked, non–Jehovah's Witness, drug-addicted elementary school classmates.

I have no idea what possessed my mother to drive me separately to *Sesame Street on Ice*. In her mind, I think, a school bus was an unchaperoned den of sin. Maybe she was afraid I might learn to swear or be given a Christmas present.

By the time my mother led me up the steps of the Providence Civic Center, the whole class was comfortably in their seats, staring at me.

The teacher had suggested that my mother might wish to give me a little money to buy a tasty snack treat when the concessionaire came barking. Taken aback, my mother explained that she had already packed some food for me, so it was *unnecessary* to give me any money.

I sank into my folding stadium seat, and Mom handed me my homemade snack: a plastic Baggie full of dates smeared with all-natural peanut butter. The peanut butter, once a solid spoonful of Teddie Natural Smooth, had, in the warmth of her pocketbook, become a sludgy paste against the sides of the bag. Reaching inside, my knuckles became coated in peanutty goo, which had threaded itself around every date as well as my forearm and parts of the chair.

I'd taken the last open seat, in the uppermost row next to the teacher. From this vantage point I could easily view all my classmates enjoying popcorn, soda, and enormous pink gobs of cotton candy. I halfheartedly asked the girl in front of me if she'd like to trade. No one wanted to trade their delicious cotton candy for a messy bag of dried dates covered in sugar-free peanut butter. What was I, *retahded*?

I replaced the twist-tie, put the Baggie under my seat, and watched an oddly quiet spectacle unfold below me. There was no story that I could follow. Big Bird was simply *skating*. Muppets were weaving in and out of one another for seemingly no reason.

Muppets plus ice rink equaled *boring*. Was this all there was to life—mushy dates, social alienation, and wordlessly skating trash cans? Sure, a giant Oscar the Grouch skated in a circle, but what was the *point*?

By the time I was in sixth grade, my parents softened enough to allow me to take a single elective: aerobics class after school. It was healthy, after all. I wore my gray stirrup pants and we purchased pink leg warmers and a matching headband so that I might suitably Get Physical. Although we lived four blocks away, my parents still drove us to school every morning and picked us up every afternoon, reducing a four-minute walk into a 14-second spin around the corner. Taking the class meant that my father had to pick me up one hour later than normal. Being a habitual everything-in-its-place kind of guy, it also made it easy for him to forget me.

Not surprisingly, one day, Dad forgot me. Four blocks and 240 seconds away from my house, I paced up and down the stone steps of my elementary school like a hyena in Roger Williams Park Zoo. I collapsed onto the grass and cried into my inside-out, off-the-shoulder sweatshirt. Oh, God, what if he never came? I prayed to Jehovah for support.

"Dear Jehovah God, please protect me from kidnappers and killers and please make my dad come and pick me up or maybe let somebody see me here or something so I can get home safely and not be killed or kidnapped or forced to lick a Smurf dipped in acid and then killed. In Jesus' name, amen."

"Why didn't you just walk home?" my father asked, when he finally arrived and finished apologizing to the hysterical, praying twelve-year-old in gym clothes who clung to his neck. Why didn't I? I was amazed. How could he not know his own rule? How they looked down their noses at all the neglectful parents with their self-walking "latchkey kids."

"Dad, don't you know? Because I'm not allowed to!"

My father's mouth grew Botox-tight again. There was only one expression on it this time, and it said My God, I raised an amazingly stupid daughter.

Dad must have had visions of picking up his grown child for the rest of his life. He surely imagined driving his 35-year old daughter to her job at the post office, four blocks away, or taking me to the mall so I could buy my husband a silver anniversary present. He must have seen a future in which I peed myself at a spelling bee every year for the rest of my life. Because starting the next week, we were suddenly allowed to walk home from school. For those whole four blocks, I was going to be like the other kids.

CHAPTER 8

Stand Back, for Jehovah Is Punishing

Those He Loves Most!

According to Jehovah, the best way to raise your children is with loving attention and timely discipline. We even had a song about it: "They are gifts from God. He says use the rod." It was one of my mother's favorite Kingdom Melodies, a song about how real Christians love their children more than everyone else. When we had misbehaved in some manner, Mom fetched the rubber-coated electric cord that wrapped around the coffee percolator and folded it over in her hand so that it formed a pointy oval for whipping. Meting out proper discipline was part of being a good Christian; in other words, it was for everyone's benefit.

In my Kingdom Hall, the boiler room was known to us kids as "the beatin' room." As in, "Wanna go play in the beatin' room?" "Nah, we can't. Carmen's gettin' a beatin' in there."

At least once during every meeting, you'd look up to see a blur of feet as a screaming child was carried into the back of the Kingdom Hall to be given a little alone time with the Lord's Rod. In fact, if your child was misbehaving and you *didn't* take her in the back for 40 whacks, people would really start to talk about your lax parenting techniques.

The end result was that Jehovah's Witness children were well-mannered lovers of God and Christ. They sat quietly without causing problems and did their homework while simultaneously memorizing the books of the Bible. They were often able to convert their teachers to the Truth simply by virtue of being so well-behaved in class that teachers would be curious as to "what makes this child so very special?" The answer, of course, was Jehovah God.

Stories like these were all over our *Watchtowers* and in our sermons. Why couldn't I be that perfect? If I could only remember to pick up my toys every day or not knock over lamps while playing in the living room, then I, too, could be mentioned in the *Watchtower.*

Some of the kids had heard tell that there was something called a "time-out," some fairy-tale punishment in which you were apparently sent upstairs to play in your room alone for an hour. We would never be so lucky. Non-corporeal punishment was for those impotent college types, the reason why their rich, blond children were always having tantrums in the supermarket.

"No discipline in this world," my father would say while watching an upper-middle-class mom with a screaming toddler attached to her leg. "You kids were never allowed to get away with crap like that."

When we misbehaved, we received a meaningful slapping about the backs of the thighs. My father's implement of choice was a ruler, while my mother preferred the electric cord. Usually the phrase "Don't make me get the cord" was enough to stop my brother and me from shoving Monopoly pieces down each other's pants.

After our punishment, we would stand facing the corner, next to the refrigerator, where we were told to "think about what just happened." Behind us on the wall was a wood cattle yoke, which one of my mother's more crafty friends had painted with a verse from the book of Matthew: "My yoke is easy and my burden is light."

Once, during a routine beating, Dad's "good ruler" broke in half while he was hitting me with it. He was so angry at the loss of his long pink yardstick that he began to hit me harder and harder with the back of his hand until his palm turned bright red. "Now you're making me hurt my hand," he yelled with each swipe. I had gone and made someone so upset with me that they were forced to hurt their hand on me.

It hurt so much while I was experiencing each smack that I always ran straight to the mirror, feeling like my wounds would be more visible than they were. Just once, I wanted a beating to leave field-hand whip marks on my back. After being punished, I took a natural-bristled hairbrush and vigorously rubbed my butt cheeks until it looked like I had rosacea of the *tuchas*.

If only someone could see the marks, I thought, I could garner some sympathy. Unfortunately, the rash faded within an hour and I had to face the fact that my name was not Luka and I did not, in fact, live on the second floor. I could not show up at school the next day and point to my ivory-white thighs and claim that I was being abused.

In my mind, I was simply—like so many children of the '80s—getting knocked around a bit. I didn't have any broken teeth, I just got smacked in the head for knocking over a glass of milk. This was not abuse—it was Christian discipline.

For the rest of the week after breaking his good ruler, my father walked around with his hand wrapped in an Ace bandage and I was glared at angrily or otherwise ignored. I scraped vigorously at my ass with the hairbrush, but couldn't make it bleed.

My father had a bandaged hand to show for his troubles, but none of my own wounds were ever visible.

God was our shining example of how a good father should treat his children. Now, here was a man who was not going to take any guff. God was no yuppie parent giving Kaetlyn and Portia a time-out next to the large-screen television. This was a father who would just as soon turn you into a pillar of salt as pat your head and take you to the ball game. It was the right way to parent.

In any case, I got smacked less than a lot of the other Jehovah's Witness kids I knew. More important, it was never random. I'd always done something to "deserve" my punishment, like not finishing my math homework, running away from my brother, or not turning off the television.

Most of the time, we got in trouble because we were doing something that would make our mother yell at our father. This might mean that she'd return home from work to discover we hadn't folded the laundry, had broken a dish, or, worst of all, had burned popcorn.

If I ever felt like initiating a good old-fashioned whupping with the wooden yardstick, burning popcorn was a surefire way to reach that goal. It wasn't that my father cared if the house smelled like burned kernels, it was that now he'd have to listen to my mother yell about it. And that was all our fault.

Unfortunately, I never could consistently get the popcorn right. We didn't have fancy store-bought microwave popcorn bags. We used a Tupperware vegetable steamer. So by the time we got a hint of the acrid cloud that was forming just beyond the microwave door, it was often too late—smoke already existed.

Immediately, wordlessly, we would spring into action.

"Shit, goddammit!" my father would yell. "You know she's gonna have a *fit* now," and he'd run upstairs to grab the box fan from the bedroom. My brother and I would immediately open all the windows and begin ventilating the kitchen with dish towels. I prayed to Jehovah for a cool cross-breeze.

While the kitchen was airing out, my father would grab the ruler from above the kitchen door frame. We were in trouble because *he* was going to be in trouble. The wood would catch the air and make a whooshing sound before it hit the back of my thigh. If we tried to run up the stairs, we'd just get it on the ankle, the back of the hand, wherever it landed.

After the beating, we'd turn on the television and wait for Mom to get home.

"Oh, I knew it!" she'd scream as soon as she walked in the door. "Disgusting, disgusting, disgusting popcorn!"

Dad would already be camped out in his office in the cellar, holding a Hi-Liter and pretending to study the *Watchtower*. The office, too, my mother found to be "disgusting." But she would still go down there to let him have what-for about the popcorn.

Our cellar was not a furnished, middle-class rumpus room with floppy beanbags and a foosball table. It was a concrete catacomb where pieces of wall routinely fell on us and it hurt to walk without shoes. There were exposed pipes encased in a white, fluffy substance with black vertical bands around them. This is now known as "asbestos," but may one day be known as "the reason I die young." Once, while I was trying to dislodge a tiddlywinks game with a silver baton, I got a faceful of toxic snow.

The cellar was clearly uninhabitable, yet this is where my father camped out whenever Mom was home. He'd run an extension cord to a small black-and-white television and kept a constant supply of Planters cheese puffs on a desk he built himself. Rather than listen to the screaming about whose turn it was to take out the trash, he preferred to sacrifice all sunlight and watch blurry television in a cave wallpapered with cancer. A set of hanging indoor-outdoor vinyl curtains decorated with ferns was all that separated his sanctuary from the bicycle pumps and jumper cables. There was an enormous oily furnace four feet to his left. It was a testament to how much he must have hated his life.

Once, Emily and I burned popcorn when no one else was home. I was old enough to know that I had only a few seconds to protect my father and the only way to help was to erase all traces of this popcorn's existence. Panicked, I ran into the backyard to throw my afternoon snack all over the lawn.

"I gotta do this or I'll be in so much trouble," I told her.

"When we burn popcorn in my house, my mom thinks it's funny," Emily said.

I guessed they treated burned popcorn a little differently over in Cumberland, but this was how we did it in Pawtucket. When my father came home, Emily and I were back on the couch, chilling in front of the television. I knew he'd be proud of me for saving him from a night in the basement.

"Hey, Daddy! I burned the popcorn," I calmly told him. "But don't worry, because I threw it all in the backyard!"

My father grabbed me by the arm and yanked me off the couch.

"You did what? You'll choke the birds with that stuff! Get out there and pick up every last piece of that popcorn before you kill all the birds!"

"I'll help," Emily offered.

"No, you won't," my father said.

"Nah, it's cool. I'll be right back," I told her. I wanted to act like this was totally normal, like I understood why I had to do this. It was *she* who didn't understand the ecological threat that partially burned popcorn poses to the United States sparrow population.

I took a towel into the backyard and knelt on it, so as not to scrape my knees on the patches of dried crabgrass and small rocks. I crawled around like a forensic detective, picking up every last piece of popcorn. I knew my father was sitting in the basement, running a pink Hi-Liter across this week's study article in the *Watchtower*. I had tried to do the right thing for everyone. I was sobbing.

When no one else was around, I could escape punishment

by locking myself in the bathroom until my parents got tired of pounding on the door. But with Emily here, I had to play it cool.

Locking myself in the bathroom was a standard self-defense tactic, until the day my father decided to take the door off the hinges. At first, he engaged in the usual fist pounding and yelling of "Open this door or I'm going to kill you when you get out." I sucked in my breath and tried to make myself as thin as a bath mat so I could slide under the sink. I knew he didn't really mean to kill me—it was just a figure of speech. Usually, Dad was funny and watched cartoons with us.

I covered myself in towels and pretended to be part of the dirty pile. Maybe an hour passed. Then the door lifted up and out, and was gently laid to rest on the hallway rug. I peered up from inside a pile of bleached-out facecloths and brown-and-orange paisley hand towels. My father grabbed my ankles and I grabbed on to the claw-foot bathtub. He didn't hit me. Instead, he dragged me onto the hallway carpet and told me to get out of his sight. He said I'd wasted his whole damn afternoon. I crawled into my bedroom as he quietly put the bathroom door back the way it had been before any of this happened.

Around the age of 11, I began to knock things over, cause trouble, and fight with my brother so extensively that my mother began to request "meetings of encouragement" in our home with the congregation elders. The elders would read scriptures about children being obedient to parents, drink a cup of coffee, tell my father to set a better example by making sure we attended all the meetings, and be on their way. Immediately after they left, I would resume fighting with my brother.

My mother called me "malicious," but my father just called me "a pain in the ass." Dad chose to deal with the problem by rolling his eyes and then locking himself in the cellar with a Genesee Cream Ale and the Celtics game.

My grandmother even took to calling me "Cain," a not-so-subtle reference to the biblical story of the first murder in which Cain, a farmer, killed his brother Abel, a shepherd. Cain was jealous because God blessed Abel's bloody sacrificial animal offering but refused to accept Cain's offering of fruit, vegetables, and macrobiotic quinoa salad with organic tahini dressing.

"You're going to kill your brother, Cain," Mom-Mom would yell whenever Aaron and I were in her presence. "Why do you want to kill your brother?"

"She really hates her brother," Mom would agree. "Why do you hate Aaron so much, Kyria? Do you know who created hate? Satan did."

"I don't hate Aaron," was all I could say in response. The real answer wouldn't have made any sense. I didn't understand it myself.

All I knew was this: Once, I had been a good Jehovah's Witness kid sitting alone on the worn living room carpet, watching cartoons. I noticed, suddenly, that there were little white painted squares that formed an old heating vent in our ceiling. For no particular reason, it occurred to me that the only way I could breathe would be to look at one of these squares. It cut into my television viewing, true, but I had no choice. I knew, without a shadow of a doubt, that I had to look at the ceiling each time I took in a breath or something bad would happen. I mean, I *knew* it, like I knew my own name, like I knew that Jehovah would one day turn the earth into a paradise. I tried not bothering with it, choosing instead to get the uninterrupted view of my afternoon Shirley Temple movie. But it felt so much better to breathe while looking at the little white square, like the difference between snuggling a down comforter and snuggling an angry badger. So I did it. It seemed easy enough. Badgerless.

As for my brother, I was inexplicably and immediately afraid to let him touch me. If he did touch me, I had to spend hours in the bathroom, washing my hands and counting and psychically wiping off what I could only describe as "bad stuff." I would chase him around the block, screaming so that each and every neighbor must have come to their window. This my parents saw as sibling rivalry gone horribly awry.

No one understood. Things were "bad" and I had to make them "good." Bad things could get inside me and dirty things could get on me, and everything in life was so tenuous that I could fall into a black pit at any second. I needed to know that I could be wonderful, perfect, at all times.

I decided to keep my new way of life a secret, a little something-something just between me and my fluctuating serotonin levels. It would be a few years before I would learn about OCD from an afternoon episode of *Sally Jessy Raphael*, when I would discover that it was caused by a bunch of confused chemicals in my head, not because I was a bad girl, or even the murderous vegetarian brother of the biblical Abel. I would even receive the small consolation that while not all smart people have OCD, a lot of people with OCD seem to be pretty smart.

Until then, I would have no response when Mom-Mom called me Cain and my father told me to "knock off this *shit* already."

I simply put my head down and said sheepishly, "I don't hate my brother. I swear I don't." Then I went in the other room to count to 11 while doing jumping jacks under a drapery.

I'd never had trouble with my schoolwork before, but with all the ritualistic counting I had to get through, I now found it nearly impossible to concentrate. Even though my grandmother thought I was an evil genius, I still couldn't do long division while simultaneously carrying out a series of complex counting and tapping rituals, several of which involved asking for a bathroom pass in order to be fully executed in private. While other kids were shading their multiple-choice dots, I stood facing a toilet in a stall in the girls' lavatory mumbling "not nine, not nine" over and over again.

The kids, of course, would taunt me. They had to—I understood why.

"Why do you always do those weird things with your hands, Abrahams?" they'd ask. "Why are you so weird, weirdo?"

"I'm not doing anything!" I'd say.

"Yes, you are. I saw you!"

I would swear to them that I wasn't doing *anything* and promise myself that next time, I would be more covert in my counting—a gentler kind of nut job.

I could have told my parents, but tell them what, exactly? That I have to . . . *do* . . . *stuff*? And I don't know why? And kids make fun of me for it? If only there had been a pop-up book I could have pointed to, something called *Mommy, Why Do I Need to Wash Words off My Hands and Sometimes Count Telephone Poles?* Then I could have opened to the last page, where a magical bar of soap says, "Hey, little crazy girl, you don't need to wash your hands again because they're already *cleeean*!" To which the little girl would respond, "You're right, magical bar of soap! Now let's go back to Non-Counting Land, where everything only needs to be counted once!"

Unfortunately, the majority of the books we owned had names like *The Truth Book* and *You Can Live Forever in Paradise on Earth*, and they weren't exactly helping me to be *less* obsessive-compulsive.

Meanwhile, my parents desperately tried to figure out why their well-behaved Jehovah's Witness daughter had been acting up on them. Math tutors were summoned, school meetings were held, and pediatricians were seen. My father was convinced that there was a demon in the basement, while my mother and an overly enthusiastic nurse-practitioner believed that I had Lyme disease.

I knew, though, that all I needed was to be locked in a sterile white room, away from worldly influences and sinful people. If I could just hold out until Jehovah turned the earth into a paradise and cleansed us all with the blood of the Lamb, nothing in the world would ever need to be fixed again.

CHAPTER 9

Be Best Friends with God First,

Mankind Second!

In elementary school, I'd been gifted only on Tuesday afternoon and only in a basement. In seventh grade, I was asked to be gifted on a daily basis. I wasn't used to being so conspicuously separated on the basis of my skill for speed-reading social studies. As sixth graders, we had a frog in a tank and learned that Columbus sailed the ocean blue. What more would life ever expect from us? We were an autonomous hive, working toward the greater good of stacking chairs and standing alphabetically in line. All I cared about then was that some kids were nice and some kids were Eric Barboza, who taped "Kick Me" signs to my back at least once a week and accused me of snorting cocaine just because I had acute snuffles.

"Why you always blowin' yo' nose, *Jehover*? You do cocaine or something? Heh-heh-heh."

"I am not some druggie," I screamed. "I happen to have severe mold and dust allergies!"

"Okay, *Jehover*. Just sayin' cuz you, like, blow yo' nose a lot or whatevah."

I was optimistic when I graduated to Falter Junior High. The classes in this school were separated into numeric groups ranging from "one" (meaning you would one day own a nice condo) to "fourteen" (meaning the teachers were happy if you managed to keep your shoes out of your mouth). I would be placed in "the ones" where, I hoped, my classmates would have heard of hay fever and would no longer accuse me of tooting nose candy off my Trapper Keeper.

Being in the ones meant that we were *wicked smaht*. The rest of the depressed school district's resources went to breaking up fights, preventing pregnancies, and teaching some of the more special students how to zipper things. But the ones were treated with all the respect the Pawtucket school system could afford. We even got homework.

Until junior high, it hadn't occurred to me that maybe I wasn't actually brilliant—maybe it was all relative. Particularly after Mrs. Remmington, the new social-studies teacher, welcomed us to her class with a lecture on how much we sucked as human beings.

"They call this the *gifted* class," she spat. "But you're no better than any of the other kids in this school. My daughter wasn't accepted into your group, and my daughter is just as smart if not smarter than every last one of you in this class. So don't think you're going to get any special treatment from me. Gifted, my *ass*. You're nothing more than average."

"What a witch," one of my worldly classmates said as we walked to our lockers. She had straight blond hair, bifocals, and adorable German dimples. Her name was Sarah Stover.

Immediately, Sarah and I bonded in intense hatred for Mrs. Remmington. I found out that Sarah had even attended the same gifted program where I learned Logo, but was a Wednesday-only genius. We sat together every day at lunch, noted our mutual crush on Jayson Winters, and became immediate best friends with ease.

Sarah's clothes were so unfashionable that kids didn't even make fun of her—they just felt empathetic. Meanwhile, I wore black spandex bicycle pants with white racing stripes down the side, fringed boots, an acid-washed jean jacket, and matching acid-washed socks. I coupled this with a shirt that fell to my knees and had a gold crest on the breast pocket as if I were the mayor of '80s Town. I was trying my hardest, and therefore, kids did not feel bad about making fun of me.

We tried our best to make Sarah look as cool as possible, considering her mother would only take her shopping at Sears. This is before Sears had MTV and strobe lights above the Juniors X-Treme Socks section, before every store in every mall was at least partially cool. Sears did not sell acid-washed fabric. Sears sold sheets and air conditioners. Any jeans purchased there usually had the words "tough" and "reinforced" somewhere on a large leather patch. Fabric was never described as pre-rip or fluorescent, but contained only long-lasting craftsmanship and sadness.

To add insult to injury, Sarah wore glasses reminiscent of Dustin Hoffman in *Tootsie* and had recently gotten a perm so tight that poodles winced. Her parents thought about pragmatic issues, such as savings bonds and clothes that would last for years. The last thing on their minds was whether or not their daughter had stirrup jeans.

But Sarah was hardly uncool to me. If anything, she was meta. She was so cool that she could like uncool things, like Dick Van Dyke and Mille Bornes, a French card game about driving a car, which you won by achieving 1000 kilometers. Never was more fun had in an imaginary Peugeot truck.

Sarah was too sweet to be unpopular. And even if she was, just a *little*, it was nothing in comparison to my most unpopular friend to date, Dora, the deep-voiced, pear-shaped girl—at school who never spoke and laughed like an ape. Actually, she wasn't so much my friend as someone my mother forced me to be nice to.

Dora walked hunchback and would always force her way into lunch tables she wasn't invited to. Instead of trying to ingratiate herself into the conversation, she'd methodically devour a sandwich while pressing her chin into the neck of her soiled Members Only jacket. Her silence was broken only by an occasional snort-laugh at an inside joke I knew she couldn't possibly have gotten, because I didn't get it either.

My relationship with Dora had been that of a satellite until sixth grade. One day, when my father was driving us home from school, we saw an underdressed hunchback walking home alone in the freezing rain. My father pulled the car over, and a rumpled, wet Dora silently skulked into the backseat. This was the year we had a talking car, so Dora's awkward entry was serenaded by a computerized voice saying, "A door is ajar." She slouched her head and looked at her lap.

"It's cold out there, isn't it, Dora?" my father asked.

Dora didn't answer. Thankfully, we knew where she lived, because I don't think we could have gotten her to tell us if we'd shot her full of sodium pentothal. She got out of the car without saying thank you. Dora made our car seem chatty.

"She's such a creeeep," I squealed.

"Doofy Dora," Aaron agreed, in a faux baritone. "I'm Dora doo-doo head."

"I think she has some problems at home," my father said, but my brother and I were too busy giggling and saying, "I'm Dora! Dur dee dur dee durrrr."

The next morning, the doorbell rang. Doofy Dora was standing on our front porch, silently clutching a single notebook. I assumed that she'd left something in our car, but the next thing I knew, she was sitting at our kitchen table and my mother was making her breakfast.

This continued every day for the rest of the year. With the exception of Saturdays, Sundays, and a *very* rare sick day, Dora was our omnipresent breakfast guest.

Soon my mother began shopping specifically for treats that *Dora* liked, and buying *Dora's* favorite cereal, and picking up extra Capri Suns to stick in *Dora's* ample pockets.

My mother told me to be nice to Dora because she didn't have anywhere else to go. I knew we were showing her Christian compassion, but why couldn't we have been compassionate to a more popular girl in school?

If I really wanted to get rid of her, I could have played the "bad associations" card. But since she seemingly had no personality, she couldn't really be an influence on me one way or the other.

My parents couldn't bring themselves to be so coldhearted as to slam the door in her face, which was why our family constantly had to struggle to be exemplary Jehovah's Witnesses.

Dora had infiltrated our mornings, become as synonymous with getting ready for school as brushing our teeth.

"Dora's still coming to school with us every morning," I'd gossip at school to Jessica and Jane.

"Oh, God," they'd say. "That's so queer. I feel so bad for you."

I didn't dislike Dora at all, but suddenly all I had to do was really *hate* her and I was able to bond with cool girls. Dora had been eating all our cereal; now she could repay me with popularity. At least until the popular kids got bored, which was pretty quickly.

"It's so crazy, I mean, I wonder if she'll keep ringing our bell once school ends," I'd say.

"Yeah, we *know*," Jessica would say, and uncomfortably look away.

Unless Dora had a stroke in the car on the way to school, I was clearly in danger of becoming a one-trick pony. Sure, the kids hated her, but they hated me too. And they no longer cared that she was in my kitchen. So, along with my Lycra bicycle pants and peer-pressure-induced love of Bon Jovi, Dora went into the pile of "things I thought would finally make me popular, but never did."

Once elementary school ended, Dora vanished. There was no forwarding address or thank-you note to my mother for all the free, homemade breakfasts she'd had throughout the year (frankly, I was surprised my mother didn't sit down with her to help her write one). I didn't see Dora once during the entire summer, not at Pawtucket House of Pizza, not at the public pool, and not in our kitchen.

So when seventh grade started, I was surprised to see Dora in the junior high cafeteria, sitting right behind me at a long faux-wood folding table. She wasn't in the ones, but I was completely amazed to discover that she was in the *twos*. I didn't even know she could form a complete sentence, let alone almost make it into my gifted class.

Dora shrugged her shoulders, adjusted her glasses, and laughed a toothy laugh.

"Hey," she said.

"Oh, hey, Dora. Uh, hey."

"Who's that girl?" Sarah asked, spinning around on a blue folding bench attached to a red folding bench.

"Oh," I said. "That's just . . . nobody."

As far as I and everyone else in school was concerned, Dora really *was* nobody. Sometimes I smiled when I saw her in the hallway, but most of the time I pretended she wasn't there.

Sarah's parents were retired geography teachers who had already raised four children and were starting on a gaggle of chubby grandchildren. They were fundamentally different from any people I had ever experienced. While my family thought of school as a way to kill time between birth and Armageddon, Sarah's family creepily thought it was *important* or something. These were people who put stock in learning about things that aren't solely in the Bible. These were Episcopalians.

Mrs. Stover had soft gray curls and several housecoats checkered in various shades of Easter pastel. She usually whistled while baking her famous chocolate chip cookies, but occasionally she would yodel. Mr. Stover was a pipe-smoking dad with both a favorite rocking chair *and* a favorite easy chair. A man who diligently crushed and tied used cardboard boxes before throwing them in the trash.

The family had bookcases with actual books in them and a dining room table that was rarely puzzle-free. In this home, I discovered that not only was there a magazine called *Games* but people actually subscribed to it. The only logic puzzle my family had was a Rubik's Cube with all the stickers peeled off. The only books we owned featured pictures of saved Christians climbing the sides of mountains into rays of sunlight.

Mr. Stover drove a mint-green Volkswagen Rabbit. Mrs. Stover drove a red one.

I began fashioning excuses to be at Sarah's house every single day. I promised Sarah that we were going to do homework together. I swore I needed help with math, then we'd spend the afternoon playing Joust on ColecoVision. I wanted to sleep over on school nights. If I didn't see Sarah after school, I would walk straight to her house, alone, and let myself in through the unlocked back door.

The modest Stover-family living room was taken up mostly by musical instruments. The family owned both a piano *and* an organ, used mainly for choir practice and set atop a braided country rug. I played the Charlie Brown theme over and over and over again—poorly. No one ever asked me to stop.

Things were calm at Sarah's pipe-scented house. There was no screaming, no slamming of chairs, no chasing of people with kitchen utensils while screaming the word "whore." I enjoyed eating her mother's cookies while thumbing through a book of world maps and secretly plotting to move in with the Stovers.

One day, without warning, I was shanghaied into sinning in Sarah's dining room. It was Sarah's brother's birthday and I was in the midst of my first birthday party.

There had been no birthday fanfare and I hadn't seen any dark cloud above the green bungalow indicating that Satan would be paying a visit to their kitchen. I had noticed that the puzzles had been cleaned off the dining room table, but there was no other indication that things were amiss until the country rug was suddenly topped with smiling German relatives.

The only birthday that is mentioned in the Bible is King Herod's feast, at which point John the Baptist is beheaded, presumably for bringing some really dry cupcakes. Since everything in the Bible is there for a reason, celebrating your birthday, for Jehovah's Witnesses, is akin to ordering a beheading. Bad things happened at birthdays. These parties encouraged debauchery and selfishness. Families went bankrupt trying to afford Corvettes for their demanding, spoiled, pagan children.

I felt like I'd graduated into doing something wrong. Now I could tell Witnesses about the time I got trapped in someone's house while they sang "Happy Birthday," and how I dealt with that in a spiritual manner. Did I pray while they sang? How frightened and concerned everyone would feel! *God, Kyria, that's just awful*.

Only, it didn't seem awful. It was kinda fun. This was not what I had been told birthdays were about. Birthdays, I'd been taught, were about murder. I watched a happy family, heads fully intact, licking icing from pink plastic forks. The closest thing to an implement of torture was the heavy paper cutter in the guest room. The presents were cheap trinkets from a 99-cent store—a book, a fountain pen. No one got a sports car with a pink bow on it. No one got a "birthday whore" or a regrettable "birthday tattoo." Instead, there was a new bell for the cat. What the hell was going on?

I chose to eat the birthday cake, but I did not sing the birthday song. In truth, having never being allowed to sing it, I wasn't entirely sure how it went. I knew it was a variant of "Happy birthday to you, Happy birthday to you . . ." but I wasn't positive that there wouldn't be a curveball in the middle. Perhaps this was some kind of extended remix version where people suddenly start counting to the person's age in Spanish or yelling "Hip-hip-hoo-birthday!" A Jehovah's Witness girl didn't know these things.

While the family sang, I stood off to the side, twiddling my thumbs in an apathetic fashion. None of the family protested or seemed to find this strange. They simply smiled sweetly and asked if I was sure I wouldn't like some cake. The nephews drank ginger ale, the adults drank coffee, then everyone hugged their grandmother and went home.

Having survived an actual "happy" birthday, I became a changed woman. To my Jehovah's Witness friends, I'd be like the quiet kid who'd once seen a dead body. In this way, I secretly began to think that things I'd always seen as *very* wrong were only *slightly* wrong. My useful habits were flickering slightly, like trick birthday candles. Lately, I'd been missing meetings at the Kingdom Hall, preferring to sit in a rocking chair and watch HBO at Sarah's. On top of it all, the entire Stover family considered themselves to be Christian. They believed in Jesus, went to church, and even did community service. It was a shame that Jehovah was going to kill them all at Armageddon.

CHAPTER 10

Recreation that Is Pleasing to the

Eyes of Our Lord

During the summer, the Stovers went on something Sarah called "a family vacation." I'd heard about this sort of normalcy, having been on a vacation of my own, once. When I was three, my whole family went to Montreal, where my mother accused the maid of stealing her Chanel No. 5, we got trapped in a self-cranked elevator, and I was begrudgingly allowed to eat Fruit Loops in our hotel room. Our family never went anywhere together again.

When I went to Sarah's house, I felt like a beloved TV-sitcom neighbor who comes over without knocking, and enters to applause. But during her family vacations I was empty and betrayed. My cat, my piano, and my never-ending supply of chocolate chip cookies had been viciously wrenched from me.

While the Stovers whiled away the sunburned hours in line at Space Mountain, I stood on the edge of my bathtub, threw cotton balls out the second-floor window, and sang a little song ("cotton,

cotton, cotton drop!") while they floated gently to the ground. I was having a hard time filling in the gaps.

So when Sarah visited Boothbay Harbor or Miami Beach, I hung out at the beach with my now second-best friend, Emily Fein.

At least once a year, Emily's mother hooked a pop-up trailer to the back of their Oldsmobile and drove me and her two daughters to Fishermen's Memorial State Park in Narragansett, an asphalt-paved campground with a swing set and a septic hookup. Sometimes my mother would tag along and make my life miserable by forcing me to wear long pants at night as protection against Lyme disease. She usually joined us only for the last day of the trip, frazzled and carrying a binder full of unpaid credit card bills.

Betty and my mom would drink instant coffee on a picnic bench and complain about their husbands, while Emily and I walked in circles around the campground, desperately looking for some crack in the pavement we hadn't seen the year before. No fathers ever came. We were strong women on vacation, driving just below the speed limit in the passing lane, doing it ourselves because the men in our life weren't taking the spiritual lead.

Emily's older sister, Maya, was 17. With her perky, attractive nose, she was the only person I knew who had actually gotten plastic surgery. On a night when my mother wasn't there, Maya met a blond surfer named Dean and his friend Corey, neither of whom appeared to own any clothing that didn't say Body Glove. Having the same fearless streak that Emily had, she invited Dean and his friend back to our campground to toast marshmallows. Betty pretended to be wary of the situation, but mostly she giggled like a suspicious schoolgirl at the two Jams-wearing surfer boys. And, because she was "the cool mom," we all drank one mini-Corona each and then waited for two hours to make sure the boys were safe to drive.

"I like your shorts," Dean said to me.

"Yeah, right," I stammered.

Not only could Dean drive, but he also had a job as a cashier at Stop & Shop. I felt completely outclassed.

"What?" he asked.

"I mean, okay."

"No, I really like your shorts," he reiterated, asking, "Are you shy or something?"

"I'm not shy!" I said. "I'm just . . . you know."

This highbrow comment about my shorts had me stumped. How could I keep up with an intense conversation like this?

"What kind of music do you like?" Dean asked as he mindlessly picked at my shorts. I giggled. My mouth was exuding glue in place of saliva. He asked again. "No, really. What kind of music do you like?"

"I listen to *cutting edge*," I told him, my voice like paste. "Like, you know WBRU? The *cutting edge* of rock?"

"Nah, I don't know it," he said. He ran his fingers through his sun-bleached mushroom cut. "I asked because we're going to a concert in Providence and I wondered if you like ska."

"Uhm. Who sings that?"

"Okay, never mind. Maybe I'll see you around First Beach."

In my diary, I wrote, "I am in love with a boy named Dean but he is so much older than me and he works at Stop & Shop and he drives. I CAN'T BELIEVE HE DRIVES!!! Maybe I will see him again though???"

Narragansett was only a 45-minute drive away, and my mother was a Sunday driver who meandered back roads in search of cute shops and ice cream parlors. So it wasn't surprising, several weeks after the camping trip had ended, to soon find myself "on the way" to Dean. Mom was deep in her amateur-photography phase at this point, and no covered bridge, waterfall, or grist mill was safe from her lens. I maneuvered us toward the shore by telling her I was really in the mood for seafood and suggesting a restaurant with a photogenic duck pond out back. We ate broiled scallops and drank tea with lemon. In my mind, every car that passed the restaurant was driven by Dean. I needed an excuse to get to Stop & Shop.

"Mom," I said. "I need tampons and I need them now."

Unfortunately for my ego, the plan was successful. Dean was standing dreamily behind a cash register and I was holding up a product that proclaimed, "I am bleeding between my legs."

"Oh, hey. What are you doing here?" he asked.

"You know," I said. I handed him my box of tampons and stood aside so that my mother could pay for them.

"Well, it was good to see you," he said.

"You too," I said as my mother glared at me viciously. My scam was up.

"Did you know that boy?" my mother asked as we walked back to the car.

"Kinda," I said, cursing my shorts, my fake period, and my inability to drive.

When I was 15, I transferred to high school and Emily got a summer job at a local bakery, ringing up almond horns in a mini-mall—just the sort of thing that would impress Dean. I seethed over Emily's ability to buy music tapes and T-shirts, that is, until she got fired because her coworkers thoughtfully baked her a birthday cake. Her spirituality was so offended by the free cake that she screamed, "I told you I don't celebrate my birthday! I'm a Jehovah's Witness!" and stormed out of the bakery. When she confided in me about the affront to her personal beliefs, I nodded my head in horror.

"I can't believe they baked you a surprise birthday cake," I said. "That's just . . . wow. What a terrible thing to do to someone."

"I know! I was so annoyed, I couldn't believe it!" she said. She didn't seem to be faking it either. It didn't seem to be an appropriate time to tell her I knew the Stovers had gift-wrapped a birthday bell for their cat.

I wished I could be spiritually strong like Emily. She was so fierce in life! I had always been the weak one, afraid of sparklers and dogs, and now kowtowing to worldly personalities. I was afraid of making a scene or hurting people's feelings, even in the face of Christian truths. What of the examples of Noah or Moses, fearless men who stood up for Jehovah even in the face of total social humiliation? Would Noah have stopped building the ark if someone showed up with Cookie Puss?

I thought of Sarah Stover's birthday party, how I wasn't spiritual enough to resist being there. I should have been like Emily, should have stood on the Stovers' piano and yelled, "How dare you have a birthday here when you know that I, and I alone, am a true Christian?" then walked right out their front door. Had I been at Herod's birthday party, would I have polished the platter that held the head of John the Baptist?

Thankfully, by the time Emily was fired, she'd already saved enough to put a down payment on a used car. As soon as she got her license, my own life changed vicariously. Suddenly my parents meant little more to me than last year's bus schedule and Dean was just a cashier who could chart my menstrual cycle. Emily would drive me to see a million Deans!

With Emily's car, I discovered Thayer Street in Providence, five commercial blocks of *Artitude!* that flanked Brown University and the Rhode Island School of Design. The independent bookstore let you sit on the floor, and the punk clothing store carried suits that said "Fuck" on them. There was even a futon store. This was a quarter mile of subversive collegiate life complete with real, live creative RISD art students in the coffee shop. Emily wanted to try Indian food, I wanted to be discovered as a brilliant artist. Either way, it was better than hanging out at Stop & Shop with my mother.

Emily would even take me to my very first concert, the Smithereens at Rhode Island College. I didn't really know who they were, and had never been to a concert, other than the day my mother surprised me with tickets to see *Cabbage Patch Kids Live* at the Leroy Theater in Pawtucket. I really wanted to go to a concert that didn't involve people wearing removable heads.

Emily nearly dislocated my shoulder pulling me through the sparse crowd at the Forman Hall facility to the front of the stage. I couldn't believe I had actually gotten to the front of the stage at my very first concert! I turned around and saw about 20 or 30 bored students mingling around in a small carpeted room. Then the Smithereens appeared, actually appeared, right in front of us! We held our ears and screamed. Not whistles or hoots of applause as our favorite songs began, but inappropriate, undirected Beatles screams. Insane, Ed Sullivan–like, *I think I just saw a man get stabbed in that alley* screams. The Smithereens looked at first bemused, then uncomfortable, and finally, began to scan the black box theater for escape routes.

After the concert, buzzed on adrenaline, we drove around North Providence with the moonroof open and screamed "Blood and Roses!" at everyone we passed. Woodstock couldn't have been better.

Emily was one of the few Jehovah's Witnesses I knew who was really into music. Sometimes she and her sister, Maya, held actual *dance parties* with actual *teenagers* at their home. Not only that, but any chaperones at the party who were of legal drinking age were actually allowed to drink.

Unlike every other Jehovah's Witness party, I didn't have to spend the night in the kitchen, having an "upbuilding conversation" with a 60-year-old Pioneer or—worst of all possible scenarios—playing Bible-based board games.

After everyone else left, Emily and I would sit on the steps with her mother and drink about a tablespoon each of Southern Comfort, speaking of it in hushed tones, like we were going into the bathroom to snort coke.

Maya invited some of the older, more mature couples from her congregation, like newlyweds Kimmy and Kevin, who, at the age of 24, had just had their first child. At one dance party, I spent most of the night bent over the baby's stroller, pinching its cheeks and trying to impress Kimmy with my innate child-rearing skills. However, the new mother seemed disinterested, and Maya gracefully pulled me out into the kitchen.

"Kevin's disappeared from the party and she doesn't know where he went," Maya whispered. "She's upset because he left her alone with the baby again and he's been doing this lately."

Emily confirmed that she, too, had heard that Kevin wasn't ready to be a father yet.

This gossip hit me hard. Weren't they almost, like, 25? How old did you have to be? And how could anyone be less than thrilled to own a beautiful, attention-grabbing child? What happened then? Jehovah's Witnesses weren't allowed to get divorced. If they were unhappy now, they'd be unhappy forever.

It haunted me for the rest of the party as I stole small secret glances at Kimmy, waiting to see her cry or otherwise express some real emotion.

At every party, Emily and I took pride in clearing the dance floor with some of our "cutting edge" music that normal people just didn't get. Still, we didn't expect to be the only two people dancing to a mainstream hit like "Losing My Religion." The partygoers were backing away from the dance area now, leaving an empty circle where Emily and I had jumped up and down and screamed, "I thought that I heard you laughing." It was halfway through the song, right around the mandolin solo, when the grumbling started. People stood with their palms against the wall, like we were in an amusement park ride that spins so fast you stick to the sides. We were all getting ready for the floor to drop out. Betty tapped Emily on the shoulder.

"We need to turn this song off," Emily whispered to me. "My mother says people are being stumbled."

"Oh, please! What, do they think they're going to actually 'lose their religion' by listening to it?" I scoffed.

"We've just got to turn it off."

I wanted to make a big deal out of it. I didn't want to lose "Losing My Religion." That's not what the song was about and I wanted to debate and discuss this like adults. It was one thing to be worldly, but this was a metaphor! What about freedom of expression?

"Let it go, Kyria. It's not our place to stumble someone or offend their conscience. It doesn't matter why."

I thought again about Sarah Stover's wicked birthday parties. Everyone there was so happy, so full of joy and cupcakes. Everyone at this party just wanted to bitch about something and turn off our music. Plus, the only cute boy here was an absentee father who left his wife sitting in a kitchen.

I would have gladly given up my belief in freedom of musical expression in exchange for meeting some cute boys at these parties. Most twentysomethings I knew were already married. There was no "casual dating" among our friends. If you went out to dinner with a member of the opposite sex, it was because you saw him as suitable marriage material. Dating was not for recreation. And since we could only date other Jehovah's Witnesses, the pickings were slim.

Unless, like me, you hid the truth from everyone in your congregation and secretly dated a worldly boy from school.

Miguel Ramirez asked me if I had a date to the Junior Semi-Formal, which, being a freshman in high school, I did not. Having already been corrupted by the worldly influence of birthdays, R.E.M., and futon stores, I accepted his invitation. I knew it was wrong, but when it came to boys, I was incapable of good judgment.

The problem, I guessed, was that my father hadn't been raised from birth as a Jehovah's Witness and he spoke of dating and cruisin' with a sly smile that made me long for bobby socks and shotgun weddings. There was always an underlying nostalgia Dad had for his teenage years, for *American Graffiti*, for Elvis,

for malt shops. My mother hadn't been raised a
Witness either, but she also said things like "I never ᵤᵤ
Beatles."

My father had a hard time hiding his nostalgia for the rockin'
'50s, and it seemed terribly unfair to someone like me, being
raised in the fundamentalist '80s. Sometimes a song like "Run-
around Sue" would come on the radio and make my father shake
his head in a way that let me know there had to be a girl attached
to it. "It's about a girl that I once knew," he'd mumble, combing
Vitalis through his hair. I wanted to bond with my dad, let him
know that I, too, could be a Teen Angel or a Fool in Love. But
when I told him I'd had a crush on Jayson Winters since seventh
grade, he gave me a stern lecture about being ready for marriage,
and the dangers inherent in being attracted to another person.

"I'll tell you another thing," he said. "Condoms don't work.
Just look at your brother for proof of that, okay?"

If Dad could have thrown me in a time machine, like his oldies station, "rolling the clock back to fabulous '55," he might have
let me innocently intertwine my soda straw with the captain of
the football team. But we were living in the last days, in the end-
time, in This System of Things Which Is Soon to Pass Away. Madonna sang about prayer in front of burning crosses, and Laverne
and Shirley lived together doing "God knows what." I was going
to stay locked in the house—not *like* a virgin, but *exactly* a virgin.

"I heard that Miguel asked you to the Junior Semi," Crystal
King said to me at school. "You know what he'll do if you go on
a date with him? He'll take you to his bedroom and claim he's
going to show you his baby pictures! And *then*—"

All the girls erupted when she said this, laughing so hard their
hair-sprayed bangs almost moved a little. Whatever! I liked baby
pictures. Maybe they were laughing because there was an embarrassing picture, like one of him being bathed in a sink.

I wanted to go on a date with Miguel, not because I was attracted to him but because he was the first boy who'd ever asked

me out. Even though I'd just gotten to this school, I knew he'd dated other girls who were older and cooler than me. It also meant that he didn't know me. He didn't know I was a Jehovah's Witness.

I figured that if things progressed well and I had to tell my parents we were dating, I'd just start a Bible study with him.

"I just need to let you know, Miguel, that I'm a Jehovah's Witness," I told him the next day. His face fell and I knew that wasn't what he wanted to hear.

"So, what does that mean, exactly?"

I told him I guessed it meant that I couldn't celebrate my birthday. It also meant I shouldn't make out with him, but I had every intention of doing that.

"I can still probably kiss, though," I told him. I wanted to play this cool and not ruin my chances.

"Well, I guess I should find someone else to go to the dance with, then."

"No, I mean, I still want to go to the dance."

"Uh. Nah. It sounds like maybe you can't go. I really don't think you can go."

"Oh, I can definitely still go! I just thought you needed to know, you know . . . I can't celebrate birthdays, I guess."

In this way, I cockblocked the perfectly attractive Miguel Ramirez at his own Junior Semi-Formal.

I told my parents I'd be at Sarah's, which I was. I just didn't tell them that I was also going to change my clothes and someone named Miguel was going to pick me up in a white suit and hand me a corsage.

Sarah didn't seem to mind covering for me, but she didn't seem especially supportive that I had a date either.

If only my fellow freshmen could see me at a *juniors'* dance, they'd change their minds about me real quick. In the high school gym, Miguel towered over me. During one of the slow dances, I tried to stand on his feet. He held his body flat against mine. I grabbed his butt cheeks and rubbed the small of his back. I wasn't sure what I was supposed to do, I just wanted to soak it all in, like a real teenager would.

I wished there were some way to share this night with my father, some way to make him proud of me for getting a date to the sock hop. Deep down, I felt that he secretly wanted me to have these experiences. But I knew that if I came right out and told him where I was, he'd have no choice but to punish me for it.

After the dance, Miguel and I went for a walk around the block. In a parking lot, he tried to put his hand up my skirt. Instinctively, I slapped his hand away. He tried it again, so I slapped his hand away again. It was, after all, what Gidget would have done. Miguel said he'd had a lovely time, dropped me off at Sarah's, and never spoke to me again. It was a shame, because I never did get to see his baby pictures.

Word of my prudence apparently didn't spread far, because a senior named Trevor Richards asked me out too. He'd been dating another senior, but she wanted to get married, so he broke up with her. To me, of course, getting married in high school didn't seem unusual at all, but I pretended to understand.

For our first date, I once again told my parents I'd be at Sarah's while Trevor took me to see my very first R-rated movie: *Pretty Woman*. I tried to act like I'd totally seen R-rated movies before. Yes, they'd been cut for television, but I knew what they were *really* saying under the bleeps.

At one point during the movie, Julia Roberts asks her hooker friend to name one woman who had a fairy-tale ending to her life, to which the sarcastic gum-chomping Laura San Giacomo answers, "Cinder-fucking-rella." The audience in our theater went wild.

Even though I was a freshman in high school, I had never heard anyone say the word "fuck" in a movie before. Yes, I had seen it on pants in a window on Thayer Street, but that was for the counterculture. It didn't occur to me that the word could be so commonplace that an audience full of otherwise normal people could actually laugh at it like it was *funny*. I wished I could find it funny too. But I couldn't. It seemed only a few years ago that my brother and I would hide in the backyard, far from where our parents could hear us, just to say "fuck" back and forth to each other.

A moment after "Cinder-fucking-rella," Trevor descended upon my face. We spent the rest of the movie like that, making out like it was the most acceptable thing in the world. With one movie ticket, I discovered that cussing could make people laugh and that seniors kissed by sticking their tongues in your throat. It never occurred to me that any decent high school student would want to have sex out of wedlock—we were only teenagers. That was for evil kids and Trevor didn't look evil. Trevor broke up with me a few weeks later to get back together with his ex, but that was fine by me. Since seventh grade, I'd been in love with Jayson Winters. And now I knew how to kiss him.

Chapter 11

And Look! In Heaven, There Appeared

a Fiery Eruption!

The first time I saw Jayson Winters, he was wearing snow-white parachute pants and a neon turquoise button-down shirt that came down to his knees. We were waiting in line for our seventh-grade homeroom assignments. His freckled face resembled that of a disturbingly sexy Cabbage Patch Kid accentuated by a highly stylish mushroom cut. I rarely saw mushroom cuts on the boys in my Kingdom Hall because our elders refused to give any privileges to boys who used a number two razor halfway up the back of their skull. This haircut was almost more than I could bear. For the first time in my life, I had the experience of being unable to stop staring at a person, even when they were onto me, even when they nudged their friend and said, "That girl's staring at me." I was transfixed, as if by a car wreck full of junior high school phero-mones. I went home and circled every Winters in the Pawtucket phone book, calling each number, then hanging up the phone.

Jayson and I were destined to be together. He wrote short stories that no one else understood but me, and listened to music that no one else liked but me. I rushed the line to make sure I could sit near him in the lunchroom and my desk was always right next to his.

Jayson ate M&Ms for lunch, and soon, so did I. Eating the sandwich that my mom had wrapped for me the night before suddenly seemed about as cool as wearing a lobster bib. I stopped hanging up the phone and started actually asking for Jayson.

Jayson was an artsy fellow, so his handwriting was a series of distinct, tiny capital letters. Not surprisingly, in about a month or so, so was mine. I'M NOT LIKE ONE OF THOSE OTHER GIRLY-GIRLS WHO DOT THEIR I'S WITH LITTLE HEARTS, I was saying. I'M JUST LIKE YOU, JAYSON. ONLY WE, TOGETHER, UNDERSTAND THE IMPORTANCE OF TINY CAPITALS!

Subtle, I was not. The entire class knew that I was harboring an obsessive crush on Jayson. I kissed his desk when I walked by it. I wrote poetry like THE OCEAN IS ALONE BUT I THINK OF YOU AND SMILE. I folded it and flicked it like an origami football across the lunch table at him. On the last day of school, I brought my camera to school and took pictures of Jayson taking pictures of me.

Jayson Winters. I heart Jayson. Kyria hearts Jayson. Kyria + Jayson 4-EVA.

Despite the fact that I stalked Jayson through two years' worth of mushroom cuts, bowl cuts, and summer-short crew cuts, he didn't hate me. By the time we got to high school, we had formed a kind of twisted friendship. That is, I was desperately in love with him and he was bemused by it. Every night after school, I'd shut myself in my room and we'd talk on the phone for hours. When he answered, music would be blasting in the background and he'd have to excuse himself to go turn it down. This led to many thrilling conversations such as "Whatchya listenin' to?" and "Oh. Who are they?" Through Jayson, I learned that you could even go to a concert while wearing *another band's* T-shirt.

"Everybody does it," he told me.

With hours spent on the phone every night, I was unable to conceal my crush on this boy from school. My parents could not forbid me from talking to him without my having a tantrum, so instead, they chose to annoy me about it.

"Hey, how's your comedian boyfriend?" my mother would ask. "You know, good old Jonathan Winters?"

"Mommmm! Come onnn! It's *Jayson* Winters!"

"Right. You know, I loved him on *Mork and Mindy*!"

Mostly, I sat quietly on my floor, fingering the phone cord while Jayson made fun of me for being a Jehovah's Witness. He pretended to have actual religious questions, so even if my father picked up the downstairs extension, he'd usually hear me quoting the tail end of a Bible verse. Jayson would laugh as I scrambled to find the perfect answer in the myriad of Jehovah's Witness reference books we had in our house. Desperate for his attention, I let him toy with me. He knew I couldn't bookmark or cross-reference fast enough. I was a fundamentalist golden retriever with a stack of slobbery *Watchtowers* sitting on the floor in front of me.

"You say you can't have blood transfusions. So what about eating meat?"

"We're not vegetarians! What are you talking about?"

"I mean, meat has blood in it."

"No, it doesn't. It's been bled!"

"But you can't get it *all* out."

"Yes, you can. Hold on . . . let me get another book. I know that's mentioned somewhere!"

I did everything I could to keep him on the phone, as if the call were being traced. Soon I'd familiarized myself with more Jehovah's Witness doctrine in the name of Jayson Winters than I ever had for Jehovah himself. Everything I knew about religion had been to impress a boy. He'd debate with me for hours. But when I told him that I was madly in love with him, he just laughed and changed the subject back to my religious proclivities.

"I heard you shut off the radio when the Morrissey song "Ouija Board" came on. What, did you think you were going to get possessed through the radio?"

"I love you, Jayson."

"I have a girlfriend."

Sure, he was dating some ditzy rich redhead who liked to ski, but I was still the girl he called to make fun of every night after school.

When Sarah signed my autograph book on the last day of junior high, she wrote, "Kyria, please don't be a gookie your entire life, okay? Please stop asking 'Do you think Jayson likes me?' and 'Do you think my hair's okay?' and do something with your life, okay?" Ever the perceptive teen, I read this, laughed, and continued to spend the entire summer asking if she thought Jayson would like my hair.

The best thing that could have happened to Sarah would have been for me to hook up with Jayson, not because she was rooting for me, but because I would finally shut up about it.

"Jayson was making fun of me for turning off 'Ouija Board,'" I told her. "Can you believe that?"

"Yeah, I can," she said. "Can we talk about something else?"

"Okay. Why don't I come over and we'll play Mille Bornes?"

"You know what, I have this friend," Sarah told me. "And she's always, always over at my house. I was wondering if you could recommend what I should do about that."

"I dunno. I guess you should just tell her that you don't like her."

"Well, it's not that I don't like her, it's that she always has some kind of problem we have to talk about. I don't want to hurt her feelings, but I can't help her."

"Are you talking about your friend Carol?"

"No."

"Are you talking about Vera?"

"No."

"Pam?"

"No."

"Who is it, then?"

"I'd rather not say."

"Right. But who is it?"

"Just . . . never mind, okay?"

Lately I'd been getting the distinct impression that Sarah was looking for excuses to be alone. This became clear after she told me that she needed to do homework—for two months.

"Can I come and do my homework with you?" I asked.

"Kyria, you don't even *do* homework. Ever."

True, by this point I was pretty much failing every single one of my classes and was in the guidance counselor's office at least once a week. But so what? I wasn't going to college, so it wasn't like I needed high school for anything.

College was at best unnecessary, and at worst atheist boot camp. My parents hadn't gone, and on top of that, we couldn't afford it. At least I'd been in the gifted class where I'd gotten "feeling smart" out of my system. With my fourth-grade knowledge of Logo in tow, I figured I already had a leg up on a large percentage of American public school graduates.

If you dedicated your life to Jehovah, he would provide for you. Taking matters into your own hands by going to school was like saying you didn't believe God could really handle the apocalypse, so you were gonna stock up on M-80s. It was the equivalent of investing in a huge block of real estate in downtown Pompeii.

I knew that Jehovah, or at least the Jehovah's Witnesses, would always take care of me. I didn't have to worry about school!

"Well, can I still come over after school just once a week?" I asked.

"No. I'm trying to get good grades so I can get into college. And I need extracurricular activities too."

I had no idea that colleges counted extracurricular activities. "What about the weekends?"

"Yeah, I mean, sometimes, I guess. I just need some time for . . . homework. I'll see you during the day at school, okay?"

Sarah was my best friend, she *had* to be! Didn't she want me over at her house day and night, eating her food and sitting on her bed and kicking her cat? She wouldn't send me back to my home, back where my parents were ripping up Dungeons & Dragons games and making fun of me for my crush on Jayson. Would she?

Later, I found an evangelical pamphlet on her shelf called "How to Witness to Jehovah's Witnesses." It contained lies about Jehovah's Witnesses being a cult and said I would get very angry if this were brought up to me directly.

"Do you think I'm in a cult?" I screamed. "Because I'm not! I'm in the one true religion! Are you trying to convert me?"

"No, no. I was just reading it because I mentioned to a friend that you were a Jehovah's Witness and someone at my church gave it to me, that's all."

"Why would you be talking about me being a Jehovah's Witness? Is this what you think of me?"

Sarah looked at the floor and didn't say anything. I couldn't believe that she would betray me like this. She'd never once insinuated that she didn't agree with my religion. All this time I thought that I was subtly converting *her*, that through my godly works and deeds, she might one day become a Jehovah's Witness herself, then I wouldn't have to lose my best friend at Armageddon.

I couldn't even sit with her at lunch for a few weeks, letting the idea of my best friend's undeniable death gently become reality.

I just . . . needed some time to do my homework.

While Sarah was readying herself for college, I was readying myself to flunk out of high school. I stayed home more often than I went to class, and my mother began making overarching threats about how I'd be taken away by the truant officer, as if a London bobby with a nightstick was going to grab me by the ankles while I scurried under the docks. Since I couldn't pass any tests, I was pushed out of the gifted program and down into the twos.

Under the influence of Jayson Winters, my lunch lately consisted of a can of Coke and an ice cream sandwich. Still undiagnosed with hypoglycemia, I crashed every afternoon. If a class was scheduled within 20 minutes of a candy bar, I would whiz through my tests like Robin Williams at an *SNL* after-party. After that, I put my head down on my desk and tried to figure out how to move my arms without falling over. Depending on the weekly class rotation, I could either be a brilliant biology student or the kind of student who dissects her own thumb.

I was also knee-deep in OCD. Most of my compulsions centered on writing things on paper, specifically numbers. So I couldn't write any math problems without in turn scribbling ritualistic hieroglyphs on the side of the paper. Every math test I turned in looked like an ancient rune, a multiple-choice *Book of the Dead*. I found a brief respite in algebra, whose much-maligned variables made it the most relaxing math class I'd ever taken.

Meanwhile, my new history teacher insisted that children learn better when it's cold and opened all the windows in January. My French teacher taught us how to say *"oui,"* then *"mais oui,"* and spent the rest of the year in the hallway flirting with saucy Cape Verdean girls. My drunken math teacher once pulled aside a student who'd repeated her class, and slurred, "You took this last year. Why don't you teach it?" and wobbled out of the room with a flask in her hand.

Many people reach adulthood with pleasant memories of a favorite teacher who changed their outlook on life. I, however, rated all my teachers on two levels: those who were completely apathetic and those who seemingly aimed to destroy the institution of public education.

About this time, I became "teenage suicidal." I didn't grasp the full ramifications of not existing, but death seemed preferable to sitting in a 40-degree history classroom, obsessively drawing numbers on my test, while my pancreas excreted mass amounts of insulin into my shivering body and a man with halitosis screamed in a Rhode Island accent, "Let's tawk about the Contahnental Cawngress!"

Death was dark and dramatic. School just sucked.

When my father drove me to school, I would pull the seat right up to the dashboard, take off my seat belt, and pray that he would get into an accident. Unfortunately, my father was a competent driver and I was very short.

It's possible I might have done well academically if my parents had sent me to an artsy private school, the type of "interactive learning environment" that grades students by asking them what score they believe they've earned. I asked my parents if I could attend School One, a private school in Providence with a lot of pottery classes.

My parents couldn't afford it, so they told me that I was failing school because "Kyria wants to do what *she* wants to do when *she* wants to do it." With this nuanced decree, the matter was considered closed. I could make art on my own time, but for now, I was going to sit in a wintery history class and I was going to *like* it.

"If you have a real problem with it, you can go to Davies Tech. At least you'll learn a skill," my mother would threaten.

A lot of kids in my Kingdom Hall were going to Davies. They became hairdressers, carpenters, and repairmen—blue-collar jobs that paid more than anyone with a master's in English could ever hope to make working at the bookstore.

I wanted to be a pianist or a cartoonist. Cutting hair was anathema to me. I wrote poetry and took black-and-white photos of graveyards. I did not, I could not, give someone strawberry-blond highlights. But Davies Vocational was as close as many Jehovah's Witness kids got to college.

One *Watchtower* article described the terrible fate that befalls those who try to better themselves through higher education. It told the story of a young Christian man in, quote, "a large city in the Far East," who went abroad to further his study. In just a year or so, the article noted, "he lost his faith completely and claimed to be an agnostic."

The bottom line was that Armageddon was coming and college would make you Asian. My high school needed welfare, I had OCD and hypoglycemia, and on top of it all, I was still a self-obsessed teenager.

So, in tenth grade, I decided I'd like to stay home from school pretty much every single day and I didn't really feel like making up a reason to do so. I planned to quit the day I turned 16.

CHAPTER 12

Excel as Students of God's Kingdom,

Not of Higher Education!

My parents needed to go to work and didn't have time to pull me out of bed by one ankle every morning. My father chose the apathetic route of dealing with this by smacking me in the back of the head and saying, "Fine, go ahead and stay here, you lazy lump," while my mother would sit on the edge of my bed and threaten me with psychiatric treatment.

"What's the problem here, Kyria? Do you think you are too good to go to school, or what? I mean, just who, pray tell, do you think you are?"

"I think I'm me," I'd say, and roll over into my pillow.

"Well, I think 'me' is going to need to see a psychiatrist if she doesn't get it in gear, that's what I think."

In the absence of a satisfactory answer, Mom began trying to find one on her own. She rifled through my room when I wasn't home, read my poetry, and found my diary where I'd hidden it inside the drop ceiling. She spent hours on the phone with her friends discussing my attitude problem and unacceptable behavior ("She's out of control and I am utterly exasperated with her shoddy attitude. I tell you, she is going to be the death of me one day!").

I spent my copious "sick" days playing the piano, watching talk shows, and eating potato salad. I tore down huge strips of the rainbow wallpaper that had hung in my bedroom since I was born and began to draw a series of cartoons on the exposed dry-wall with a Sharpie. Sarah, who had recently visited Germany, came over and wrote a harrowing poem called "Auswitch," that I thought was a joke. My bedroom wall was soon covered in song lyrics and Monty Python quotes. It smelled of indelible markers.

The more my parents ineffectually yelled at me, the more I became convinced that I was doing the right thing with my life. School was lame, parents were lame, and the Jehovah's Witnesses would take care of me until Armageddon came. In my mind, there wasn't a single reason not to quit high school. My mother would be angry, but then, she was always angry.

I can't say I had big plans for my free time, I just preferred playing 1940s jazz standards to playing volleyball with a group of angry students. If not for the constant threats that the truant officer was going to take me to juvie, I could have sat at the piano bench and tinkled out "Misty" for the rest of the semester.

One evening, I came home from a solitary bike ride to find Sister Emery, a gray-haired Pioneer, sitting in our kitchen. She was drinking coffee and awkwardly holding a photocopy of a note I had recently written my mother. The note said: "My damn room IS clean you stupid bitch so LEAVE ME ALONE!"

A second copy of the note had been pinned to the refrigerator with magnets. The word "bitch" was circled in red pen. At the bottom my mother had written: "Haughty, disobedient to parents, unthankful, disloyal, having no natural affection, not open to any agreement, slanderers, without self-control" says 2 Timothy 3:1–5!! What kind of CHRISTIAN daughter calls her mother a BITCH??"

I walked past my mother and sat at the top of the stairs while Sister Emery was given pastries and questioned as to what *she* would do with a daughter like me.

My mother spoke loudly, knowing I was listening. She said she had tried absolutely everything, but I just refused to cooperate and now she was absolutely, positively at her wit's end.

"Kyria wants to do what *she* wants to do when *she* wants to do it," my mother said. This was a stock phrase, her go-to definition of me. Independent, selfish, without regard for others.

"You know, I remember reading about something called 'school phobia,'" Sister Emery said. "I didn't like school much myself as a kid. Maybe it's possible that Kyria has school phobia."

"The only phobia Kyria has," my mother responded, "is to being a decent daughter."

I yelled from the top of the stairs that I thought I *did* have school phobia, and my mother responded by telling me to mind my own beeswax.

"You see how she is, Sister Emery? Listening in on our conversations like that. How am I supposed to help a girl like that?"

The next time I saw Sister Emery at the Kingdom Hall, she put her hand on my shoulder and asked how I was doing. "Think about that 'school phobia,'" she told me. "I bet you a dollar to a doughnut you have that."

My mother made an appointment for our whole family to see one Dr. Vogell—an angry, ruddy-faced family therapist with a lot of macramé owls in his office. Jehovah's Witnesses were allowed to seek mental assistance if necessary, but the organization warned us to be very careful. Many therapists, guided by Satan, had used the opportunity to convince their already mentally weak patients that they were in a *cult*! So it was imperative to keep on guard and ensure that when a therapist took away our nervous tics and agoraphobia, he didn't also take away our access to eternal life.

My father refused to see Dr. Vogell. He'd been through the

same *shpiel*, he said, many times when my mother called the elders to come over and pay the family a visit of encouragement. These visits usually ended with my father getting up in the middle and saying something like "I don't need to sit here and be crucified," then heading into the basement. My mother was just looking for someone, anyone, to corroborate her story against Dad's.

My brother and I were unable to escape. All three of us sat on the same leather couch, with Mom in the middle. Immediately, she burst into tears. Seeing my mother cry always made me cry, even when I wasn't feeling sad, like the fumes from peeled onions. I began to cry too.

"Why are you crying?" the therapist asked us.

"Because it just *sucks* that we even have to be here at all!" Mom said. When she said "sucks," her voice cracked and got far too loud.

For the rest of the session, Mom talked about how my father was so irresponsible he couldn't even be bothered to be here for his family and how she was *trying, trying, trying* to keep everything together but got no support from anyone.

"It all just *sucks*, quite frankly, Doctor. It's all a big, smelly bunch of BS!"

I marveled at the decorative choice of dark wood paneling matched with an intensely thick bright orange shag rug. This man had the deepest pile I'd ever seen.

My mother continued to see Dr. Vogell weekly, until he told her that she should stop caring so much about what other people did and start concentrating on herself. She then declared him a quack and an a-hole who just wanted to get people hooked on medicine. She said he wanted to get rid of her as a patient because she was onto him and wouldn't take drugs.

"Do you know how much money a doctor gets if they can hook you on those drugs?" Mom would ask anyone who would listen. "It's not nothing!"

At this point, we began to see a series of family counselors, whose reactions ranged from mildly disinterested to obviously annoyed. We'd see someone for a few weeks at most; then my mother would declare him to be a quack and a "worldly influence." One of the therapists was accusing *her* of needing to change *her* behavior, while another dared to suggest that our religion might be making things difficult.

To my mother, all you had to do to be a good therapist was agree that her children were lazy and disrespectful, that her husband wasn't taking the lead, and that she got no recognition for being the only one who held our family together.

There was one woman I really liked, named Denise. She showed me how to relax my whole body just by doing breathing exercises. After seeing her for about a month, I decided I trusted her enough to tell her that I was crazy. I called her on the phone and asked if she knew what obsessive-compulsive disorder was.

"Yes, I have heard of that," she told me.

"Well, don't tell anyone, but I have that," I said.

"Okay. We can talk about it the next time you come in."

"Don't tell anyone!"

"I would never do that."

"Please don't tell my mother. I'm begging you!"

However, the next time I was scheduled to see her, I refused to get out of the car. My mother tried pleading with me, yelling at me, tugging on me, and finally, went inside to get Denise. I had no way to explain that I'd simply changed my mind about telling the truth today. I didn't want to be crazy, I'd rather stay *Cain*.

Denise tapped gently on the car window.

"Don't feel like coming in?" she asked gently.

I shook my head no. I was certain that the jig was up. Now she would take my mother aside and tell her that I, Kyria Abrahams, was a complete idiot. I was a fool and a moron because I thought I could stop bad things from happening by counting trees. I had no trust in Jehovah. I had no grip on reality. I was really stupid.

My mother got back into the car. "Well, the therapist said that she's sad she can't talk to you today. She'll be glad to have you back whenever you feel up to it."

Mom took me out to lunch at one of our favorite restaurants, J&B's Bistro. We ordered cheesecake. We took our time. Mom never asked me why I didn't want to go back and never forced me to see a therapist again.

After that, I was taken to a regular physician, who, in the absence of anything more compelling, determined I had a mild vitamin B deficiency. This was after I, unfortunately, had tested negative for Lyme disease. He brought me into his office to discuss this in private. This was the first time I had ever been in a doctor's office and not in an examination room. I was surprised to see that there were guest chairs and a hanging plant. The wall behind his desk was covered with plaques that proved you could trust him.

"Does your mother seem overbearing?" he asked me.

This was completely out of nowhere. How did he know?

"What? Yes. But why?"

The doctor came out from behind his huge, dark desk and sat in the chair next to mine.

"Your mother. Is it like she's always telling you what to do?" he asked, leaning forward and looking into my eyes.

I turned around in my chair to see if my mother was in the room or if there was otherwise some kind of recording device aimed toward me.

"Uh, yes?"

"Do you feel like you can't do anything right as far as she's concerned? I mean, does she yell at you a lot, does she look down on you?"

How did he know these things? How could anyone know these things about my mother?

"Yes, oh yes! Absolutely! She is constantly yelling at me and telling me I'm a bad person and I'm lazy, and I'm really not!"

"That's what I thought. Tell you what, why don't you wait outside for a minute, and I'm going to talk to your mom, okay?"

I was not expecting this line of questioning, but I was overjoyed. For the first time in my life, someone had seen through what was happening. My mother, who acted *oh, so put-upon*, was not the innocent martyr she made herself out to be. If a real medical doctor told her to stop yelling at me, surely she'd have to! Now she *had* to respect my feelings. I didn't know how or why or what gods had sent me a vitamin B deficiency to make my mother shut up, but I wanted to praise them. Thank you, lack of almonds in my diet, thank you!

It took about 30 seconds before my mother came storming out of the doctor's office. Her coat half on, she grabbed my hand like a kidnapper and rasped through her teeth, "Come on. We are getting the *hell* out of here."

"What happened?"

"Just move it, okay? I have never been so disgusted in my entire life!"

I turned around briefly, to see the doctor peering gently out from behind his office door. He gave me a small wave.

Since my failing grades had nothing to do with an omnipresent Armageddon, a miserable school system, the overabundance of insulin in my pancreas, the lack of serotonin in my brain, or a dysfunctional home, my mother deduced that it clearly must be a brain tumor and scheduled me for a CAT scan.

Now that I'd been dragged from congregation elders to psychiatrists to school guidance counselors, the hospital was my last chance for redemption. Was I really lazy and a bad person, or did I just have cancer? Once they scanned my brain, everyone would know for sure.

Getting a CAT scan if you're an adult who has been suffering from debilitating migraines is, I imagine, something of a relief.

Having a CAT scan because you're a teenager who is failing math and hates her life was not something I welcomed. I handled the situation with typical detachment and annoyance. I complained to my friends about having had my brain scanned for tumors, saying, "My mom is like, so crazy!"

In the hospital, I was told to lie *perfectly still* inside an impressive-looking metal tube that happened to tell people if they would die from cancer. The technician smiled and told me not to be scared.

"Some people do get scared," she said.

I didn't want her speech to be in vain, so I pretended I'd been a little nervous until her voice calmed me. In reality, I felt nothing but resignation. I lay on the slab of machine where she reminded me to remain *perfectly still* with the compelling argument "Or we'll end up doing this all over again."

My mother sat somewhere outside during all this, I guessed, in a waiting room or in the cafeteria with a large black coffee. Maybe she was catching up on the pile of unpaid bills that she carried in her pocketbook at all times. She would spread them on her lap or a coffee table whenever a free 30 minutes presented itself.

I found being trapped in the machine to be rather cozy. Save for the occasional *bink* or *ping*, the machine was eerily silent, like submerging your ears in the bathtub. There was a little mirror right above me, reminiscent of the ones in a parakeet cage, to give the patient a comforting, otherly face. At this point, I had two options: keep my eyes shut tight, or take a good, long look at myself.

I saw a thin, stupid face, with big blue eyes. When I was a little girl, people used to stop me in public to tell me what beautiful eyes I had. "I know," I once answered, much to my mother's horror. I was four years old, and I thought that knowing things for sure was what made you a grown-up.

I had no inner guilt about not doing my homework or any

number of things I should have been doing but wasn't. I couldn't do anything but lie still and stare at myself.

I liked the CAT scan better than having Lyme disease, better than 1970s shag carpeting, and much better than gray-haired men with bookmarks in their Bibles. It seemed completely normal to hold my arms perfectly still. Lying still and waiting was what I did every night.

I rarely saw Sarah anymore, so when she called to let me know that she and a friend from school were going to see the Fourth of July fireworks at the PawSox stadium, I let bygones be bygones and accepted the invitation—especially because Jayson had broken up with his girlfriend and was driving us in his parents' station wagon. This was my big chance to make Jayson fall in love with me. It was also my first chance to see a real fireworks display.

My parents hadn't given up on attempting to tell me and my brother what to do; we'd just stopped caring. They would yell, but they always yelled. What had stopped us in our tracks as kids was now just a bothersome speed bump. I told my mother I was going out and listened to her screams of "good for nothing" and "What about the Book Study?" become more and more muffled as I closed the door behind me.

My clever plan to seize control of my star-crossed lover's heart during the fireworks display would utilize the seductive power of music. I would bring a tape of The Cure's *Disintegration* cued to "The Same Deep Water as You"; then I would give Sarah a predetermined signal to leave the premises, pop in the tape, and allow Jayson to fall moodily in love with me. I hadn't really gotten further than that.

Five minutes after we parked, I brought Sarah and her friend Vera into an exceedingly conspicuous huddle.

"Okay, so you guys are gonna find an excuse to leave, right?"

"Yes, Kyria! We told you! We'll take off, don't worry!"

"Please. Please just do this for me." I was wringing my hands like an old Italian woman begging a saint not to take her only son. "I'm. Begging. You."

"Jesus, Kyria. I said we'd do it like five times already!"

A tense half hour passed before Sarah announced that she and Vera were going off to find a girls' room. Jayson protested because the fireworks were about to start, but I glared at Sarah and told her to take her time, really. As if hitting my mark on a movie set, I curled up next to Jayson on a blanket in the back of the station wagon, just like I'd imagined it.

"Hey, you like The Cure, right? Put this in," I ordered, pulling the tape nonchalantly out of my pocket and leaning over him to turn up the volume.

The song itself is over nine minutes long. It begins with the sound of rain, then thunder, then soft guitars. Robert Smith shudders out the line "Kiss me goodbye," as if *"goodbye"* is the only way anyone ever kissed.

The fireworks started and I touched his face with my hand. Robert Smith sang about the twist of a lover's lips, and I did too. Jayson kissed me. Held my hand. The sky bloomed with shiny soot and everything around me was exploding. We kissed for nine minutes and 21 seconds. Just like I'd imagined it. Robert Smith sang, "I'll kiss you forever on nights like this." I agreed.

I'd waited the last four years for this Hollywood-perfect nine minutes. All the Trevors and Miguels were just rungs on a rickety ladder leading to the furnished roof deck that was Jayson Winters. With the exception of being born, this was the first time in my life that I'd gotten what I wanted. When Sarah came back, I gave her the thumbs-up and told her that Jayson was in love with me too.

"We missed the fireworks while waiting in line at the Port-A-Potty," she said.

There was some initial discussion on who to drop off first, which surprised me. Wasn't it clear that Sarah and Vera should go home first? Obviously, Jayson would want some alone time with his girlfriend.

"Want to go somewhere and make out some more?" I asked.

"Nah, I mean, I gotta get home."

God, he was so cool.

"Oh. Well, what do you want to do this weekend, then?"

"I think I'm busy this weekend," he said.

"Uh. Do you want to sit in the car and listen to that song again?"

"I think I'm fine for now."

"Okay, well, I'll see you at school, then. I'll call you tomorrow! Or you can call me tomorrow! Well, you know. I love you! I'll talk to you tomorrow!"

"Okay. Good night, then!"

Jayson kissed me goodbye with the strangest twist upon his lips. I walked into my room and lay on my back on the floor, rewinding "The Same Deep Water as You," pawing at the air. Knowing everything, finally, was perfect.

When my new boyfriend/love-of-my-life called me the next day, I was so hyped up that I could barely keep myself untangled from the phone cord.

"I can't see you again," he said. "Think of it this way. Say you have a really nice white dress that you don't want to soil . . ."

"What? You. . . . But you kissed me."

"You're like a white dress, Kyria. Do you know what I mean? You're a clean white dress and I don't want to get you dirty."

I was simultaneously confused and insulted. Why would Jayson have a dress? How could he dirty it?

"I am not a white dress! I'm not! I am in love with you and you kissed me and it was good. Please, just be my boyfriend, please! I promise you will love it if you give it a chance! Just don't do this to me."

"Kyria, trust me. You are too *clean*."

I protested until there was nothing left to say. But I made him laugh, I said. We had all these great conversations. Other girls wouldn't make him laugh like I did. I *got* him. I'd felt the way he kissed me. Why stop now? What would he do without me?

Jayson said there was nothing left to discuss. I was a white dress and he hung up on me. When I cried, it sounded like fireworks.

My mother was screaming at me because I had forgotten to close the refrigerator door. It was hanging open, cooling the whole house. She spat the usual litany of my sins at me. Not only was I ungrateful, lazy, and malicious, but I'd finally gone and failed all my classes and would have to repeat the tenth grade.

"That's what you wanted, isn't it?" she yelled. "You tried and tried and tried to fail and you finally got your way. Kyria always gets her way! No regard for anyone else, that's what you have! Kyria does what *she* wants to do when *she* wants to do it!"

I decided, at that moment, that I was tired of being screamed at. I walked to the bathroom, locked the door, and opened the medicine cabinet. I chose a full bottle of store-brand antihistamines. I noticed that they were yellow as I swallowed them. They worked, because I immediately stopped wanting to die. The weight of my impulse-suicide lay heavy on my chest like an X-ray apron.

"Selfish, selfish, selfish!" my mother was repeating.

I opened the bathroom door. Mom was still screaming, pulling blankets out of the cedar chest, saying "Goddamn kids," and "Nobody helps around here," and "Damn, damn, shit!"

"Mom," I said, handing her the empty bottle.

"What is this?"

"I don't know."

"Kyria, what is this? Did you swallow these?"

"Yes."

She took the bottle from me and walked down the hall to where my father sat on his bed, polishing his shoes for the Kingdom Hall. I backed into my bedroom and curled up on my canopy bed. My father opened the door.

"What the hell are you trying to do, you idiot? Are you trying to kill yourself?"

"I don't know."

"You idiot," he said. "You stupid idiot!"

I stayed in the bedroom for a while, with the door closed. I shuffled to the top of the stairs, and strained to hear my mother on the phone, whispering. I heard her say "Yeah," and "Mm-hmm," and "Okay, bye." I went back into my room and turned on some music. I closed my eyes and fell asleep for a little while.

I woke up feeling like I'd been punched in the tongue. I ran to the bathroom and puked in a way that can only be described as "majestic." A perfect arc of still-whole pills emanated from my throat. It tasted like I was gargling aspirin. I needed to breathe, needed to stop this fire-hose burst, but nothing short of a throat tourniquet would stop it. I could only stand there as if this were happening to someone else, continuing to watch the stream leave my body and wait until I could breathe in. I thought I might asphyxiate.

I pulled a stack of towels from the shelf and collapsed onto the bathroom floor, wondering if I was going to die. I couldn't lift my head and I couldn't drink water without puking. Frankly, this failed-suicide thing was all getting on my last nerve. My stomach wasn't playing fair. We needed to talk. There is nothing left in you, stomach, I said, There's no need to send my uvula flying into the wall. Can't we work this out like adults? I fell asleep hugging a pile of starchy towels, porcelain sweating above my head.

I slept on the floor for several hours, expecting an ambulance or at least a glass of water. But no one ever came.

When I awoke, it was already getting dark. I managed to pull myself off the floor and staggered downstairs. The house was eerily empty, shuttered like an unused time-share. I surmised that my father was in the basement, but couldn't be sure.

I grabbed a container of yogurt from the refrigerator and brought it back to the bathroom. I ate one spoonful of yogurt, waited about ten seconds, and barfed. For the rest of the evening, I lay on the bathroom floor, with a quart of yogurt next to my head, wondering where everyone had gone. Had they left to go buy a coffin?

I surmised that my parents were so annoyed that I'd "pulled this stupid stunt" that it was now my punishment to deal with it alone. I was glad that I didn't have to look my parents in the eye, but it was so hard to lift my head. I didn't want to deal with my family, but I wished I didn't have to be completely alone—if only someone could just hold the back of my head while I dry-heaved. If only someone could tell me I wasn't going to die.

Eventually my stomach stopped contracting and I crawled to bed. I woke up three days later. Bored, I decided to stencil a border of roses around my doorway with some craft paints. My mother came into my bedroom with her camera and, crying, snapped the whole roll of film. This was the only acknowledgment I had tried to kill myself that I ever received—a tearful series of photos in which I look like I have two black eyes. Other than that, we never spoke of it again.

Not only had I flunked out of the tenth grade, now I had failed at committing suicide. Jayson thought I was a white dress and Sarah saw me as a deterrent to college.

This, it seemed, was a good time to make some new friends.

Zelda was an artsy, nonconformist chick, who I had seen but never talked to because she was one grade behind me. She carried a lunch box instead of a purse, matched combat boots with ripped prom dresses, and showed a general disdain for everyone we knew. I wasn't entirely sure that Zelda didn't have a great disdain for me as well.

"You're such a poseur," Zelda said to me as we sat alone together at lunch. "I mean, look at you. You bring your sandwiches wrapped in wax paper just because I do. You never used wax paper before you met me, did you? *Did you?*"

Even though she was probably an atheist, I thought of Zelda as Jehovah's Witness by proxy. She had two cousins, Josh and Pete, who attended a Kingdom Hall in Springfield, Massachusetts.

The first time I met Josh was at Zelda's house. He had come to visit his cousins carrying a skateboard and a videotape of *Harold and Maude*, which he said was "the saddest movie ever made." Josh was like a ruddy-nosed Keanu Reeves. He was sort of freckly, sort of cute, a little dopy, and about as punk rock as a Jehovah's Witness could possibly be on his off days without someone reporting him to the elders.

Zelda spent that night dressing in costumes from their "costume bag" and jumping on the couch. Josh made inside jokes about the Violent Femmes song "Blister in the Sun."

"Remember what Chuck said that meant?" Josh would squeal, at which point his brother Pete would become incapacitated from laughter and fall across the back of the couch, slamming pillows with his fist.

"What, you guys? What does it mean?" I'd ask.

"Never mind!" Josh would say, making a fist at Pete as if just *daring* him to stop punching the couch and let me in on the joke.

Then Zelda put a tutu on her head.

A week later, Josh asked me on a date. He wanted to know if I'd like to go to Wes' Rib House with him and his brother, then watch while they skated on a half-pipe. In the parking lot, he presented me with a mix tape and immediately became my boyfriend. The romance of the tape, coupled with the fact that he was a Jehovah's Witness capable of standing on a board that had wheels on it, sealed the deal.

The half-pipe was in an old mill with leaky pipes, sweaty walls, and all the ambience of Mad Max's Thunderdome. The mill also housed the studio of a RISD student who made stickers that told us "Andre the Giant Has a Posse." We were greeted by a man with yellow dreadlocks and an eye patch, who walked with a cane and was probably named something like "Crazy Jack" or "Herpes Pete." He pointed Josh in the direction of the other skaters, tapped his cane against a rabid-looking dog, and led me to a catwalk high above the skating action. For a brief moment, I thought I might be asked to walk a plank.

The dank mill echoed with deafening skate-rock anthems about punks and skaters and skate punks skating. I was shivering and dizzy, filled with BBQ pork. In between songs, there was the crashing of boards and a few choice grunts of agony, mostly from Josh. For two hours, I watched as Josh and his brother landed repeatedly on their asses. When he finally put his arm around me to lead me back to the car, I felt like I'd been rescued after spending days trapped in a well.

To my family, I denied that Josh and I were dating, even when he came in to use the bathroom. Of *course* we weren't dating, I assured my mother, because only people who are seeking a suitable marriage mate actually go on dates. But she knew that I was trying to hide the fact that I was happy, so as revenge, she decided to make my life miserable over it.

"When's your boyfriend *Rick Springfield* coming over again?" she'd taunt.

"Don't call him that, Mom!"

"Rick Springfieeeeeeld. Rick Spriiiiingfield!!" she'd sing. "I'm onto you. You and your *boyfriend* from Springfield!"

She said the word "boyfriend" as if she were saying "Hitler!" or "Your goddamn secretary!"

"Why do you hate him, Mom?"

"Oh, I don't hate him," she'd say. "I just think it's funny to see you get so upset!"

In truth, I found him boring. Once the novelty of "skater" wore off, there wasn't any huge connection between us. The only thing he ever talked about was this "awesome married couple" in his congregation named Matthew and Susan who were really cool and spiritual, even though they were, like, 30. "I swear, they are so cool," he'd tell me. "You'd just have to meet them to understand."

I'd see him once a week, and we'd make out in his car. He rarely shaved and kissed like he was trying to Brillo my face off. I threw my lips onto him like a retarded leech. Since there was nothing else to do, nowhere else to put our hands, we had marathon sucking sessions that lasted for hours and resulted in a semipermanent cherry Popsicle–stain rash around my lips.

When Josh went on a family vacation for two weeks, I didn't miss him. I was relieved that I didn't have to spend my weekends getting thrown out of parking lots on the charge of mediocre skateboarding. When he returned, he gave me an R.E.M. postcard along with a wallet-size copy of his high school photo, on the back of which he had written:

Dear Kyria
This time I ~~think~~ KNOW it's real.

Love, Josh

He then told me that he had bought a pair of sunglasses for the hip 30-year-old married woman and how awesome she was and how she didn't act old at all. Mostly, we talked about how much he hoped she'd like the sunglasses.

In order to get him to shut up, I grabbed his neck with my tongue and sucked it like a vampire. I wasn't sure what the point of this was, but I heard that people liked hickeys. Then he drove back to Zelda's house to say goodbye to his aunt.

Twenty minutes later, the doorbell rang. He was back! How romantic!

"Why did you give me a hickey?" he yelled.

"Why? What do you mean, *why*?"

"You should have told me. My aunt saw it. They're mad. They're mad at you, Kyria!"

"It's just a hickey or whatever!"

"They think I should break up with you now," he said, before adding, "But I'm not going to. Not yet."

Several weeks passed before my parents were both out of the house and our hard-core kissin' party made its way onto the daybed, which had replaced my now childish canopy bed and all its memories of "playing fort." Josh scoured his face into mine, pinning me down against my decorative pillows. Soon he stopped kissing me and began moaning and throwing himself against me. His whole body was convulsing, each leg having its own independent seizure. I felt like I was vicariously receiving electroshock therapy. He jumped off me and ran into the bathroom.

About 15 minutes later, he emerged with his head down and a huge wet spot on the front of his jeans.

"I have to go," he said.

"Why? What happened."

"I got in the sink."

"*In* the sink? How?"

"The sink. I . . . turned the water on too hard."

"Do you want a hair dryer?"

"I have to go home and change my pants!"

Josh kept repeating that he had to go home, had to change, didn't want to talk about it. I didn't understand why he was so embarrassed by getting "in the sink." What was so bad about having wet pants?

A week later, Josh broke up with me on my side porch.

"I talked with Matthew and Susan in my congregation about

it. You know, they're older, so I told them what happened," he said. "I was really close to sinning, Kyria."

"Close? You can get as close to sinning as you want to, as long as you stop."

"No! You don't understand. The things that we were doing are for married people to do. We're not married!"

"So?"

"Kyria, I can't marry you now. And I want to make it to the New System. So I can't see you anymore, okay?"

At this, I tried to make myself cry.

I called Emily and told her that Josh had broken up with me. I was actually relieved not to have to watch him skateboard again, but, used the opportunity to soak up just a little sympathy.

"God, what a jerk-off!" Emily said. "He's just a real jerk-off!"

"I know!" I fake-cried. "I hate him!"

"Did he say why he was breaking up with you?"

I told her I had no idea. He hadn't really explained it very well.

CHAPTER 13

Taking the Lead as Friends of Christ

Lisa's blue Dodge Colt ran on Holy Spirit, not gas. We knew this because Lisa was a Pioneer in our congregation who spent 90 hours each month knocking on people's doors to proclaim the imminent arrival of God's Kingdom. In order for the end of days to occur, Jehovah needed her Colt to have a working clutch.

Most Pioneers I knew were housewives who had spare time to volunteer as temporary Auxiliary Pioneers. Lisa, however, was the real deal. Single and 24 years old, she pioneered full-time, worked part-time, and prayed until her starter clicked. No husband supported her; no one took her out to lunch to celebrate when the month was over. For as long as I knew her, she never seemed aware that she didn't *have* to do this.

Although Lisa couldn't hold down a full-time job while Pioneering, she was not overly concerned about money. The Watchtower Society said that as long as we were serving Jehovah, he would provide for us.

God worked in mysterious ways, and with Lisa it was mostly through other people's checking accounts. For example, after a week of borrowing rides to the meeting, Jehovah may have moved another sister to let Lisa borrow $200 to get her car fixed. Sometimes the Holy Spirit interceded with her landlord to allow her to be a month late with the rent.

Not only was Lisa incredibly spiritual, but she also had a great sense of humor, made evident to me by her collection of irreverent greeting cards with cranky old ladies on the front. On top of that, we both loved Dunkin' Donuts and had a crush on Earl, a cute blond boy in our congregation. Lisa was like a cool aunt who teaches you about boys and also happens to think the world will end any day now.

Lately, my whole family had performed especially below-par as Jehovah's Witnesses. My parents loved Jehovah and knew birthdays were sinful, but they also worked all week and had high blood pressure. As a compassionate Christian, Lisa took me under her wing. She never chided me about the times I stayed home from the Kingdom Hall to watch television; rather, she nonchalantly called the house and asked what time she should pick me up. She acted as if it were a *given* that I'd be going.

Due to the immense pressure from our congregation to make every single meeting and go door-to-door on the weekends, my father was constantly racked with guilt. After all, what sort of role model lets his children run free outside on a sunny afternoon instead of dragging them through four-story tenements to talk to strangers?

Dad's spirituality ran in cycles. We waffled between being go-getting Jehovah's Witnesses and wanting to stay home and nap. I'd spend several weeks getting used to hanging out at home on Tuesday nights. Then Dad would suddenly act as if there had been no reprieve and demand his kids get dressed immediately, before we made him late.

Our family was never considered "inactive" in the organization, just in need of some gentle encouragement. Every now and again, a well-meaning ministerial servant would "be in the neighborhood" in his dress clothes with a Bible in his bag and would pop by to passive-aggressively see how we'd been.

One thing we never missed were District or Circuit Assemblies, and after each convention, Dad would become so motivated that he'd practically pin his name badge directly through his chest.

"That's it! Time to get it in gear," he'd swear, clapping his hands together in cheerleading fashion. "End-time is coming fast. Peace and security, they'll cry! Yup! Peace and security, and then that's it. All gone. The end. *Boom!*"

His voice would trail off: "You can see the signs, you can see the signs . . ."

For a month or so after each convention, Dad would become official head of the household, and schedule a weekly family study with my brother and me. We'd bring colored Hi-Liters and underline key passages in books like *Questions Young People Ask—Answers That Work*. We'd prepare answers to recite during the Tuesday night Book Study and draw an asterisk next to the paragraphs we planned to raise our hands for. As much as Aaron and I hated studying the *Watchtower*, it felt good to be a part of something with Dad. It was the only time I ever felt like we were a healthy family.

Inevitably, though, Dad would have a headache and our family study would be derailed.

Lisa said my father wasn't doing enough as head of the household. She recognized she had a duty to save my spiritual soul, and even though I lived a three-minute walk around the corner from our Kingdom Hall, she'd pick me up for every meeting. She didn't even want to *look* at my father, so she'd park outside, honking the horn of her idling Colt.

When I hung out with Lisa, there was no guilt or fear. I was pleasing Jehovah *and* having a good time. It never occurred to me that perhaps there might be something a bit off about a 24-year-old who has a 16-year-old best friend. I figured I was so totally mature that she had mistaken me for someone who knew how to drive and hold down a job.

Under Lisa's tutelage, I regained near-perfect attendance at the Kingdom Hall, qualifying me for the position of holiest person in my family.

Lisa helped me to take solace in the fact that it was common in dysfunctional families for the child to take on the role of the parent. She said she had the same problem with her father and that's why she left her home and moved to Pawtucket. I tried to be like Lisa and encourage my family members in the Truth whenever possible, taking care to remind everyone that I had been at the Kingdom Hall at 9:00 AM on Sunday while they had stayed home and overslept.

In fact, Lisa told me that she had also moved to our congregation to escape memories of childhood abuse. She talked about it as freely as my Jewish great-aunts talked about how their favorite restaurant, had recently gone downhill, because they "must have gotten a new chef." At the time, I thought "inappropriate touching" was a topic that all well-adjusted adults discussed while sitting in an idling car in a Dunkin' Donuts parking lot and rocking back and forth compulsively.

Eventually, hidden molestation became Lisa's catch-all analysis for everyone we knew. If you had an allergic reaction to pecans it was because you were clearly dealing with a sordid, abusive past. Any brother complimenting our hair was a pervert and a rapist. Once, someone in the apartment laundry room moved a load of Lisa's socks and underwear from the washer to the dryer and she nearly called child welfare.

"That Lisa sure does have it in for me," my father would say, after he'd wave at her from the front porch and she'd quickly roll up the window and slump down in her seat. "I don't know what I did to that girl, but she hates me!"

Around the holidays, Lisa would sit in the Kingdom Hall with tears rolling down her cheeks. Halfway through the service, she'd bolt to the bathroom, curl into a ball, and let loose a series of expansive sobs.

"Every Thanksgiving, we went to *his* house." Lisa wept as I crouched beside her. "And he . . . At night . . . In my room. Every holiday we spent there."

This dramatic show was just one more reason I thought Lisa was, like, the *coolest*. What horrors in my life had I forgotten so that I, like Lisa, could justify freaking out and leaving the Kingdom Hall early on Thanksgiving?

Lisa confided in me and I confided in her, or at least tried to. It was hard to compete with her incomprehensible trauma. She was older, she was wiser, and she was on Prozac. All I had were some vague memories of an old family friend that touched me once. I told her that I always felt like *something* might have *kinda* happened to me once, but I couldn't remember it.

Americans were gaga for a new trend called "repressed memories." Since I remembered suspiciously little about my own childhood abuse, Lisa thought I, too, might be repressing. Home from school on one of my myriad sick days (which I had long since stopped feigning sickness for), I watched Sally Jessy Raphael listen intently to a semi-famous soap opera star recount the time she had been sitting in hair and makeup getting her lashes curled when all at once she remembered her mother had savagely beat her.

I longed to fit in with this horribly abused young woman. So one afternoon, I walked into the living room, where my father was sitting shirtless on our sofa, watching television with a canister of Planters cheese puffs. The slipcover was bunched around his baby-blue checkered polyester shorts and his slippers angled skyward, pushed halfway off by the ottoman. For dramatic effect, I studied him for a moment before screaming at him across the room: "I know what you did."

My father stared at me. His cheese-powdered forearm was frozen, a handful of puffs halfway to his mouth. He blinked a few times, then crunched his salty snack treat and went back to watching television. I walked proudly out of the room, leaving my perplexed, chewing father thinking he'd forgotten to feed the cat that morning—and I *knew it.*

I was on a Lisa-high. This was my year to live forever! I'd flunked out of school, was unlucky in love, and couldn't even kill myself properly. I was tired of sneaking around with worldly friends who wouldn't think twice about getting a blood transfusion and wanted to convince me I was in a cult. Finally, I knew for certain that what I was doing with my life was *the right thing.* God approved, and so did Lisa.

I wasn't a Pioneer, but I was a Pioneer *groupie.* Lisa thought I'd come so far that it was time for me to dedicate my life to Jehovah in baptism, and I liked the way she thought.

I became a baptized member of the Jehovah's Witnesses during the "Lovers of Freedom" District Assembly in Providence. I was "cleansed in the blood of the Lamb," or more precisely, I was doused in the chlorine of the Providence Marriott hotel pool.

I was mature enough to dedicate the rest of my existence to Jehovah, which meant I totally didn't have to sit with my parents. As soon as they dropped me off, I found Emily, and together the two of us climbed high up into the top row of the arena seating— the *blue* seats. I had a snack and a pair of folding plastic binoculars. I waved to Lisa. I watched cute boys.

I drew circled asterisks around "Enter Into Freedom by Dedication and Baptism" in my convention program. My baptism would come right after "Keep Yourself Free to Serve Jehovah" and right before "Song Number 13 and Intermission." While the rest of the 3,000 attendees were eating lunch in their seats, I'd be entering freedom.

In the corded-off shallow end, I was ushered into a line of penitent Christians adorned like me, in modest, unmemorable swimsuits and starchy hotel towels. Our bathing suits all had thick linings and had been bathtub-tested to ensure that they did not become immodest when wet. The throng of people at a large District Assembly was unmanageable, so no friends were allowed to watch. The baptisms took place simultaneously, with as many people as could reasonably stand in the pool. Several moist, appointed men stood in the shallow end, wearing Hanes Beefy-Ts, ready to dunk whoever came in close contact with them like American Gladiators fending off a foe.

Unceremoniously, a brother I did not know wordlessly took my hand and led me down a set of concrete steps. He helped me to hold my nose and pulled me into a backward "trust fall." Without fanfare, I flopped underwater. Unspeaking, the strange brother pushed me out of the pool.

Someone grabbed my hand to pull me toward the showers. I cocked my head and pulled back a little, eager to smile at the next person in line and share this life-changing moment of being filled with the Holy Spirit. No one smiled back. No one applauded or told me I was a better person now. The next person in line looked positively glum, like this was the chemical shower after a deadly experiment.

I had just dedicated my life, blood, and soul to Jehovah's Promised Kingdom, and it was positively the most underwhelming experience I'd ever had. Ordering Cinnamon Crispas from the Taco Bell drive-through gave me more of a rush.

I never told anyone how depressing dedicating my life to God had been. I towel-dried my hair, stapled on a smile, and asked everyone I knew to come to the Mon Kou to celebrate my big day by sharing a pupu platter. My parents and friends congratulated me and I savored my one chance to be somewhat "celebrated." Inside, I felt completely unchanged, but I knew that couldn't possibly be the case—I must have just been imagining things.

CHAPTER 14

Placing the Mark of Jehovah upon
the Homes of Unbelievers

Not much changed for me as a baptized member of the congregation, except for the looming knowledge that I could now be marked as an apostate. If I had never publicly dedicated myself to God, he couldn't penalize me for betraying him, like some random Hebrew who accidentally kissed Jesus on the cheek the night before his execution.

Now that I was officially extra spiritual, I also needed to knock on doors more regularly, lest I be marked as "inactive." Before going door-to-door, congregation members met at the Kingdom Hall, where a designated brother would distribute area maps known as territories and assign partners to those who showed up alone.

I partnered with Lisa, not only because she was my best friend, but because my one experience with being otherwise partnered had been most regrettable.

My blind-date partner had been Sister Preckle, a circular

middle-aged woman with gastric issues and a stained peach poly-ester suit. She managed to creep out the very first householder we visited by cackling about Armageddon until he wordlessly slammed the door on us. Humiliated, I ran out the front gate, assuming she was following me. But the gate did not click shut a second time. By the time I turned around, Sister Preckle had vanished.

I scanned the sidewalk for a minute, then moved to the side of the house. I noticed a rustling of bushes and called out her name.

"I'm here," spoke the bushes. My partner stood up, wiping her mouth. Then she lowered herself back into the foliage, leaving only the unmistakable sound of someone puking into an irate stranger's bushes.

I studied the windows of the home, trying to discern any shadowy figures watching from behind flickering drapes. Since there were none, I fled back to the car, leaving Sister E. Coli to projectile-vomit the unsightly image of Jehovah's Witnesses onto someone's front yard.

Five minutes later, Sister Preckle came waltzing around the corner, merrily swinging her arms as if nothing had happened.

"Are you all right? Do you need to go home?" I asked.

She laughed. "I'm fine! I just have this . . . condition . . . where I need to throw up."

"So, maybe you should go home, then?" I urged.

"Oh, no," she assured me. "This happens all the time!"

I never tested whether this was true or not. From then on, I only went in service with Lisa.

After the Field Service meeting, Lisa and I would head to the Dunkin' Donuts drive-through to purchase two coffees. We ordered ours "extra large, extra-extra," which, in Rhode Island, is a perfectly acceptable way to request that your drink be equal parts sugar and heavy cream, with a tablespoon of coffee thrown in for flavor. As part of our routine, we'd sit in the parking lot and examine our territory while we waited for the sugar high to come on.

Lisa motivated and mentored me the way my father had during his inspired, manic bursts of family studies. I was mortified and I hated every single moment of it, but nothing could compete with the smug satisfaction I derived from my internal sense of accomplishment and superiority. Knowing I would live forever wasn't a bad perk either.

God told us we had to speak to everyone on earth or Armageddon would be sabotaged. We knew that *not one single person* would be left on this earth who hadn't heard the name of Jehovah before the end came.

When people didn't answer the door, we made a note, marking them as "Not at Home." Once you were assigned a territory, you were not allowed to return it until all your Not at Homes had been Homed. If no one answered the door on Sunday at 10:00 AM, you tried again at 6:00 PM, then on Monday at 10:00 AM, and then Tuesday, and so on, until someone, *anyone*, in the house had been reached. If no personal contact was made, you would write a letter and slip it into the mail slot with a topical issue of the *Watchtower.* Like the FedEx employee who'll take anyone's signature to drop off a package, we needed to be freed of liability before moving on. We were supposed to talk to everyone.

Everyone. At one home, a man answered the door wearing nothing but tight white underwear. He had accessorized this ensemble by draping an enormous boa constrictor across his shoulders.

"Would you like to touch my pet boa constrictor?" he asked Lisa. "Her name is *Sally.*"

Never one to back away from confrontation, Lisa just laughed. She knocked on strangers' homes 90 hours each month and could do it with her eyes closed. She was used to freaks, or maybe someone just trying to freak her out. A boa constrictor wrapped around a semi-naked guy was child's play. Lisa's need to advance

God's Kingdom message could not be derailed. She ran her hand against Sally's cold-blooded belly. Maybe Sally would like a home Bible study?

The man's face fell. He had clearly wanted us to run screaming, to get a good story for his friends, but it had backfired.

"Would you like to see her cage?" he asked, trying so hard to appear menacing that he may have actually started to laugh.

"You bet we would!" Lisa countered. "Would you like a copy of *You Can Live Forever in Paradise on Earth*?"

"You know what, I think it's okay," he said, and closed the door.

"Let's go check up on Angela, my new Bible study," Lisa said to me. "She hasn't answered the door the last few times I've been by and I don't know what's up with that girl. If she's playing games with me, I don't have the time."

Lisa had no qualms at all about entering the private home of strangers and forcibly engaging them in conversation about the evils of celebrating Halloween, but I was intensely self-conscious. I didn't want to make people talk about paradise if they were hiding from it. It seemed . . . *rude*.

"Sure. Sounds great," I said, praying that Angela would leave us on the front porch in the cold.

The unspoken consensus among Witnesses was that rich neighborhoods made the worst territories. The rich were materialistic, had no need for God, and never answered their own door. The upwardly mobile residents of the nearby town of Lincoln, Rhode Island, were satisfied with life, and much to our amazement, seemed to actually enjoy their own religions. They had finished basements and therefore very little need for living eternally in paradise.

We proved this by quoting from the book of Matthew: "It will be easier for a camel to fit through the eye of a needle than for a rich man to enter the Kingdom of Heaven." Barring the invention of a nano-camel, it seemed the rich were done for.

The residents of financially depressed Central Falls, however, were likely to greet us with open arms, then ask if we'd watch their children for a minute while they made a run down to Pappy's Liquors to get their paycheck cashed. Everyone wanted to preach in the poor areas, where residents were not blinded by satisfaction with their lives and actually wanted the world to change.

We liked the four-story tenements of Central Falls, where unemployed single mothers were happy to bring us into their kitchen at 2:00 PM on a Tuesday for a Capri Sun and some second-hand smoke. These were the kind of people who had the time to accept a stranger into their home to discuss religion on a weekly basis. They didn't have a whole lot of extracurricular activities, unless you counted looking out the window with a cigarette in their hand.

The immediate goal of knocking on a stranger's door was to find a willing heart who would agree to a weekly, free, home Bible study. This person then became your ward and companion—like an AA sponsorship—and was known as your "Bible study," as in, "I am late to the Bible study with my Bible study."

The ultimate goal was to have the person continue his education until he, too, became a baptized Jehovah's Witness.

After blowing us off several times, Lisa's absentee Bible study, Angela, finally answered the door of her fourth-floor walk-up. We hauled our book bags up to the top of the rickety stairs, where her apartment door was wide open, revealing a small child wearing nothing but juice stains standing in the middle of the kitchen.

"Where you been, Ange?" Lisa asked. "I came by two weeks in a row and nobody was here."

"Oh, Leez, you don't even *know*! It's been frickin' crazy!"

Angela sat us down at a wobbly metal folding table with an empty Lucite picture frame as a centerpiece. She began by telling us how much her picture frame cost. She pronounced it "pitcha frame," dropping the final *r* in her Rhode Island accent.

"Do you know how much this pitcha frame cost? This pitcha frame cost fawty-seven dollahs. This is a wicked-expensive frame."

I estimated the actual cost was approximately three dollars. "It's beautiful," I told her.

"You bet it is! A fawty-seven-dollah frame, that's what that is!"

Lisa interrupted, "So, would you like to get your Bible?"

"Lisea, one of the neighbas called the cops on my sista yestaday. She went to the packie to get Camels and left the winda screen up. So the neighba seen her kid in the winda and called the cops. Jesus Christ, right? It's not like the kid fell out or anything but you'd think that the neighbas didn't have anything betta to do than lookin' at windas fah somebody's kids all the time."

This was the entire Bible study. We vacillated between a discussion on the economics of pitcha frames to complimenting the only piece of furniture in the living room (a giant-screen television from "the Rent-A-Centah"). Under the table, my feet stretched up and down against the sticky brown linoleum, and a tiny, dirty hand reached up and stained my skirt.

Back in the car, Lisa said simply, "I have a hard time getting her to focus."

This was what saving people with Lisa was like. One day, I spent an hour in a strange kitchen watching an annoyed Ethiopian girl eat Cream of Wheat–covered chicken with her hands after a wobbly drunk had asked if we wanted to go for a ride in his "limbo." The next, nobody answered the door, so we gave up and drove to the Dunkin' Donuts parking lot to talk about boys.

Once, after failing to make any new disciples in Pawtucket, we saw a group of three seniors from my high school. One of them was tall with a Mohawk and tattoos. One was chubby with long hair and a leather jacket that said "The Misfits" on the back. Years later, I'd learn that The Misfits are a crooning rockabilly punk band with few songs longer than 120 seconds. Back when my irony meter only reached two, I was certain they were earnest

Satanists. A virgin-sacrificing death-metal cult bent on causing teenagers to commit suicide via sleeveless T-shirts and melting pompadours. The third kid was the "normal" friend, but he still had leather wristbands.

"Gosh, I go to school with those kids."

Most Jehovah's Witnesses do not approve of the words "gosh," "golly," or "gee," as these are clearly derivative of taking the Lord's name in vain. But Lisa was cool; she was down with the gosh.

"You know them? Great! Let's go talk to them!"

This was not what I meant. I meant, I go to school with them, therefore, let's *not* talk to them. Let's head back to the car in as inconspicuous a manner as possible. I know them, so let's totally not talk to them ever. It's *Dunkin' Donuts time*!

The next thing I knew, I was standing next to Lisa in a modest, flowered, yoke-front dress, and talking to the Satanists from Charles E. Shea high school.

"We go to school with you," one of them said in a surprisingly articulate tone. I expected fake blood to come pouring out of his mouth at any moment.

Lisa introduced us as two friends who had gone out for a stroll and also happened to be talking to people about the coming Kingdom of God. The punks then proceeded to debate the beliefs of Jehovah's Witnesses in the most articulate way I had ever experienced.

"You can't prove a scripture by quoting another scripture," said the chubby, long-haired guy.

"And how do you know there's only one religion?" the tattooed one countered.

"Yeah, how do you even know God is Christian?" asked the normal guy, who was still probably a warlock.

I nodded in stunned agreement. Not only were they not vomiting blood, they had excellent talking points. Because I felt obligated to speak, I made one feeble attempt to respond with something or other that I'd memorized from the back of our *Reasoning from the Scriptures* book, which gave a pat, one-paragraph retort for every dispute ever uttered in the history of religious debate.

"Well, according to Leviticus, Jehovah God says, 'You must not profane my holy name, and I must be sanctified in the midst of the sons of Israel.' And, um, therefore we know that the *true* religion will, uh . . . recognize that God's name is Jehovah?"

They didn't purchase a *Watchtower* and *Awake!* combo, nor did they accept a free at-home Bible study. We left without converting them, but that was normal. Not everyone became Jehovah's Witnesses immediately—what was important was that the seed had been planted. Patience was the key.

When I next saw the Satanists in the hall at school, I smiled and waved. We'd had, like, a debate. They now knew that I wasn't just any Jehovah's Witness—I was a Jehovah's Witness who stood awkwardly and smiled while her friend did all the talking. I hoped they'd think I was cool for not pressuring them to become one of us. Instead, they looked confused that I was even saying hello to them at all and turned back to their conversation.

Because Lisa was outgoing and personable, she had tons of Bible studies, although some of them were admittedly of dubious value. I felt more pressure than I ever had to find myself some good sheep and bring them into God's fold. My opportunity arose when, while out with Lisa, a girl my own age answered the door. Lisa elbowed me to take the lead.

"Hi . . . hello," I stammered. "My name is Kyria and this is my friend Lisa and, uh, we're just in the neighborhood today asking people if they feel that, you know, there's a reason for all the wickedness in the world?"

"I don't know," the girl said. She had gentle eyes.

"I could show you from the Bible, like, where it says why bad things happen."

I opened my Bible to a bookmarked page and read aloud how Satan was the cause of suffering, not God. The girl tilted her head onto the porch and read along with me.

"If you'd like, I could come back another time and, you know, we could talk about it more."

The girl trusted me. I was a kindly teen on her doorstep, I was holding a Bible. She gave me her phone number and agreed to have me come over and talk with her.

In a sudden moment of complete clarity and introspection, I realized that I actually knew very little about the Bible. Although I had always *intended* to, I'd never managed to force myself to read it from cover to cover. We had books and magazines that always *quoted* the Bible, so I didn't really need to read the book itself. I got by with highlighted passages that I read straight from our publications without truly knowing what they meant. I zoned out at the meetings, and like in my phone calls with Jayson, I didn't truly understand half of what we were supposed to believe in without consulting our literature first.

I never called the girl or went back to her house. On my monthly time card, on the line designated for reporting Bible studies, I lied and wrote "one."

After that, I stuck to giving people the *Watchtower* and quickly running away. That way, the householders would be witnessed to, and I would never, ever have to talk to them again.

Proselytizing, however, is not all about high school Satanists and people screaming at you to get off their property. Sure, getting doors slammed in your face is a great adrenaline rush, but most people don't even open their doors wide enough to slam them. Most often we'd see the rustle of a curtain, and then hear a dog bark and a disembodied voice telling the dog to *shut up!* After a second rustle and a second muffled bark, we'd pick up our book bags and walk away.

It's amazing that Jehovah's Witnesses earned the reputation of bothering people at home, because as far as I could tell, very few people were ever home to bother. For every resident who threatened to sic a boa constrictor on us, there were 114 who were smart enough to simply not answer the door.

To pass the time, Lisa and I had a game we would play. It was called "That's Gonna Be My House After Armageddon."

It involved driving around a suburban Rhode Island neighborhood and pointing to the quiet, shuttered home of an unsuspecting, doomed Episcopalian family. These families had brightly colored, durable plastic play centers in their yards and appropriate holiday decorations on their ample front porches. Their front lawns were landscaped with perfect oval bushes. The inhabitants were clearly sinners deserving of destruction on the day of our Lord.

Lisa's fantasy house was a brown-and-cream neo-Tudor, which I found lacking a certain *je ne sais quoi*. I was partial to 1950s ranch houses in the town of Lincoln, which I revered as "kitschy." I loved their June Cleaver cleanliness, the chimneys that actually connected to a fireplace. Since I'd grown up in a poo-brown duplex with mismatched carpet swags, these postwar dollhouses were my idea of paradise. And if God saw fit to spare the concrete goose in the raincoat on the front lawn, all the better.

The burning question was: Once God judged these people, what would happen to their postwar bungalows? We imagined a fundamentalist *Trading Spaces*, in which we'd get the chance to knock down a wall for Jesus, then move on in. It would be our favorite new reality show: *While You Were Out, Forever*.

For example, would Jehovah destroy the adorable white ranch with turquoise shutters? The people who lived there were Jewish, but on the other hand, Jehovah *did* create turquoise.

The post-Armageddon housing buffet wasn't an official Jehovah's Witness doctrine. We didn't really know what would be left standing after the apocalypse. We had no Sunday sermons about moving into the houses of the judged, no street maps with colorful flags sticking out of them like a Domino's delivery route. We true believers knew only this: After Armageddon, the earth would be transformed into a fertile paradise of giant grapes and friendly tigers, on which Jehovah's Witnesses would live forever. Everyone else would be—to borrow a phrase from corporate America—downsized. From that, Lisa and I extrapolated that we could take their houses. The specifics had to be filled in by our furtive, fundamentalist imaginations.

Everyone who wasn't a Jehovah's Witness was going to die; we accepted this fact. It wasn't about being a nice person, it was about becoming a baptized Jehovah's Witness. We never thought of this as unfair, since we weren't the ones who were doing the killing—we were doing the saving. We were warning people that they were going to die, telling them to stop being evil Buddhists and get on the Jesus bandwagon!

Yes, it was a shame that people would choose death over worshipping Jehovah. It was very sad that unborn babies in the womb of a Jewish mother would be devoured by lava. It was unfortunate that Adam had sinned and that Armageddon had to happen at all. But it was *really* a shame if the houses had to go too, especially when they were so much nicer than ours.

Chapter 15

Behold! The Poetry of Creation

at Work in All Living Things!

In the Dunkin' Donuts parking lot, convinced that we were going to live forever, Lisa and I talked about Alan Brody, a 24-year-old brother in the congregation who had a huge crush on me. Alan was, for all intents and purposes, a stinky nerd. That is, as he was a nerd and he also didn't like to bathe, he often exuded a pungent aroma of onions. He wore thick glasses and looked like a cross between Rick Moranis and Barney Rubble. He played ragtime piano. And since he'd never been married and therefore could not have partaken in the privileges of the "marriage bed," he was still a virgin. So, he was an extremely horny, stinky, eccentric, Mark Russell–ish Jehovah's Witness. He needed to get laid.

Alan also liked to wear a rubber laboratory tube as a belt and imagined himself as the Val Kilmer character in *Real Genius*. He had a crush on all the girls in our congregation, as well as every other girl in every other congregation that he could manage to visit. He mainly had a huge crush on me.

I asked Lisa if she thought I liked him or not. She said she didn't know, but that I sure did talk about him a lot, so there must be something there. I knew I felt *weird* when he was around, but I couldn't tell if I was repulsed by him or attracted to him. Did I like his "dancing Snoopy" tie, or did it make me uneasy? What were you supposed to feel when you were attracted to someone? If he loved Jehovah, did it matter?

I'd never met anyone before who had as much personality as Alan. I'd never met anyone who watched *Mystery Science Theater* and could recite pi to the fortieth digit and had a T-shirt of the universe with an arrow that said "You Are Here." Alan had a Post-it note that said "Buy More Post-It Notes." He had an *Oxford English Dictionary*. All I had were multiple copies of Funk & Wagnalls Volume 1 (A to American Elk) because they cost a nickel in the supermarket.

Alan was also the only Jehovah's Witness I knew who dared defy the elders and seek extra learning in the form of attending Rhode Island College. He was a math major, but his education was not limited to numbers. He'd written a paper entitled "I Camus—Can You? The Existential Dr. Seuss." I didn't know what existentialism was, but I had once read *Marvin K. Mooney Will You Please Go Now!* (which also probably cost a nickel in the supermarket) and knew that writing a paper on Dr. Seuss in a philosophy class seemed cheeky.

Because of his college education and his cartoon-character neckties, he wasn't in very good standing with the congregation. They never let him have any special responsibilities such as mowing the Kingdom Hall lawn or holding the microphone for feeble sisters to speak into during the Sunday *Watchtower* discussion.

Lisa said Alan didn't seem very spiritual. She worried about his love of Jehovah. He often spoke of listening to worldly music or mentioned seeing a movie we all knew was rated PG-13. Above all else, he didn't think he had to go to all three meetings every week in order to be a good Witness. We were horrified.

Finally, we decided to cut the poop and get to the bottom of Alan's immoral intentions. We invited him for coffee. Lisa and I sat in the Colt's two front bucket seats in the Dunkin' Donuts parking lot while the head of Alan Brody stared up at us from the stick shift. To illustrate his irreverence, he lay on his back with his feet dangling into the rear window of the hatchback and one hand gripping each seat. He'd become the first outsider to drink coffee in the Colt with us.

There was a spiritual intervention taking place. Lisa was insisting it was important to go to all three meetings. Alan was saying if he missed a few here and there, it wasn't the end of the world.

"I go to the meeting on Sundays and Thursdays. I just have class on Tuesdays," Alan said.

"You have coffee breath," Lisa said, winning the argument while handing him a mint.

Although I had often missed meetings, I never debated whether or not it was actually *okay* to do so. I felt guilt-ridden when I stayed home and would never dare to justify the habit to another Jehovah's Witness.

The Watchtower Society said we had to make all three meetings and anyone who disagreed with the Watchtower Society was an apostate. But here was someone who disagreed with the society, yet still wanted to be a Jehovah's Witness.

I was entranced, yet repulsed.

Eventually Lisa got Alan to agree to start attending the Tuesday night Book Study in addition to the Thursday night Ministry School and the Sunday morning *Watchtower* Study. Satisfied, we allowed him to exit the car.

After much deliberation, we agreed that as long as Alan was going to all the meetings, it was okay for me to like him. By "like," we meant "date," and by "date," we meant "get married to."

That day, on the edge of the parking lot, my fate was sealed over coffee and a Field Service territory. Alan Brody was going to be my husband.

It's very validating, at age 16, to have a 24-year-old boyfriend. Especially if you are way too mature for high school because kowtowing to some rigid concept of education is for lemmings and conformists. Especially if you're a poet, an artist, and your favorite member of *The Breakfast Club* is Ally Sheedy. Especially, then, if your 24-year-old boyfriend is a part-time math professor at a local college, you have therefore received validation that high school is lame.

Around this time, I took to shuffling through the cafeteria in ankle-length skirts and doing the unspeakable—eating lunch alone. Not because I wanted to be alone, but because I wanted the other kids to know I was *capable* of being alone. It was one thing I'd seen adults do, but never teenagers. I brought a disturbing lunch, usually cold spaghetti in a stained Tupperware container. Beyond "uncool," this was just shy of saving bread crusts for pigeons. I opened a copy of Otto Rank's *Art and Artist*. I drew a skull. I was officially above it all.

My first step to being above it all was to write poetry in a cemetery located on a well-trafficked main road next to an elementary school. But this was no ordinary modern cemetery on a well-trafficked main road next to an elementary school, oh no! This was my own Secret Garden, and the empty Zima bottles and discarded grocery store circulars were but keys through her enchanted gates! Surely, some dashing young rebel would find me here, the quirky loner, the deep and solitary artist, splayed out in the grass like the heroine of Andrew Wyeth's *Christina's World*— not going forward, yet not going back. Would that I might *bewitch* you?

I wasn't alone. No. I had my poetry.

On Ladders, Still Reaching

Visions of Moonlight, and the mud of this
open grave
My body separates
fixed on a face
I used to call my own
Am I moving?
I create and observe
every pulse of my death
circled with a swirling
carving heat
Imploding from lack of
or too much
reality
And I long to escape
to be above and below
take me
take me
to the edge of my dreaming
to hold myself dying
and get on with my life

Sadly, Christian Slater's character in *Heathers* never arrived, and I eventually grew bored with churning out dark-wave free verse while sitting on empty Styrofoam cups. I bought black-and-white film to take photos of crying concrete angels. I forced my brother to come to the cemetery and pose for me. However, due to both his wacky poses and his insistence on wearing jean shorts and an Ocean Pacific T-shirt, the photo shoot was not the New Romantic *tableau vivant* I had hoped for.

While on my self-imposed lunchroom exile, I wrote long letters to Alan on college-ruled notebook paper. I told him that I wasn't doing my homework because I was just way beyond homework:

Like, I'm so anachronistic, you know. It's like I belong in some other time, right? I should be in the 1920s or something and just, you know, wear flapper dresses and go to jazz clubs. I mean, everybody thinks you need to graduate from school to be smart, like some piece of paper means that you know what two plus two means. Like there's no other way to learn something than to have a diploma.

Then I quoted Otto Rank.

Alan owned a single suit—gray polyester with strategic condiment stains. The bell-bottomed legs were short enough to show off his yellow-and-blue-striped tube socks. The ripped jacket pocket flapped off his waist like an unfashionable flag. He was the congregation joke.

He would run over to me immediately at the end of every meeting, practically jumping over seats to corner me between the wall and the aisle. We were kinda dating, but that didn't mean I wanted to be seen talking to him.

"Have you ever seen *Mystery Science Theater 3000*?" Alan asked, the dancing Snoopy tie cascading gently over his polyester knee.

"Have you ever thought about getting a new suit?" I asked.

"Why does it matter what I wear to the meetings as long as I'm here? Do you think Jehovah really cares about how much money I spend on my suit?"

"Well, the congregation cares about your suit. And anyways, why look ugly?"

"Kyria, when I was on campus one day—"

"That's another thing. College, I mean—"

"Fine, whatever. College is, whatever. The point is, I was on campus and my belt broke, okay? Snapped in half. My pants were falling down and I had no belt. Now, I could have left and bought a new belt, but why should I? Here's what I did. I went into the science lab and I got a piece of rubber surgical tubing. Do you know what that is?"

"Whatever. I guess so."

"No, I don't think you understand. It's a rubber tube, okay? And I wrapped it around my waist and I knotted it and then cut it. I wore that as a belt, and I still wear it as a belt. It's perfectly practical and I got it for free! Everyone on campus was looking at me, but you know what? I didn't care!"

"Why not just get a real belt?"

"Kyria! Listen to me! I just told you why! I was wearing rubber tubing as a belt. Because it worked, okay?"

I should have been disgusted by Alan. Actually, I was. He was creepy and geeky, and not only that, he was self-righteous about it. But he was also 24 and the only Jehovah's Witness I knew who actively read books that weren't put out by the Watchtower Society. He was also trying to make me jealous.

When I asked him why he hadn't been at the meeting the week before, he told that he'd gone to visit a girl in the Framingham congregation, some gothy slip of an Auxiliary Pioneer on antidepressants. Her father beat her.

"She's the smartest person I've ever met," Alan said, mindlessly fingering his flapping pocket. "She's twenty years old and I think she's probably in love with me."

Immediately, I invited Alan over to my house to hang out. I was not going to be usurped by some existential high school graduate on Prozac. My main long-term relationship experience up to this point had been with a skate rat who broke up with me for giving him an erection. It didn't occur to me that trying to make someone jealous by claiming you have another love interest was a popular and overused tactic. I was 16—I was exactly who jealousy tactics are made for.

Alan arrived at my apartment smelling of onions and wearing a T-shirt that said:

WHAT PART OF

$$\frac{dy}{dx} = \frac{dy}{du}\frac{du}{dx} = g'(u)\,f'(x)$$

DON'T YOU UNDERSTAND?

My parents were charmed by his sense of humor and seemed

pleased to know that I was dating someone intelligent who would have the ability to support me. He was, after all, a math teacher.

Alan brought a grocery bag filled with videotapes of *Mystery Science Theater 3000* and we spent the afternoon on the couch, fast-forwarding through local commercials for the New England Tractor-Trailer Training School. We ordered a pizza and Alan attempted to order one with extra cheese and every single topping on the menu, especially anchovies. When Nicholas Kyklades at the Pawtucket House of Pizza refused, Alan ran his fingers through his greasy hair and gloated as if he were the ultimate Merry Prankster. My brother could not have been more impressed.

This was the entirety of our date: my nerdy brother fawning over Alan while my mother drank rum and Pepsi in the kitchen and occasionally popped her head in to sing, "Love is in the aaaaaair!" It was as much as Alan and I needed to know about each other. He loved Jehovah well enough, and he had the kind of job that only smart people can do. He was, as the Jehovah's Witnesses were fond of saying, "a suitable mate."

It wasn't uncommon for God-fearing youths to get married as soon as they turned 18. None of us could have sex until we were legally bound together, and we had to bind with a Jehovah's Witness. Unless you met someone at a large convention, you had a dating pool just slightly larger than that of *The Blue Lagoon*. Thankfully, it was unacceptable to marry your own cousin, otherwise Jehovah's Witnesses might have found it hard to hold a *Watchtower* in their congenital flippers.

Since divorce was not allowed, none of the teen marriages ended unhappily, or at all. Couples ate dinner in silence, slept in separate bedrooms, prayed to Jehovah to "put love in their hearts." Husbands grew to hate their wives, to hit their wives. Wives put steaks on their black eyes and called the elders the next day for a visit of encouragement. The elders read scriptures, husbands cried sincerely, the family prayed together, and children thought that things would change.

After a night of pizza and videotapes, Alan and I concluded our first date. I saw him through the cold front hallway, where we stood on a dirty carpet next to my mother's brass umbrella stand.

"I'm in love with you," I told him as we kissed for the very first time.

He kept his eyes closed. "I don't know what love is," he said.

Cute. I'd seen this kind of thing done in movies before, like *Star Wars*. Alan loved me but had too much pride to admit it. Whether or not I loved him back was not my problem. The point was that I was almost 17, I wanted a boyfriend, and I didn't know any other Jehovah's Witnesses who liked me at the moment.

"Of course you love me," I explained. "You just don't know it yet."

"No, really," he said. "I'm not sure what I feel."

Alan kissed me with his breath full of onions and drove home, where he lived with his parents and the one of his three brothers who still lived at home, Jeffy. I immediately picked up the phone to call Lisa and tell her that the rest of my life was all mapped out.

"I thought you didn't even like him," Lisa said.

"I don't like him," I told her, "but I think I do love him."

"I'm coming to pick you up. Be waiting on the porch for me."

I positioned myself on the front steps in a suitably brooding semi-fetal crouch and waited for Lisa's Colt to pull up. I got in the car, expecting her to drive to Dunkin' Donuts. Instead, she started driving in the direction of Alan's house.

Lisa pulled into their driveway and told me to stay in the car. I watched her walk up onto the porch, past a folding table covered in empty beer bottles, ring the doorbell, and walk straight into the house. This is what she was good at.

A minute later, she emerged, but not alone. I rolled down the passenger-side window to come face-to-face with Alan, wearing a huge grin and filthy bunny slippers.

"Get out and talk to your boyfriend," Lisa told me as she pulled her seat belt over her lap. "I'll be back to get you in an hour."

As the Colt pulled away, Lisa pointed her thumb at Alan and yelled to me through the window, "And make sure you encourage *this one* to stop missing meetings, all right?"

Alan's house could be described, among other ways, as "sticky." The counter was littered with country-rooster pepper shakers and country-pig cookie jars, all coated with dust stuck to a gummy layer of grease. You could scratch the kitchen cabinets with your fingernail and spell your name in dried corn oil. This was country living at its most viscous.

Alan's brother, Jeffy sat in the living room, his legs crossed over the arm of a mauve La-Z-Boy rocker. He was watching Jerry Springer, reading the *Weekly World News*, and drinking screwdrivers. Jeffy had hair-sprayed dirty blond bangs and a layer of bronzer that would put Fabio to shame. He wore fluorescent green Jams and a blousy linen shirt that revealed a tan, stubbly, shaved chest.

As far as I could tell, he was probably not into girls.

Alan's mother, Barbara, sat beside him petting their dog and talking long-distance, to her own mother in South Carolina.

"Oh, my lordy-lord, have you seen this?" Jeffy squealed, handing me the tabloid. "It's a Bat Boy T-shirt! Oh. My. God, girl. I *so* need this Bat Boy T-shirt!"

"Oh," I said. "Is Bat Boy some kind of a . . . thing?"

"Totally! They had him on the cover and now they're, like, bringing him back again. I buy a *Weekly World* every time I'm at the supermarket! Isn't it the funniest thing you've ever seen in your entire life?"

"Alan!" Barbara yelled in a Southern drawl, moving her neck forward so the receiver locked under her chin. "Go on over to D'Angelino's and pick us up some pockets."

"Shhh, Momma," Jeffy scolded. "You'll miss Jerry's final comments!"

"Oh! He is *so* good," Barbara said, snapping to attention. "Such a smart man the way he sums everything up at the end of each show. It is just such a shame that he is a homosexual."

"Mmm-hmmm," said Jeffy, fluffing his Sun-In'd mane. "Such a *damn* shame."

Alan explained to me that Jeffy wasn't allowed to drive. He'd lost his license in some very disturbing accident, which the family never, ever spoke of. Now Jeffy ran errands in the big red van with Momma, unless Alan was home. In which case, Alan ran errands in the van by himself.

"Don't forget an extra number nine pocket, Alan!" Barbara yelled as we walked through the kitchen. "Sheba's hungry!"

"Whenever we order sandwiches from D'Angelino's, we always get an extra sandwich pocket for the dog. She likes the number nines," Alan told me. "I have to make sure there's no hot peppers in it, though. That was a day I don't want to repeat."

Alan's father, Jake, was sitting on a country-style butcher-block stool in front of his country-style butcher-block kitchen table, drinking out of a highball glass. His head was pointed down as far as it is humanly possibly to point your head down while still ingesting whiskey. Digging into an open purse, Alan pulled out a key chain decorated with a rubber "pooping cow" and a bell the size of my fist. We jingled off to buy a grilled pita sandwich for the family dog.

When we returned, Lisa was parked outside.

"You kids work out what you need to work out?" she asked.

"I guess so," I said. Did watching Springer and giving indigestion to a family pet count? I slipped into the Colt, waved to Alan, and let Lisa drive me home.

The next time I visited Alan, his family was in the process of cooking an enormous cauldron of Manhattan clam chowder. Every Sunday afternoon, Barbara and Jeffy would go shopping at BJ's Wholesale. By Sunday evening, industrial cans of tomatoes and whole-bellied clams lined the kitchen counter, their lids protruding upward like buzz-saw blades.

At the butcher-block table, Alan showed me how to mix a whiskey-liquor called Yukon Jack, which tasted like the alcoholic equivalent of maple syrup. "It's called a snakebite," he said, squeezing a brown lime into a glass. "It's the best drink ever invented."

When we were suitably buzzed, or at least sick to our stomachs, we took Sheba into the backyard to relieve herself. So far, there had been zero skateboarding involved, and that officially made this the best date I'd ever had.

Betty and Jeffy were watching television. Jack had finally fallen under the table or otherwise disappeared. No one was watching us. So Alan took me into his bedroom to show me his college textbooks.

"Ever listen to Queen?" he asked, and began to rewind a tape of "Night at the Opera."

I thumbed through the hefty volume of *An Introduction to Mathematical Modeling*. Alan gently removed the book from my hands, placed it on the bed, and began to kiss me. I wanted to show him how mature I was, so I immediately pulled his hand to my breast, which he fondled for so long that it eventually became boring. It didn't feel like much of anything and I wanted him to stop, so I pulled his hand to my crotch so he could rub me through my pants. I didn't expect his fingers to end up inside my underwear, but when they did, I didn't protest. He was a Jehovah's Witness, after all.

I didn't feel guilty, which, in turn, caused me to feel an immense amount of guilt. Shouldn't I feel bad about this? I wasn't masturbating or stealing a warm beer from my father's shelf, but

I had something inside me that wasn't a tampon or a Pap smear. Was it really sinning to half-lose your virginity to your future husband's index finger?

I fake-moaned like I'd hear people moan on television.

Afterward I looked for blood or hymen residue or some visible sign of having been finger-banged, but my Jockey for Hers looked just the same as they had when I'd arrived.

The majority of conversations with Alan's family centered on how bizarre it was that Alan was smart. They called him "the little professor." This was a hardworking, blue-collar family. So when Alan was three years old, they were surprised to learn that he had taught himself to read. The next thing they knew, he was demanding college.

"We always say that Alan belongs to the mailman," Barbara said to me. "We just don't know *where* he came from!"

Barbara was a whiz with a hot-glue gun and she ran a successful flea market craft table business out of her basement. The entire home smelled like a Vermont craft store, like plunging headfirst into a pile of freshly raked leaves. She and Jeffy, who was nearly 30 years old, arranged silk flowers around ceramic geese, glued summer hats to teddy bears, and garnished them all with countrified touches like ribbons and dried leaves. In turn, this paid for long-distance calls to South Carolina. Alan's father had dropped out of the fourth grade to support his family. Now he worked in a factory, bringing home leftover cans of Lori Davis hair spray—the kind Cher hawked on infomercials—and wondering why his son was so excited about it. He must have also wondered why Jeffy had a separate razor just for shaving his chest. These were honest folk, not people who expected to sire a math teacher with a predilection for wearing rubber tubing around his waist.

When I quietly refused to use the family's bathroom on the grounds that the oak toilet seat was cracked and covered in white stains, Alan grabbed the pooping-cow key chain from Barbara's purse and drove me home. No one in his family suggested a chaperone.

Alan parked outside my house, but I didn't want to go inside yet. Instead, I asked him to park the car. We'd already been on two dates now, and today, I'd been fingered.

"Marry me, Alan!"

Alan looked scared, so I repeated myself. "Marry me. We're getting married, right?"

"Look, you're not even eighteen yet. I could really get in trouble for this."

"So what? I'm almost seventeen and I'm just as mature as an eighteen-year-old. We'll get my parents' permission. We can get married so long as they agree to it."

I needed Alan to marry me because I wanted to have my own life already. I was bored and I was so *over* being a virgin. He was a Jehovah's Witness, and most important, he was a teacher, which was an actual *career*. While I knew people who worked in bakeries and cleaned houses, I didn't know anyone with the kind of career you needed a degree for. On a teacher's salary, we could be rich enough to have a nice apartment. Maybe even buy a house. I could stay home and bake cookies and have a Tuesday night Book Study at my very clean home. And wouldn't this just prove to everyone what I'd been saying all along? I was way too mature for high school.

"Kyria, I could really get into trouble for this."

"But we're *supposed* to get married. And I told you already, I'm really mature for my age. Let's go tell my dad."

"I don't know about this. Are we really gonna do this?"

"We're gonna do this," I said. "We have to do this."

Alan was the man I was going to marry because this is what adults did, and I was an adult. I violently flung open the front door like I was part of a highly orchestrated bank robbery.

"Dad!" I screamed into the house.

My father was shuffling about in the kitchen, trying to open a jar of pickled herring. I could hear his slippers flapping, scraping on the linoleum.

"What is it now?" Dad yelled from the kitchen, expecting a broken lamp or a request for money.

"Alan and I are getting married," I announced.

Dad burst into the living room, holding a fork like a trident while cream sauce dripped down the handle. The house smelled like microwave popcorn, and the television was on.

"You most certainly are not."

"We're getting married and there's nothing you can do about it!"

My chin was high and dramatic, like a poster of a soaring eagle. Beneath me, in bold serif font, was written the word "determination."

"You're in school!"

"I have school phobia! And I already know, like, everything they want to teach me anyway."

Alan stood motionless, silent. He was supposed to be defending me, declaring his intense need to take my hand in marriage or threatening a star-crossed suicide. He was not supposed to be backing against the wall with his arms crossed, looking scared. Did his stage directions not Xerox correctly?

"You are not getting married," Dad stammered. "I am not letting this happen."

"You have no right!" I yelled. "I hate you! I hate you!"

"Knock it off right now," Dad said, turning to Alan as if to say, This brat is your problem now.

"I'm old enough to make my own decisions," I yelled. "Fuck! You! Asshole!"

At that, my father swung for me, a flapping of fingers limply brushing my coat. He had hit me. He had tried to hit me! I immediately began screaming. Yes, he had hit his own daughter, his grown daughter. Nearly 17 years old, and he had attempted to hit me as if I were a child. Who knew what he was capable of now?

"You can't hurt me anymore, Daddy!" I screamed. "You can't hurt me *anymore*!"

I ran into the kitchen, leaving Alan and my father to work it out between themselves. Since Alan wasn't defending me, I called Lisa. I spoke loudly, so that my father would hear me call someone who really loved me. He would see how people who care about other people don't say *no*.

"Welcome to the nuthouse," Lisa answered. "How may we serve you?"

"Lisa," I sobbed, "he . . . he hit me."

"Kyria? Oh, no! Oh, my goodness. Are you okay?"

"I don't feel safe," I said, trying to use hot-button phrases that I knew she'd respond to. "I told my dad that Alan and I are getting married and he totally lost it. He got *violent*."

"Wait. You're getting married? To Alan?"

"Yeah, he just proposed to me tonight. Please come get me. I don't feel safe here right now!"

"Pack your stuff. I'll beep when I'm out front."

I dumped mothballs out of a vintage suitcase lined with shredded purple silk. I packed all my underwear and clothes for the Sunday meeting. Alan was downstairs with my father and they were both at a loss as to what to do with me.

I had it all planned out. I was going to move in with Lisa. I left home.

CHAPTER 16

Remaining Clean in the Eyes of Our Neighbors

It was easy for me to move right in because there were already two beds in the one-bedroom apartment, in case Lisa had a flashback in the middle of the night and needed a change of scenery.

"Sometimes I scream while I'm sleeping," Lisa said. "Just ignore it. I'll stop eventually."

I chose the bed closest to the door. The ceiling of Lisa's apartment was slanted like one of those "mystery spots" where you look taller on one side of the room than the other. Standing up too fast could necessitate several stitches. L'eggs panty hose spilled from open drawers. Boxes of winter clothes were hidden in a closet with a curtain for a door. The room was not merely crowded, but filled with the strangeness of an inexplicable extra bed, as if part of a very poorly run orphanage.

Since this was an attic, I had to crouch to look out the window. At the tenement across the street, an older Italian couple hosed down their concrete lions and pruned a makeshift grape arbor above their driveway. A yellow Camaro with a Cape Verdean flag attached to the antenna drove slowly up the block for the fifth time that day, blasting "ethnic music" at peak volume. Earlier that day, a man had approached me on the sidewalk holding two three-pound freezer bags and asking, "*Pssst* . . . Wanna buy some shrimp?"

This was Central Falls, Rhode Island, the city that in 1986 was crowned "Cocaine Capital of New England" by *Rolling Stone.*

Lisa lived in a four-story, vinyl-sided building that was owned and occupied entirely by Jehovah's Witnesses (except for the second-floor tenant's son, a soft-spoken boy who occasionally had random car stereos for sale). The tenement next door was boarded-up, having been recently raided as a crack house. Unfortunately, just as I moved in, they kicked out all the squatters. This was a shame because I had started telling a story to my friends called "I Totally Live Next Door to a Crack House." Between that, and the fact that I had quit school to get married, I was getting a lot of attention lately.

Lisa set the wind-up alarm for 4:00 AM, and the digital alarm for 4:15. She made an extra $30 each week delivering the early morning edition of the *Pawtucket Times*, and with the extra money, we sometimes ate a crab-stuffed breaded chicken breast at a restaurant with a wood-paneled ceiling.

For the first week that I lived there, I left my pajamas on and climbed into the front seat to deliver papers with her. Together, we were disseminating information to the good people of Pawtucket, letting them know that nasty pothole on Smithfield Avenue would be getting fixed but Mama's Pizza would be closed for two weeks. Lisa wondered, at Christmas, if Jehovah would approve of her accepting an extra tip if placed in a nondenominational holiday card. She was poor, and she was sleep-deprived, and if I didn't know better, I could have sworn she'd taken the job to punish herself.

After her paper route, Lisa climbed back into bed to sleep for another 20 minutes, then drove 45 minutes to work at a facility for mentally disabled adults. She was the first person to tell me that retarded people masturbate.

Lisa said they called the people there "workers," and never "retards," which wasn't considered appropriate. Although Lisa didn't come into direct contact with the workers, she said that sometimes they escaped and came out to the front desk to talk to her.

"The thing you don't think about is that just because they're retarded doesn't mean they're not adults. They still have sexual desires like the rest of us. And you don't even want to imagine the mess that happens when they get their periods. One worker walked right out into the front office, her hand dripping with blood. Guess where that hand had been?"

One of the first things I did upon moving in was scrub the bathroom with baking soda and an old toothbrush. Cleaning the house from top to bottom would show that I was mature and had good manners. Since Lisa had let me be her roommate, the least I could do was be the poster child for the classic self-help book *The Boy Who Couldn't Stop Washing*.

"Golly. You need your bathroom to be really clean, huh?" Lisa asked.

"Sure do!" I said. "There's tons of mold in the corner!"

I stopped going to school and spent all day sitting in her kitchen. Sometimes I got dressed and took a walk, but strolling by the tenements of Central Falls while a drug-filled sports car circled the block didn't make for a relaxing constitutional. Once, I made it as far as my old high school, admired it wistfully, and then walked back to Lisa's.

Alan would visit me after work, and we'd sit in the driveway and talk about how great it would be to get married so we could finally be alone together. We'd drive around looking for an empty parking lot where we could make out. I'd make him stop at the liquor store and buy me a bottle of apricot brandy, which I hid in one of the dresser drawers Lisa had cleaned out for me. Sometimes Alan would refuse, saying, "My dad and brothers are all alcoholics and I don't want it to happen to you," but I would cry until he gave in. I was a teenager and still freshly practiced at pleading. I whined that I *needed* it, claimed I'd *kill myself* if I couldn't get it. Sober, I couldn't sit still.

For entertainment, Lisa had a basket full of Kingdom Melodies and one Bruce Springsteen tape. With this selection at my fingertips, I could have thrown the lamest Christian rave in history. I turned up the Kingdom Melodies and stood with the cold aluminum volume knob pressed into my stomach. Trebly, tinny orchestral sounds fell to the rug and lay there. The music was as moving as listening to a child practice his scales.

Kingdom Melodies were purposely written so as not to arouse sexual feelings. Minor keys were a big problem with modern worldly music like Madonna or Billy Ocean. Music could be used to turn you on.

I turned on Kingdom Melody number 82, "The Women Are a Large Army," and stood facing the wall, rubbing the sugary corkscrew of an open brandy bottle. The bland music was working. I felt nothing.

As a means of employment, Lisa's workers were given balls made of yellow rubber strips to peel and separate for a wage of three cents per pound. Not only did this employ the otherwise unemployable, but it also gave them something tangible to keep their hands busy. And, if they ever left the home, they could always get a job working at a taffy pull.

Lisa brought home unsanctioned bags of this tangled rubber, like she was stealing papers that needed to be filed. We would sit in her living room, eating Smartfood brand cheese-flavored popcorn and watching *Fresh Prince of Bel Air* while we finished a job meant for people who needed to be "integrated."

When Lisa laughed at *Fresh Prince* or *Roseanne*, I knew that I was supposed to laugh. I waited for my cue, like someone pulling a string on my back; then I made noises that sounded like laughter. I wondered if anyone had noticed this slight time-lapse in my emotions of late. Was I still capable of recognizing humor? Everything felt like listening to Kingdom Melodies. Nothing had made me feel happy in so very long. Maybe, I thought, there was something kind of wrong with me.

I told Lisa I would find a job, which I did by sitting in the kitchen and drinking. My mother left a message on Lisa's answering machine saying that if I didn't go to school, they were going to arrest me. Lisa encouraged me to go back to school. It was the only time I felt she didn't totally get what I was trying to do with my life.

I met with my guidance counselor and told him I was a Jehovah's Witness and that I was getting married so he would know that I had a good reason for quitting school. He stared at me uncomprehendingly, as if I'd told him that I felt I had an extra limb that needed to be chopped off.

Before I quit, I spent one semester getting *A*s in all my classes, so that no one could ever accuse me of quitting because school was too hard. School was for conformists, and I would have far better things to do, like sit alone in an apartment all day and wait for my husband to come home.

When I told my mother I was done with school, she immediately decided it was because Lisa had told me to.

"Why are you quitting high school?" my mother screamed. "Did Lisa tell you to quit high school?"

"No, she didn't."

"Lisa told you to quit high school, didn't she? You're quitting because Lisa told you to quit!"

"Actually, Lisa told me to stay in school."

My mother carefully took in this information.

"You care more about what Lisa thinks than what your own

mother thinks," she said. "I always knew she was a bad influence on you."

Since I was going to be a married woman, I figured this was as good a time as any to do something about my mildly debilitating obsessive-compulsive disorder. It was still manifesting itself as a series of almost-cute facial tics and other random eccentricities, which I only got away with by batting my large, blue-ish eyes. I was cute enough, but the truth was, I was creeping people out. I would tap and mutter, stare off into space, then suddenly run to the bathroom like I'd been eating frozen cherries for breakfast.

It was all very "Japanese businessman" the way I dealt with it—internalized, shameful, and very, very secret. I could spend the rest of my life hiding it from Alan, telling therapists, and then running away in humiliation. Or I could finally do something about it.

From watching *Sally Jessy Raphael*, I knew these rituals were caused by chemicals in my brain that had gone all wrong together, like baking soda and vinegar, like bleach and ammonia. I also latched onto the rumor that people with OCD were highly intelligent. We might be able to cure cancer together, if only we could stop counting the petri dishes.

From a pragmatic standpoint, I was sick of it. I was doing things that had a directly negative impact on my life in order to thwart something that had never happened and that may or may not happen in an imagined future. I was casting magic spells, forwarding chain letters, refusing to walk under ladders. This wasn't an illness as much as it was a superstition that had gotten out of control. It had started with a few sage smudges and ended with a full-time witch doctor on call. I wanted my life back.

So I bought a book called *The Freedom to Live: Conquering Obsessive-Compulsive Disorder and Tourette's Syndrome,* which I tactfully hid inside a book about furniture reupholstering.

"Planning on re-stuffing the couch?" Lisa asked.

"Yeah, you know, it's a lot cheaper if you can do these things yourself," I said, walking away before she could ask me any more questions.

The next day, after Lisa went to work, I locked myself in the apartment with *The Freedom to Live* and a bottle of apricot brandy. I didn't actually open the book; I just needed to have it near me. The brandy, I opened. Then I watched television and waited. It would only be a matter of time before someone said something to trigger a burst of guttural grunts and Isadora Duncan–esque arm movements.

When I was finally triggered, I refused to count, tap, or let myself mumble even the smallest mantra. I curled into a ball, and rocked back and forth like a mentally ill acrobat. It felt like my whole body was covered in fire ants. A raw egg was being poured into my ear. My fingernails were being pried off, one by one. I'd never felt so horrible in my entire life.

I held myself in that position for half the day, ball-shaped and shuddering, before allowing myself relief. I then launched into the most intricate and time-consuming series of rituals this side of a final World Series pitch. By the time Lisa came home, I was serenely sitting on the couch watching *227* and cross-referencing the latest *Watchtower* article with the book *Is This Life All There Is?*

"Welcome home!" I said, as if nothing unusual had taken place. "Want some Smartfood?"

I didn't kick OCD that weekend, or that month, or even that year. But that afternoon, I lasted longer than I ever had before without giving in to my need to protect myself from imaginary dangers. Now it was just a matter of going a little bit further each time. One day, I hoped, I would be free to spend my day counting telephone poles, not because I *had* to but because I *wanted* to.

If I'd been aware that people actually take medication coupled with years of behavioral therapy to recover from OCD, I probably wouldn't have been able to stop. As far as I knew, I was a freak and this was something I needed to deal with alone, by myself.

The apartment on the first floor of Lisa's building was opening up. Since one room had photo-realistic wallpaper of a deer grazing near an idyllic mountain stream, Alan and I decided to move in as soon as we were married. With wacky Lisa on the top floor, it would be just like living in *The Honeymooners*, only with more deer.

The family that was in the process of moving out asked if I'd like to babysit their two daughters. In this way, I was able to feed myself with store-brand macaroni and cheese while watching their children watch a videotape of *Grease* on a nonstop loop.

Their mother, Natalie, noticed that I didn't have an engagement ring yet, and on my last day of babysitting, instead of paying me, she handed me a gold setting with a diamond chip in it. She said it was her first ring, back when she and her husband were poor, and that Alan could give her $25 and call it even.

I called Alan to let him know that I had a ring in my pocket and he should come right over with a celebratory bottle of apricot brandy. Then we went for a drive to try to find a parking lot where he could finger me.

I liked being fingered because it wasn't actually fornication but still made me feel like I was pretty knowledgeable about sex. When I went to the gynecologist for the first time and he asked if I was a virgin, I said cockily, "Kind of, you know, I've had fingers in me." When the cops blinded us with a light for making out behind my old elementary school, I told them it was okay because we were engaged to be married.

One night, after some routine, parking-lot finger-blasting with my fiancé, I came home to find Lisa sitting on the floor, cross-legged, rocking back and forth and whimpering. Her waist-length hair was flipped upside down, creating a waterfall over her knees. She had a yellow legal pad on her lap and was writing, "I am not good enough for god I am not good enough for god I am not good enough for god I am not good enough for god" over and over and over again.

I tried to hug her, but she pushed me.

"Go away," she said through her teeth. "Trust me. Go away."

A bird had been squawking nonstop since I got home and I really wished Alan hadn't already driven away. I walked down four flights of stairs and sat on the hood of the blue Colt. The squawking bird turned out to be a squirrel, now standing in the middle of the driveway and screaming at the top of his little lungs like Brando yelling for Stella. The otherwise fluffy little acorn-hugger was wobbling around the driveway, hissing. The yellow haze of the garage light made the blue car look green and the crazed squirrel look exceedingly dangerous. I hoped it might hop the fence and go freak out the crack whores, but instead it trained its gaze directly upon me and began to keen. I jumped off the car and ran back inside.

"There's a really scary squirrel out there," I told Lisa. She stopped rocking for a moment and looked up at me, mildly confused, before returning to her nervous breakdown.

The next day, the squirrel was lying on its back in the driveway, dead. On the kitchen table, under a keychain, was a note that said "Please leave before I kill you—Lisa."

Had she found the brandy? Did she know that Alan and I had been fooling around? Was I being framed for squirrelicide? I had cleaned the bathroom, pulled apart rubber twine balls, and had even been going to most of the meetings! What had I done to warrant being killed?

If Lisa thought I would still be there when she got home, she'd underestimated me. You can't fire me, I thought. I'm moving downstairs! But first, I needed to steal about five large trash bags from under her sink. I kicked my belongings down four flights and dragged them like murder victims into the un-locked, empty apartment. I needed to hide everything in case the landlord decided to check in on the place, wash his hands in the kitchen sink, or jerk off.

I checked the closets for rabid squirrels, and then lay my body across the floor. I couldn't call Alan to tell him what had happened, because there was no working phone. I lay on a still-plush strip of dark green bedroom carpet, below where Natalie had placed her waterbed. I hugged my head to my thighs and wept.

For possibly the first time in my life, I wasn't weeping for attention, I was weeping for myself. I didn't want my parents to rock me to sleep or to let Alan know that I was "sensitive." I wept because I won my wedding ring while babysitting and my best friend wanted to kill me and the apartment was dark and empty. I was completely alone and there was nothing else to do.

The next morning, I holed up inside the apartment, like a really lame and harmless Unabomber. I drank water from the tap and splayed out like a starfish in the middle of the kitchen floor. Eventually I bored myself right out of being depressed. I waited until school was getting out, then walked to Sarah's house. It was about two miles away, so I wandered in the ebb and flow of various groups of students on their way home. I passed the Catholic school, then the public elementary school as groups split and reformed, some in plaid Christian uniforms, some in tight Lycra jeans and Velcro high-tops. I rang Sarah's bell and told her I had nowhere to live.

"Can't you just go home?" she asked.

"No! Home? My dad tried to hit me! Your mom knows how my parents are, right? I mean, she knows my parents are wicked crazy!"

"I don't know," Sarah said. "My mom kinda likes your mom, I think."

For that night, I was placed in the guest room, where they kept the board games, puzzles, and books on geography with cal-

ligraphic nameplates inside the cover. I curled up in a pile of knit-
ted afghans and down-filled quilts. There were extra comforters
at the bottom of the bed in case it got too cold and a box fan in the
window in case it got too stuffy. When Sarah went to school the
next day, I sat in the kitchen with her mom and watched a black-
and-white television and said things like "I love your cabinets—
they're so kitschy!" and "How do you make your cookies taste
sooo delicious?"

"You can't stay here, you know," Sarah said after three days
had passed. "My mother is concerned that you seem to be moving in."

"I know I can't stay here, like, *forever*!" I said. "But it's okay
if I stay here for a little while, right? Like two months or something?"

Sarah put her head in her hands.

"This is hard for me to say, Kyria, but you really need to go
home."

I couldn't believe that I'd been kicked out by two friends in
the same week. It's not like they had anybody else staying in that
room! It had never occurred to me that the whole world wasn't
under some kind of obligation to take care of me, to pick me up
and rock me when I cried.

I tried to come to terms with the fact that my foray into adulthood wasn't going to involve curling up in Sarah's family's comforters and letting her mother cook dinner for me. Then I decided
to move back home.

CHAPTER 17

Adorning Ourselves as Brides of Christ

The following weekend, I found myself leaning my forearms on a metal TV tray in my parents' living room, addressing RSVP envelopes for my wedding while watching television. My parents had let me come home, no questions asked. My father even agreed to pay for the wedding. After all, Alan was charming and had decent career prospects, while I was a high school dropout with a tenuous grasp on the world outside my Kingdom Hall. If they didn't pay for the wedding now, they'd be walking in on me masturbating until I was 60.

I chose the invitations myself. They were Victorian-style and looked very classy. I was, at that time, really into things that were *classy*. For the last two years, I'd had a subscription to *Victoria* magazine, and I would settle on my bedroom floor with a ruler and a blue Bic pen to draw brownstones, cobblestones, and Dickensian oil-fueled streetlamps as if I were an illustrator for Penguin Classics. For the wedding, I planned to wear a vintage dress and carry a single white, understated lily. This was all part of my vision.

My vision, however, did not include addressing the invitations so soon. This was stupid, like homework. We had *months* before the wedding, and I wanted to go to the mall. Mom was having, like, a nervous breakdown or something.

"We have to give people time to RSVP so we know how many meals to have, okay, *Kyria*?" ·

Lately, she said my name like it was a curse word, like it was "fatty" or "jerk-off."

"Um, Mom, *whatever*. We can just pay for the extra dinners if nobody shows up. Why does it matter? We'll have leftovers."

"No, *Kyria*. It doesn't work like that. Do you know how much each one of these dinners is even costing, *Kyria*?"

I had to admit that I didn't. So I settled onto the polyester slip-cover over our couch and begrudgingly printed the names of all the people who my mother said would be insulted if they didn't receive an invitation.

The invitations included an explicit request, printed below directions to the Marriott and just above a border of roses: "The bride and groom ask that there be no smoking at the reception." It was Alan's idea to get this printed directly on the invitations, saying he had worldly family members who sucked down cigarettes like candy.

"If we don't put it in writing, those animals will show up and start smoking all over the place. You don't know how they are."

Smoking was a dirty habit, and could even be considered a disfellowshipping offense. Additionally, I was allergic to Siamese cats, dogs, and goldenrod and therefore it was decided that I would probably be allergic to cigarettes as well. I'm not sure who started the rumor that I became paraplegic in the presence of Pall Malls, but I suspect it was my dad. He was also convinced I was allergic to seafood and I never had the heart to tell him otherwise.

"It can't be good for you! All that shellfish," he'd say. "Makes people swell right up."

The wedding ceremony itself would take place in our newly erected Kingdom Hall, a building so new that the drapes hadn't even been delivered yet. Alan and I would be the first couple to enter into the marriage bond there. I would be the first virgin to stride down the virginal industrial carpeting. Everyone commented on the fortuitous timing of the construction. Not only would we have an attractive setting, but the toilets wouldn't overflow and no old rusty chairs would cut anyone. Already, Jehovah had blessed our union.

Alan's mother and Jeffy were making wedding bears. She decorated a country mailbox, into which the guests could place their cards quoting First Corinthians: "Love *bears* all things, believes all things, hopes all things, endures all things." Meanwhile, my father kept shaking his head and wondering where all this party money was going to come from.

"Just let me know the damage," was all he'd say.

I didn't know where the money was coming from either. For as long as I'd been made aware that it takes money to buy lemonade at the zoo (when we had a perfectly good container of Country Time back home), I'd never dared to ask for anything expensive. But begged, borrowed, or stolen, my father was getting me the hell out of his house.

Earlier in the week, I'd sat at a desk at the Marriott hotel, across from a woman in a peach suit, and confirmed what I'd like to be eating on the day I got married. I wanted roasted chicken and green beans almondine. Mom agreed, but overrode my initial dessert choice for a less expensive selection. "We'll already have wedding cake," she said. "People can eat *that* cake."

Then papers were being rustled and signed and I was no longer needed or asked any more questions. Grown-ups with savings accounts were handling what things would cost. I just needed to look pretty and show up for my big party. I wandered off through the hotel's event rooms, running my fingers across stacks of modular wall panels soon to be installed for a silver anniversary, a birthday, or someone otherwise celebrating the forward movement of time.

We drove to Filene's, where I'd won a spot on the Showcase Showdown they call a "wedding registry." Now I could ask for anything I wanted without having to look people in the eye. I chose a $300 neo–art deco porcelain statue and a numbered, hand-blown crystal paperweight, while my mother chose things like Teflon pans and oven-to-fridge serving dishes. My great-aunt Ruth came along for the ride and bought me a Noritake fine china service for eight, which my mother decided we should keep at her house, stacked next to her four other sets.

"It's too much money invested in place settings, *Kyria*. We can't take the chance of letting it get broken. You know how you are."

Aunt Ruth, who was a traditionalist, thought that a wedding gift should be kept by the bride and leapt to my china-keeping defense.

"Let your daughter keep her own dishes, would you?" she said, mumbling something derogatory in Yiddish like *knish-for-brains*.

My mother, who lusted after fine china, stammered and back-pedaled as I defiantly stacked $500 worth of fragile saucers and soup bowls on the dresser in my bedroom, under Sarah's poem still written on the wall in Sharpie about the dead souls who ask for vengeance from the gas ovens of concentration camps.

Jehovah's Witnesses are allowed the freedom to invite whomever they'd like to their wedding ceremony at the Kingdom Hall, even worldly family members. After all, these non–Jehovah's Witnesses, having never attended a proper Christian wedding before, would be impressed by our godly reverence and application of biblical principles. In a world with no regard for God's laws—where brides weren't virgins, gays claimed to be "couples," and people took the marriage bond so lightly as to exchange vows while jumping out of airplanes—a Jehovah's Witness ceremony would be a refreshing change. Everything in our lives was considered an opportunity to witness to people about the good news of Jehovah's Kingdom.

If our conscience allowed, we could also invite these same worldly people to the reception after the ceremony. We just needed to keep in mind that people who do not have Jehovah's blessing usually indulge in recreational drugs, premarital sex, and alcohol. Some Jehovah's Witnesses, we had been warned, found their ceremonies quickly fell into chaos after they invited neighbors or coworkers who did not subscribe to godly principles. The understanding was that if you wanted your wedding to turn into ancient Babylon, with guests snorting coke off the mother of the bride's cleavage while the DJ played backward death metal, by all means, invite plenty of worldly people.

"Bill and Paula aren't coming to the wedding," Alan told me when the RSVPs started rolling in. The returned invitation was covered in angry cursive scrawl that said:

> As you are aware, Alan and Kyria, your uncle and I are both heavy smokers. If you had concerns about smoking during the wedding, we would have gladly gone outside the reception hall. Because you included the instructions on the wedding invitation itself (which is tacky and we just DO NOT UNDERSTAND) we have no choice but to take this as a personal attack. Clearly, you would be much happier if we did not attend your wedding!

"Good," Alan said. "We don't need that kind of bad influence there anyway. They would only come for the free booze."

A few other worldly relatives boycotted the wedding in solidarity, but that was the last we heard of it. All the Jehovah's Witnesses were pleased as Punch to know that they would not be subjected to Satan's nicotine. Alan and I would celebrate our holy union before Jehovah by eating chicken stuffed with ham and cheese in a classy, smoke-free environment, with as little worldly influence as possible.

Choosing a maid of honor was easy for me. Sarah was Episcopalian and therefore unfit to grace our Kingdom Hall aisle while wearing taffeta. Only Jehovah's Witnesses were supposed to be a part of our ceremony, unless you had a worldly twin sister who was also terminally ill (and even then, you'd get dirty looks).

A rule like this was not in place to cause friction, because no Jehovah's Witness should have any worldly best friends anyway. So I asked Emily to be my maid of honor, but made sure that Sarah understood she was my first choice. Lisa wouldn't be in the wedding at all, as she and I hadn't spoken since she kicked me out of her apartment via her kitchen-table death threat. In order to avoid hard feelings, I had no other bridesmaids.

Emily and I went shopping for my wedding dress at a used-clothing store in downtown Providence called Zuzu's Petals. I had what people in my congregation called a "unique" fashion sense. After seeing *Annie Hall* as a freshman, I'd worn men's ties for a whole month. There would be no boring bridesmaids, no wide-eyed three-year-old throwing rose petals while old ladies had an aneurysm of glee, no ostentatious cathedral train. The last thing I was going to do on my wedding day was don a headdress that looked like the encore outfit from Cher's farewell tour—even if I did have 14 bottles of her hair spray.

Emily and I found the perfect wedding dress. It was thick, creamy silk with butterfly sleeves and was hanging on the wall above a Providence postcard that said "The rich live on Power Street and the rest of us live off Hope." A dour rockabilly chick pulled the dress down off the wall for me, and I imagined myself as Doris Day and Sandra Dee and Audrey Hepburn all rolled into one. It was $55, which was more than I'd ever paid for any dress in my life, but my wedding seemed worth it. Emily found a periwinkle-blue cocktail dress with a matching pillbox hat. Together, we couldn't have looked more '60s suburban kitsch if we'd been holding a tray of cookies below a giant sunburst clock.

"You're not wearing that dress," my mother said when I returned home to model my find in our kitchen. "Why didn't you kids tell me you were going dress shopping?"

"But Mom," I whined. "I paid for it myself!"

God, I couldn't believe that she was doing this! It wasn't fair!

"You can't wear that dress. It's off-white. It's almost gray. People will think you're not a virgin."

"Mom! The dress is *cream*. What are you even talking about?"

My mother called Emily's mom, Betty, to tell her what we'd done behind their backs. She asked her to explain to me the kind of girl people would think I was if I wore a funky vintage wedding dress.

"If you don't believe me, maybe you'll believe Betty," Mom said, handing me the phone.

"Just let your mother take you shopping," Betty said. "Humor her and get a more *appropriate* dress, please?"

I was totally pissed off that my mom was being such a bitch and wouldn't let me wear the wedding dress I wanted, but I knew I had no choice. We compromised, so Emily was allowed to wear her vintage bridesmaid dress as long as I went dress shopping with my mother.

We bought a new dress, which I did not totally hate and other people described as understated and classy.

I promised Emily that after we had the "regular" wedding, we would have another, super-cool wedding just for me and my friends. We'd have a potluck reception in the park and make up our own funny wedding vows. My parents and their weird, elderly friends would not be invited. More important, I would wear whatever I felt like wearing. No one would hold me down.

The next week, my mother cleared a pile of past-due utility bills off the dining room table so that Brother Wentz could come by and have a pre-wedding chat with me. My mother prized this piece of furniture more than all of our other possessions;

it was simply the most expensive thing we owned. The table had been purchased at Moda Italia, a modern-furniture store in North Providence that sold ceramic statues of leopards and mirrored four-poster beds decorated with cherubs holding lightbulbs. Mom removed the tablecloth to reveal—for the first time in months—the beveled glass top, which was only uncovered when guests were over. The glass was supported by a chunk of pink granite so heavy that the ancient Egyptians could have used it to build a spare temple.

Brother Wentz sat across the mega-table from me, wearing a polyester tie the width of his chest and clutching a large-print Bible. The same elder who had given me entrance into the Theocratic Ministry School when I was eight years old was now going to give me a heart-to-heart about what it meant to be a good wife. I waited for him to recite scriptures about respecting my husband and keeping a godly home, or to at least mention how impressed he was by our furniture.

"Kyria, you're very young," he said. "So tell me. Are you just getting married in order to get out of an unhappy family life?"

Apparently he'd decided to go off-script.

"What? Absolutely not!" I was indignant and humiliated. Wasn't he supposed to tell me how to wash my kitchen floors?

"Because from the outside, it might seem like marriage is a good way to escape. But marriage presents its own set of problems. You see, if you're trying to escape an unhappy home, marriage is not the way to do it."

I looked around my mother's impressive dining room, where guests like Brother Wentz were offered bowls of salted nuts and free coffee. What more did he expect from me?

"I'm getting married because I'm in love!"

Brother Wentz sighed. "Look, I've been to your house many times to resolve issues in your family by using biblical reasoning," he said. "It would not surprise me if you were looking for a quick way out."

"I'm almost eighteen and I know what I'm doing," I spat. "The law says I can get married at eighteen!"

I was mature; the problem was that no one seemed to have noticed yet. Brother Wentz certainly wasn't going to tell me what I should and shouldn't do. He was as bad as my mother, who I began to wish was in the room to defend me.

"I know what the law says," he responded. "I'm talking about what Jehovah says. Do you really think that *Alan* is the most spiritual mate you could find? After all, he's twenty-four and hasn't yet earned many responsibilities at the Kingdom Hall."

I was dumbfounded, blindsided. This was a messenger from God sent here to tell me off. I expected to be blandly lectured on how to cook and lay out Alan's ties for Field Service, not to be talked into living at home by a man who used to beat his wife for coughing too loud.

"Kyria, I'm not saying that these things are actually the case. I'm just saying that you should think about it. Don't rush into a marriage just to get away from home."

"Okay," I said, pretending to smile because I needed him to leave immediately.

"Promise me you'll think about it?"

"Yeah, yeah, sure. I'll think about it, promise."

Brother Wentz looked concerned as he put on his coat, which I saw as a condescending ploy to make me do what he wanted. I led him out the front door just as Mom came into the room with a tray of coffee and Cool Whip–filled ladyfingers, surprised that he had come and gone so quickly.

I specifically asked for a single white lily to carry down the aisle as a new bride. On the morning of my wedding, however, my mother presented me with an enormous, tacky bridal bouquet, spray-painted with sticky gold sparkles. I tried to scrape off the sparkles and pull out an individual flower, but this professionally built bouquet was engineered like a suspension bridge. This *so* wasn't what I'd asked for. Neither was my headpiece, which was made out of a silk headband that my aunt finished sewing pink flowers onto while I was still getting dressed. The dress wasn't the one I'd chosen, the headband was dumb, and now my single white lily was missing. It was all too much to handle.

Maybe this is why, during the ceremony, I burst into sobs so huge I couldn't even open my mouth to say "I do." Or maybe it was because Alan's brother Jeffy was wearing an International Male–style blouse with a ruby brooch at the collar and kissing all the elders on both cheeks. One photo of me in front of the Kingdom Hall looks like I put on a bridal veil just to discover that someone had stabbed my hamster in the heart.

"You okay, K?" Dad asked, putting his dressed-up father-of-the-bride arm around me. I knew I had to go inside and walk down an aisle and get married, but tears were uncontrollably streaming down my face. "Are you having second thoughts about this wedding or something?"

"No, Daddy, I don't know why I'm crying," I said. This was true. I really didn't know. This whole thing was so overwhelming, it was like asking your cat why it flipped out when you put it into a plastic carrier.

"Well then, let's not cry," he said, hugging me really, really hard. "Let's be happy."

Only songs written by Jehovah's Witnesses could be played inside a Kingdom Hall. Worldly songs such as "Jesu, Joy of Man's Desiring" by pagan composers such as Bach were not allowed to sully our wedding. I would walk down the aisle to "Have Intense Love for One Another," a tune with lyrics given to us directly from the Holy Spirit.

My father accompanied me down the aisle of our Kingdom Hall and onto the carpeted stage, from which I'd later give several public talks. I was crying and shaking uncontrollably—not gracefully tearing up but wailing as if at a wake. At first, my nervousness was sweet, and I could hear the older sisters in the congregation releasing emotional sighs. However, it quickly became a liability, as I actually could not speak. I couldn't repeat the words I had to repeat, that magic spell that binds two people together forever and ever into Jehovah's eternal paradise. Alan looked concerned. The older sisters' sighs turned into uncomfortable throat-clearing.

Somehow I managed to get it together long enough to promise to be an obedient Christian wife. Because I stopped crying, Alan and I could now be joined in the perfect bonds of matrimony. *What God has joined together, let no man tear apart.* Even if we died, we'd be resurrected together into eternal life in Jehovah's promised paradise. Now we were married, and always, always would be.

After the ceremony, Alan and I stood in the lobby of our Kingdom Hall so a receiving line of strangers could shake our hands and congratulate us on our blood pact with Jehovah. I didn't know what to say to any of these people. I said things like "Hi, who are you?" and "Nice dress." The simple, appropriate phrase "Thank you for coming" was beyond my grasp. No one had told me what to say.

Alan and I were whisked off to the reception, where I sat at a special table and was served my very first public alcoholic drink from an actual bar. Before this, my alcohol consumption in front of other people had been limited to thimbles of Jack Daniel's at Emily's parties. I was racked with anxiety that I might get carded at my own wedding.

"I can't believe you actually served me," I told the bartender. "I'm not twenty-one yet! I guess it's just because I'm the bride, huh?"

I still had to be introduced to half the guests, who were mostly old family friends. I met people like Lucy and Harold, who owned a health food store in Florida. Lucy said she "really couldn't have been more pleased" to be invited to my wedding, a phrase that she repeated several times while cracking every bone in my fingers with an overly excited handshake. Lucy was also Connie Sellecca's second cousin. The last nice event she had been to, she said, was when Connie married John Tesh. She assured me that my wedding was much nicer. She didn't go in for big affairs.

"After Connie's wedding, Harold and I were invited back to their home, back to John Tesh's home," Lucy told me. "Well, John has an absolutely gorgeous grand piano sitting in the living room, and I wanted Harold to play for us because he plays with a lovely tone. Unfortunately, there was a man sitting on the bench. He looked very small and pale and sickly and I said to Harold, 'Harold,' I said, 'look at that man on the piano bench. He looks so small and pale and sickly' and Harold turns to me and he says, 'Lucy, that's no man, that's a dummy.' It wasn't a real man, it was a dummy! Can you believe it? And when I got up closer, sure enough he was about four feet tall and it was a real dummy. Isn't that a riot? I wonder how much he paid for that! But such a gorgeous woman, that Connie. I mean I'm telling you, such a beauty!"

Alan and I fed each other cake, kissed when people clinked knives against their water glasses, and danced to Bryan Adams's "Everything I Do, I Do It for You." Since we were no longer in the Kingdom Hall, it was now acceptable to play inoffensive worldly music such as "The Locomotion" and "The Chicken Dance." I didn't dance, because we couldn't play the kind of music I liked, and no one wants to dance to The Cure's "The Same Deep Water as You" in a Marriott reception hall.

I didn't know many people at the reception and wasn't sure what else to do with my time. Ever since Alan and I had finished shoving cake in each other's face, the party had gone downhill. The room was now filled with strangers and old people pinching my cheeks—more like a bar mitzvah than a wedding. I wanted to take my presents and go to my room.

Even though I'd only had one screwdriver with an umbrella in it, I pretended to be drunk. I was too afraid to actually get drunk in public, but acting drunk seemed like a good way to absolve myself of any responsibility for what I did.

I played the stereotypical 1950s Hollywood lush, wobbling around like Dean Martin and called everyone "darling" and "sweetheart." If there had been a lamp shade nearby, it would have ended up on my head as I professed my undying love to a coatrack.

"I don't know why you said you couldn't have baked red velvet," I told the friend of my mother's who had labored on my wedding cake. "I mean, you could have just found a recipe or something. That's the cake I really wanted."

I told the chair of the math department from Wheaton College that I was going upstairs to have sex for the first time. I told Lucy that my mother had made me wear this dress and carry those flowers. For our honeymoon, Alan and I would only get to spend one night in the hotel. I told everyone how much that sucked.

All week long, my father had joked about the wacky things Jehovah's Witness couples do as soon as the ceremony is over. He said they were like rubber bands pulled so tight that they shot across the room the second you let them go. His pre-wedding advice mostly centered on Alan and me losing our virginity.

"Lots of couples never make it from the Kingdom Hall to the reception, if you know what I mean!" he said, laughing. "And if you're gonna give each other hickeys, make sure you have some turtlenecks to wear to the meeting on Sunday."

I thought of the couple who had been instructed to elope because they couldn't wait until their wedding to have sex.

Alan and I believed that leaving the reception early to lose your virginity was appropriate—this was what all Jehovah's Witness couples did. We rudely left our guests dancing to the Pointer Sisters and took the elevator to our upstairs hotel room so we could *do it*.

"I really wanna *do it* with you," I said.

"Yeah, I wanna *do it* with you too," Alan said.

"Yeah, let's *do it*!" I said. "Why don't you *do it to me* right now?"

In truth, I had no idea what "it" would be like or what the "doing of it" would entail. I didn't realize I should be excited in order to facilitate the entry of his "it" into my "it." Foreplay was not something either of us considered. What was the point of kissing when we were going to have sex? It would be like decorating a house before it was built. Could people even kiss and have sex at the same time? I was pretty sure they couldn't.

At the age of 24, Alan wanted nothing more in life than to know what it felt like to stick it in a lady. I was curious myself, despite having suffered through the comedic winks of my father all night. Because there's nothing like your dad egging you on to lose your virginity to make a young girl feel pretty.

I had no particular longing to have sex with Alan, specifically. He could have been anyone. This is why we'd tied the knot, after all—to have sex. If we could have sex at any time, why would we have needed to get married? And, as long as we didn't do something sinful in the eyes of Jehovah like have sex while I was on my period or watch porn and have anal, we would be able to share a mutual Christian orgasm and still live through Armageddon.

I changed into my sweet white Victoria's Secret wedding nightie, which covered more of my body than a one-piece snowsuit. Without speaking, Alan threw me down on the edge of the bed and separated my legs. I had to look away from his body, as the small hairy belly protruding over his crotch made him look gross, like a grown-up. Half standing, half smothering me, he fumbled with a condom, and without touching, kissing, or looking at me, he attempted to penetrate with all the romance of a child pounding a peg into a wooden toy workbench.

Finally, I discovered what I'd been waiting for since I was old enough to rub myself on my yellow beanbag and then pray for forgiveness, I found out what real sex felt like. It felt like premature ejaculation.

I put my wedding dress back on and sat in a wingback chair. Unfortunately, unlike what my mother had me believing all those years ago, Alan's penis stayed completely attached to his body.

"Maybe next time will be better," I said, stunned that it was over so quickly.

Alan went into the bathroom. "What do I do with this condom?" he asked.

"Oh, you flush those down the toilet," I told him. "Can we get room service tomorrow morning?"

"It's kind of expensive," he said. "We should just go to Bickford's."

CHAPTER 18

Remaining No Part of This World While

Still Collecting a Paycheck

Alan taught math part-time at two different colleges because he couldn't get hired as a permanent staff member without a better degree. The congregation elders had put up with just about enough from this budding "little professor" as it was, and Alan promised them that he was done with higher education. We feared what they might do if Alan dared learn a single new thing. Would they hold his head under a baptismal pool until he swore to forget everything he ever knew about mathematical modeling?

Before I was married, my social life had been limited to avoiding the high school prom and hanging out in Sarah's mom's kitchen. Now I took on the jet-setting life of the wife of a part-time algebra teacher. Alan was invited to attend a meet-and-greet picnic thrown by his new colleagues. I was nervous and excited at the opportunity to mingle with real teachers, to experience what would surely be stimulating, cosmopolitan conversation.

"So, what do you do?" one teacher asked.

"Nothing," I said. "What do you do?"

"Well, we all teach math here, dear," the man said. He had gray hair and a gray mustache.

"I play the piano during the day," I said, thinking this would impress him. It clearly didn't, and I didn't speak again for the remainder of the picnic.

One of the teachers, Bran, told a story about how he had sent invitations to a BYOB party. "So this girl comes up to me and asks, 'What does BYOB mean?' and I said to her, 'Sweetie, it means *bring your own brains!*' I mean, okay? Am I right?"

I laughed along hysterically. He *was* right! I had no idea what BYOB meant. Later, I found out that Bran was gay.

"He confided in me about being gay," Alan told me. "He feels very guilty about it. He *admitted* it. He even said to me, 'Alan, you don't know what it's like to let another man put his penis in your, um—you know—*rectum*, and then break up with you.' He's conflicted and he agreed with me when I told him that being gay is wrong!"

"Oh, good," I said. "Maybe Bran will become your Bible study! I hope you can convince him to stop being gay."

I thought about what a coup a gay man would be for our spirituality, how many accolades we would receive at the Kingdom Hall, how Alan's college transgressions would be overlooked. If Alan could get a Bible study and convince him to stop taking it in the behind, our congregation would finally give him more responsibilities and we'd be able to host a Book Study at our home. Every Tuesday, I'd put up clean guest towels and make brownies. Or maybe I'd hold off on the brownies and let Bran bring something ex-gay, like homemade madeleines.

It seemed that I needed a job. Alan's colleagues reacted strangely when I told them that I stayed at home all day, you know, going for walks and watching television. Sarah worked part-time with Happy Housecleaners to help pay for college. I asked her to introduce me to the world of spray cleaners and extra house keys. I didn't have to interview for the job or fill out any paperwork, because Sarah vouched for me as her partner. Even when we stopped by the office to refill our bottles, I wasn't sure who my boss was.

The closest I'd ever come to having my own job was the month I decided to volunteer at the Pawtucket Children's Museum because I thought it would look good on a résumé. The museum was located in a refurbished Victorian home, and I remembered the layout from school field trips. It featured an old-fashioned kitchen and a puppet room. It also housed an empty, wood-paneled room filled with child-size medical supplies for the disabled, such as leg braces and room-darkening glasses. Next to each device was a wall card, describing what would be wrong with the corresponding child. We were supposed to be learning that it's *okay* to be different, but what we took away was that being in a wheelchair was as fun as riding a bicycle you didn't have to pedal 24 hours a day.

When I was 15, I volunteered at this museum for a month, cleaning paintbrushes. After one really tired-looking girl let me borrow her copy of *Go Ask Alice*, it dawned on me that the other kids around me were not volunteering for fun, they were doing community service. The job no longer seemed like something that would look good on a résumé, and I was at a loss for charting my next career move.

I'd always thought housecleaning was a sweet job if you could get it. There were tips and an $11 an hour paycheck, more than you would ever make at a record store. It also afforded me the opportunity to explore the homes of complete strangers. Perhaps because I hadn't actually interviewed or filled out an application, it didn't feel like a real job to me. It was more like hanging out with my best friend while wiping off tables and looking in people's cabinets. I'd joke with Sarah about lame family photos or unfortunate decorating choices. One seemingly vacant home was done entirely in 1970s neo-lodge style with a wagon-wheel chandelier, real wood paneling, and a refrigerator with nothing in it but a box of crackers. Upstairs, a row of tiny and clearly unused hospital-tucked beds gave the impression the room had once been used to film a live-action *Goldilocks*.

We cleaned a white-carpeted luxury apartment in downtown Providence that featured a marble fireplace and two enormous commissioned portraits of mentally retarded identical twins in wheelchairs. We thought we were alone, until we realized there was a man lying in one of the bedrooms, unmoving, unspeaking, and watching *A Current Affair*.

I made Sarah clean around him while I concentrated on cleaning the girls' bathroom—a tiled, handicap-accessible room with no distinguishable shower and a drain in the center of the floor. It looked like a prison shower. The sink was overflowing with colorful bottles of makeup, and I became neurotically fearful of moving them. What if these two poor disabled girls with spurious vision were later unable to locate their sparkly blue nail polish and begin having simultaneous twin seizures? I methodically took each individual bottle off the counter and arranged it in the exact same pattern on the floor, like I was disassembling a car engine. Meanwhile, Sarah cleaned the rest of the apartment while I spent two hours playing cosmetics "Concentration."

Most of the clients were onetime deals, like the delusional elderly man who sat in the center of his kitchen on a folding chair for an hour yelling, "When are the girls gonna get here?" His apartment had no furniture except for one filthy, pee-scented folding cot, a rocking chair, and a transistor radio. The stove was exceptionally clean, as was the clearly unused refrigerator—empty except for a single bowl filled with mold. The bathroom appeared normal until I noticed that the tub was coated in a thin layer of dust. I ran my finger across the bottom, as if writing "Wash me" on the back of a pickup truck.

"Oh, Sarah, look at this bathtub! What the hell?"

"Yeah, I saw that, Kyria. Can you help me clean it, though? We only have 45 minutes left in here before we have to be to the next house."

"What do you think is wrong with that guy?"

"I don't know. Let's just do this, okay?"

I started to get the distinct impression that Sarah didn't think I was working hard enough.

"Kyria, don't take this the wrong way, but I really need you to work a little harder," she said as we ate lunch in the parked car. "We only get a certain amount of time we're supposed to be in these places."

"Hey, that's not my fault! Happy Housecleaners underestimates the amount of time it will take to clean a house so they can grab the client for cheap."

"I still need you to help me out, okay? Can you move a little faster? Not look so long at every little knickknack?"

"I guess, but I can't believe they'd want me to do a *worse* job. I mean, if that's what they *want*."

Three weeks after I started working, Alan asked me to quit my job.

"I don't want my wife to have to work," he said. "I'm the head of the household and I should be able to provide for us."

I called Sarah and asked her to tell them that I wouldn't be working there anymore.

"No. It's *your* job. You need to call and tell them yourself," she said.

"Why can't you do it? You're going to see them."

"No, honestly, I really think you need to call them yourself."

I called Happy Housecleaners to tell them that my husband didn't want me to work anymore, so I was going to have to quit. I didn't know who my boss was, so I just asked for "the owner" and told her that I wasn't coming in to work that day, or ever again.

"Oh. Okay," said the woman who may or may not have hired me. "We would have liked a little notice."

"Sorry," I said. "There's nothing I can do about it. It was my husband's decision."

I felt a *little* foolish, but I knew she couldn't be mad at me. It obviously wasn't my choice.

In the absence of dusty bathtubs and twin wheelchairs, I began sitting at home and drinking. The first thing I did every morning after Alan left was open a bottle of potato vodka. I wouldn't eat breakfast first, because that would dilute the alcohol. Later in the day, I'd heat canned peas in the microwave, but in the morning, it was straight alcohol landing on a shiny pink stomach. I poured four shots into decorative glasses and lined them up on the counter, like I was ready to serve a bachelorette party and I was all the bridesmaids at once. My bathrobe slipped off easily as I brought the bottle with me to the bathroom—a staggering, fundamentalist Andy Capp enjoying another uneventful weekday afternoon at home.

After a while, drinking alone lost its initial luster. So I decided to mix it up and start cutting myself. I must have read about cutting in Lisa's copy of *The Courage to Heal*, which illustrated the symptoms of women who have suffered through traumatic sexual abuse. It helped Lisa to better understand her existing behavior, while I considered it to be my how-to guide for living, my *Zen and the Art of Motorcycle Maintenance*.

I discovered that cutting myself had an interesting side effect—it momentarily distracted me from soul-crushing depression. The razor blade was a sneeze that jerks you awake after driving all night on the highway. I had pressure inside me that needed to be released, needed to trickle out. Otherwise, the pain would be trapped in my body like a wounded cartoon character pushing down a bump on his head, only to discover it popping out from his foot.

I pulled a clean razor blade from its hiding spot at the bottom of the hamper and wiped it down with rubbing alcohol. I was trying to dramatically slice myself here; the last thing I wanted to do was end up with a staph infection. I sat naked and unemployed on a closed toilet seat and slashed at a thigh with an old-fashioned shaving implement.

Now this, I thought. This is living.

I plopped down at our console piano, which really belonged to Alan's mother. The blood formed a segmented line of bobbles on my skin. If I sat still, it would coagulate in the same pattern. If I put pants on, it would stick to my clothes, then painfully peel apart when I stood up. I played the piano for an hour or two, using whatever sheet music was sitting in front of me, jazz standards like "Moonglow" and "In the Mood." Ever since Alan had told me I was technically proficient but had "no style," I refused to play the piano in front of anyone, not even my parents. People asked, but I always refused. I told Emily that I'd been emotionally scarred by what Alan had said to me, but mostly I was waiting for someone to beg. It was about the time that Alan made fun of my musical skills that I went from being constantly annoyed by him to hating his guts. At all times, I had a sort of low-grade fever which manifested in an intense, barely controlled urge to punch him in the face.

I began to notice, too, that there were black shadows in our apartment. At twilight, I sometimes saw demons crossing the walls like passing headlights. Alan and I were fighting. We were choosing to stay home and rent movies instead of attending the Kingdom Hall, which the Witnesses referred to as "slipping away." This could only mean one thing: The gorgeous set of vintage glass dishware I'd recently purchased at a yard sale had been possessed by Satan. I asked Alan to place the orange cups and plates in a paper bag and smash them into tiny pieces with a hammer while repeating Jehovah's name for protection.

I wanted to move, in case the demons had gotten into our water supply or our deer wallpaper. Alan had grown tired of living in Central Falls next to a former crack house anyway. So after someone stole my goose planters filled with geraniums right off the front porch, we moved one town over, to Lincoln. If Central Falls was where you went to buy cocaine, Lincoln was where you went to snort it. Our new apartment, in a one-story brick attached home, had a slate roof and French doors and could not have been any more quaint if it had a skating pond and a snowy red sleigh parked out front.

The house was situated on about a quarter acre of land along a main road next to a self-service car wash. Despite this, the landlords decided that they would like to own a peacock, several different types of fowl, and three shaggy red Highland cows, all of which escaped with alarming frequency. The backyard barnyard also made it difficult for me to utilize the existing clothesline. Every time I stepped outside to hang my laundry, I found myself being charged by an angry, soulless rooster. One day I answered my doorbell to find a perturbed woman standing on my porch.

"Your peacock's in the street," she said.

"It's not *my* peacock," I responded.

"Well then, whose peacock is it?" she asked incredulously.

"Not mine," I said, quickly and fearfully shutting the door. Through my window, I watched the perturbed citizen walk back to her car, her civic duty for the day still unfulfilled. The peacock watched her too.

Some days, I walked down the hill to Ann & Hope, an affordable department store housed in an old factory in Lincoln. I wandered through groups of old ladies buying paper-thin housecoats and moms with new lamp shades balanced on the back of baby strollers. There were no security cameras in the basement, so I grabbed a bottle of vitamins and put it in my purse.

I liked walking through the masses of "normal" people with my stolen merchandise. None of these people knew that I had cuts on my leg, and I had done it myself. None of these people

had the balls to hurt themselves like I did. I was invincible because no one could hurt me more than I could hurt myself. I
walked home and threw the vitamins in the trash.

This was how I spent most of my days. In addition to making
Jackson Pollock paintings out of my skin, I'd also take advantage
of my time alone to rent R-rated movies, which I hid under the
couch until I could return them. I rented movies like *Raging Bull*
and *The Doors*, but I never told a Jehovah's Witness soul that I
knew Val Kilmer had given a stellar performance. Later I'd throw
some ingredients in our bread machine, so that my husband
could have a sandwich on whatever was left of the loaf when he
got home. If he was eating, he'd at least stay in one place and I
could avoid him for another fifteen minutes or so.

The mantel of our non-functional fireplace also took up a large
portion of my day. It was lined with music boxes, collectible bon-
bon tins, and velvet-clothed porcelain dolls that Alan's mother
found at the flea market. With great consideration, I nudged and
coerced my *objets* into the most artful position, as if arranging a
imaginary photo shoot for *Victoria* magazine.

Alan and I didn't exactly have a jam-packed schedule. When
Emily or Lisa called to see how I was doing, I told them everything
was great. I told them how lucky I was not to have to work.

Most nights, Alan and I ate dinner in front of the television,
sitting on our overstuffed brocade couch, flanked by neo-Victorian
end tables. The couch had set us back almost $500, but we had
charge cards. Alan also had a moneymaking scheme in which he
switched banks every time we got an offer of $75 in exchange for
opening a new account. We bought furniture, stereo equipment,
and coffee table books—all on credit. Alan even bought a desktop
PC, although I didn't know what we would possibly need a
computer for, seeing as how we already had an electric Brother
typewriter.

We even charged a new family pet, a small lizard who I named
Timothy. We gave Timothy a sunlamp and live crickets to eat.

We gave ourselves radiator heat and fresh bread. All three of us remained well fed and under glass.

At night, I'd come up with excuses to miss the meetings. I'd claim to be sick, noting that I had a tummyache, or maybe even a temperature. By not feeling guilty, we enabled each other into falling by the wayside.

The problem with using razors was that the cuts weren't deep enough to look important. I tried using a serrated bread knife, but couldn't get it to break the skin.

"I cut myself today," I told Alan as we watched television on the couch. I showed him a thin, self-inflicted paper cut of a wound on my arm, hoping he'd be horrified.

"Yeah, don't do that," Alan said apathetically. "What's the point of it?"

To supplement his part-time teaching salary, Alan began purchasing and reselling baseball cards. I found myself wandering through depressed VFW halls and hotel convention rooms, learning the intricacies of biweekly sports memorabilia shows in order to spend quality time with my husband. While he'd obliviously chat up some suicidal junk-shop owner, I desperately searched for anything of interest spread out on one of the long folding tables. At the most, Alan would leave the shows with a stack of Topps packages, which he'd rip into in the hopes of making his fortune on the next Mickey Mantle rookie card. I spent copious weekends sitting alone in the parking lot of hobby shops with names like Ultimate Games of Warwick, trying to hold my breath until I passed out.

I begged Alan to take me out on the town some night. "I'll go anywhere," I told him. "Just please, take me somewhere fun!" He told me he didn't know of anywhere fun, but if I could suggest something, he'd consider going with me.

This annoyed me. I was 18. How was I supposed to know how

to entertain myself? My last boyfriend had taken me to a parking lot to watch him skateboard. I didn't even know what my options were.

Alan told me I had a skewed view of what people did in their spare time and I was expecting something that didn't exist.

"I mean, I'm not going to go hang out on Friday nights in a bar like my father and brothers," he told me.

Instead, we watched television. When friends came to visit, they watched television with us. Sometimes, for a change of scenery, we went to visit Alan's parents and watched television there.

I had a bread machine, a doll collection, and a neighbor's peacock. If I wasn't bored, lonely, and miserable, I would have been brilliantly content.

Anniversaries were one of the few celebrations that Jehovah's Witnesses could guiltlessly partake in. Still, I only saw my parents celebrate their anniversary on one occasion, and that's because I initiated it. I was ten years old and didn't fully understand that my parents hated each other, so I lit candles and set the table with the good china. I wrote a shopping list for my mother, including lamb chops and cake mix, which I then asked her to help me cook. I found an old vase in the basement to wrap in contact paper as a gift. My parents seemed both bemused and depressed by the whole event. By the next year, I'd grown wise enough not to repeat it.

With this shining example, I looked to television and movies to guide my impression of what people in love should do to celebrate their undying happiness on a yearly basis. It seemed that couples went to rotating restaurants or took carriage rides through a park. So on our first anniversary, I couldn't wait to see what kind of romantic balloon ride Alan had planned.

However, I quickly discovered that Alan hadn't made any reservations involving oysters or even front-row tickets to Blue Man

Group. Instead, he was asking me what I was in the mood for. Pizza?

When I confronted him as to why he hadn't made any plans for our anniversary, he blamed me. I should have told him what I wanted, he said. How was *he* supposed to know that I expected to do something special on our anniversary? My constant, barely controlled urged to punch him in the face now morphed into the urge to watch Blue Man Group throw him headfirst down a never-ending tube.

"Besides," he said, "I don't want the pressure of choosing some restaurant only to have you not like it or something! I never know what you're going to like."

This was Alan—math teacher and baseball card collector, with no idea in the world what kind of food his wife of the past 12 months might eat. I married him because he was 24 and was therefore equipped to show me the world. Instead, all I saw was television, the Kingdom Hall, and parking-lot flea markets. Not only was I bored and unfulfilled, I hated Alan for not seeing it. I hated Alan for everything.

"What about Applebee's?" he suggested. "I mean, it's too late to do anything fancy right now."

"I don't love you anymore," I said. It had been exactly 12 months, but with all the time I had taken off my life by sitting in parking lots at baseball card shops, it felt like I'd been waiting years to say this. I said it quietly and succinctly.

"Yes, you do," he responded, as if I'd told him I no longer liked soda. "Come on, it's our anniversary!"

"I don't love you anymore and I want a divorce!" I insisted, plopping myself down on the overstuffed couch. I felt light, knowing that my days of housewife-dom were finally coming to an end. I could find someone who not only knew what my favorite drink was, but would put a diamond ring in the bottom of the glass.

Alan laughed at me. Please! What was I going to do, divorce him and get myself disfellowshipped?

"Well, I'm not going to give you a divorce," he countered. "You married me and told me you loved me. Were you *lying*?"

He was grinning now, pressing his fists into a throw pillow on his lap.

"No, I wasn't lying. Don't call me a liar."

"Then you must still love me now."

Alan was using his math professor skills to trick me into staying. Either I was lying, or I was in love with him. He knew I didn't have the education to deal with logic problems.

"I hate you and I hate being married and I hate *everything* and I want a divorce," I screamed. "You're boring and I hate living here! I hate it!"

"So what?" he asked. "Where else are you gonna go? You don't have a job. How do you think you're gonna move?"

"Give me some money to move, then! Why would you want me to stay here if you know I don't love you?"

This was all beginning to strike me as a little bizarre. I had told him I was unhappy, but he didn't seem affected by it.

"You're not leaving me," he said. "You love me and you're staying."

I collapsed onto the floor, kicking my feet like a child in short pants. I could not believe that Alan wasn't going to let me have this. I wanted this. I wanted to get a divorce. He was such a fucking *jerk*!

I grabbed the car keys and jumped into our shared 1960s Chevy Malibu extended station wagon that Alan had bought from an elderly sister in our congregation. I sped—inasmuch as one can speed in a vehicle roughly the size of an elementary school—to Emily's house. I knocked on the sliding glass door until their dogs barked. I thought for a minute about forcing tears into my eyes, but I didn't have the time to be anything less than matter-of-fact. Emily answered the door.

"I need to come in and talk," I said as she slid the door sideways. "I don't love Alan anymore and I don't know what to do!"

"Oh, no, Kyria!" Emily said, distressed. She called to her mother, Betty, to come up from the cellar, where she had been trying to organize her husband's "boxes of junk." We made tea and sat on the couch so I could get permission to stop being in love.

Betty had recently gone through hell with her congregation elders because she wanted to divorce her husband, Terry—my old friend from the circus. The elders thought she should stick it out. They chose to see Terry as pathetic and in need of Jehovah's guidance.

"Are you in love with someone else?" Betty asked.

"No," I explained. "I just don't love Alan and I don't want to be married."

"I'll be honest, Alan's the best man you're ever gonna find," Betty told me.

True, if Terry was your standard for judgment.

"Yeah, I guess so," I said. "But he didn't even make reservations for our anniversary dinner."

"Men are dumb," Emily chimed in. "You have to treat them like children."

Betty agreed. "He doesn't hit you. He has a good job," she said. "Love will come. Plus, your father paid for that whole wedding and we all had such a nice time. You don't want to ruin that, do you? You should at least give Alan a chance."

I began to wish I really was in love with someone else. Then I'd have a better reason to leave. But I trusted Betty, who had always been the coolest mom I knew, to give me solid advice. Maybe Alan really was the best man I'd ever find.

"You really think I'll never find anyone better?" I asked.

"Trust me," she said. "You'll never find *anyone* better."

Emily agreed. "Men are dumb," she said. "Don't hold it against him."

We finished our tea; then I drove home and told Alan what my decision was.

"I've decided I might as well stay with you because you don't hit me," I told him. "But you better take me someplace nice for dinner."

Alan called to reserve a table at a swanky Mafioso-type Italian joint on Federal Hill called the Blue Grotto. I was served a glass of wine and wasn't carded—the second time I'd been served alcohol in public including my wedding. I wore a lace-collared silk dress, which I accessorized with my great-grandmother's ivory cameo brooch. The couple sitting next to us were both wearing khakis, and I was horrified at how underdressed they were. Didn't they realize where they were? Worldly people really were animals.

I ate risotto with seafood, and we opted not to have dessert. There was nothing else to do after that. Where else could you go on your anniversary?

"I know, we have to go to the beach," I said. "We have to go to the beach at night! It's *so* romantic!"

We drove 45 minutes to Narragansett. On the dark beach roads, I opened the passenger-side window and stuck my head out like a puppy.

"Now what?" asked Alan.

"Now we have to have sex on the beach," I said. "Come on! Sex on the beach. It's like, you just gotta!"

We parked and headed down the boardwalk. Alan pushed me under a bush, put on a condom, and pumped about eight times. He finished and I had sand in my hair, and that was all there was. We got in the car and drove back home. I couldn't wait to whisper to my closest girlfriends that my husband and I had sex on the beach. It was such a good, juicy story.

Whenever Alan and I had sex, we usually left half our clothes on. It added a false sense of urgency and kept me from seeing Alan naked. He had pretty much never been able to last long enough for us to finish undressing anyway. I chastised him every time we had sex, saying things like "You're not going to come too fast this time, are you?"

He'd always promise me that he wouldn't, but I could tell he just wasn't trying hard enough.

"Why don't you go to a doctor or something?" I suggested. "Maybe you, like, have some kind of premature ejaculation or whatever. I think something is wrong with you."

"There's nothing wrong with me," he said, zipping up his pants. "You expect too much."

"Whatever. Doing it with you is gross."

"You just don't understand how sex is supposed to be," he told me. "This is what it *is*!"

I was always dry and couldn't get penetration unless we used a lubricated condom. Sex felt like trying to thread a needle made of Velcro. It snagged. It hurt. It took longer for him to penetrate than it did to make love. It was as hot as watching scrambled porn while listening to the national anthem.

Eventually we came to a kind of compromise: When we finished having sex, I yelled at Alan to hurry up and get out of the room so I could masturbate.

Betty had told me that I was going to learn to love Alan because he was the best man I'd ever find. But I was getting tired of waiting for the happiness to kick in, and I still longed for a divorce. I needed my husband to cheat on me so I could be free. I began begging him to do so—daily.

"Alan, can't you just have an affair?" I whined again and again.

"I told you before, I'm not going to have an affair, Kyria!"

"Pleeeeease? Just have an affair so I can divorce you! I promise I'll forgive you and you won't get disfellowshipped. It shouldn't be a disfellowshipping offense anyway."

"Well, it is, and I'm not going to. So stop asking! And even if you forgive me, that doesn't mean that Jehovah will."

"Why would Jehovah forgive a murderer and not someone who accidentally got married?" I asked. Alan just rolled his eyes.

"You made a *commitment* before God," he said. "You had time to think about it. You knew exactly what you were doing."

"I didn't know what I was doing!" I yelled at him. "I was just in high school! I had school phobia! I made a mistake!"

"You didn't make a fucking *mistake*!" he screamed. He was really pissed off at me now. "You told me you were mature enough! You *promised* me you were mature enough to get married. You gave Jehovah your word. We're holding you to your word."

It didn't make sense to me that getting a divorce should be wrong. I was 17 when I agreed to get married, and now I was 19. Couldn't God understand that I'd changed my mind? How was it a sin to change your mind? That's what teenagers did, right? I mean, I didn't even dress the same or listen to the same music anymore. Alan didn't like my music, anyway—the Sugarcubes, the Smiths. I threw all my tapes into the trash. I was a married grown-up. Now I listened to Lyle Lovett.

Jehovah was supposed to be loving and forgiving. The point of being Christian was that no matter how you sinned against God, there was always a way back. Thievery? Murder? Stabbing a baby with a chopstick, then spinning it acrobatically between two plates? Just say you're sorry, really mean it, and God's gotta give you a second chance. If Jehovah could forgive a thieving, raping, baby spinner, why should it even *be* a sin for a teenager to want a divorce? I wanted a second chance at being a grown-up; how was that grounds for disfellowshipping? Why was this even anybody else's business?

No one could give me an answer.

CHAPTER 19

God's Spiritual Feast Has Been Waiting

on the Table for Years!

Back before car dealerships had MySpace pages, before it was possible to talk on the phone and check your e-mail at the same time, there was America Online. It was an idealistic melting pot of personalities, like America itself, but with goofier names.

After waiting a fortnight for your modem to beep and whir you into a connection, you had 13 seconds to read and reply to all your e-mail before a telemarketer would call and disconnect you. Awesome! We were living in the future! In just six years, we'd be writing "2000" on our checks. "Where's my flying car?" we asked. "When do I get my robot maid?"

Whenever Alan left the house, I booted up Windows 3.1 and transformed from teenage housewife into deadparrot3@ aol.com. This was freedom, equivalent to hopping in a Bel Air convertible and cruising down Route 66 while cranking *Pipeline*. I could smile and wave flirtatiously at strangers, all with the safety of metal and glass between us. I was meeting people I couldn't see, a feat previously available only through CB radio or 1-900-PartyOn. My in-box was filled with messages from people who told me I was funny and probably cute. Everyone appreciated my ability to win any flame war that was posted on the poetry message boards. My out-box, on the other hand, was filled with stories about how I didn't love my husband, felt trapped, and needed someone to give me a good orgasm. But not really. Just through glass.

When the lines were too busy, I became apoplectic. What if Alan came home while I was in the middle of writing, "And your pic is really cute too!"? I felt like I was trying to masturbate in a bunk bed before my camp roommate got back from brushing her teeth. I prayed out loud, beseeched my God, "Please connect, please, please connect. Use an alternate phone number if you have to. Please, Lord, I need to check my e-mail."

I couldn't believe that three years prior, I'd actually thought it was stupid for Alan to buy a computer. This information superhighway was the best thing that had ever happened to me.

As was customary with the local AOL-ers, I was invited out on online "dates" that consisted of simultaneously signing into the same chat room. Lately, I'd been meeting FrankBee in the Coffee Haus. When your date didn't show up, you knew it was because of some emergency, like his roommate needed to use the phone. Then you just typed stuff to yourself, knowing that no one would be able to read it.

> **deadparrot3:** I've been waiting. For a girl like you.
> **deadparrot3:** Anyone? Bueller? Anyone?
> **deadparrot3:** Echo. Echo. Echoooo.
> FrankBee has entered the room.
> **FrankBee:** Hi Parrot! Sorry I'm late.

I had recently e-mailed Frank some of my writing and couldn't wait to hear what he thought of it. I'd sent him a fake *TV Guide* with silly shows that I had made up myself, like *Doctor Quinn Kook-aburra Saleswoman*.

> **FrankBee:** What was that thing? Your weird!
> **deadparrot3:** It was just supposed to be a funny takeoff on TV Guide, you know?:-)
> **FrankBee:** Ha ha. You like tv?

Frank wasn't like the other guys I knew. He was stupid. Unlike Alan, who had initially won me over through his intellectual curiosity, Frank didn't seem to be curious about much of anything. He'd dropped out of college, joined the Army Reserves, and was currently crashing in a friend's basement in Somerville, Massachusetts. Frank told me that he wanted to kiss me. No one had ever been so forward with me before. So I gave him my phone number.

He called several times, and I'd lie on the throw rug, looking up at the computer, saying things like, "I wish we could be together." It was just something to do while my husband wasn't home.

One of my favorite AOL sections was a comedy portal sponsored by Budd Friedman's Improv. Everyone there was hilarious, and you could tell because they even started threads just to make fun of people. I watched A&E's *Evening at the Improv* on cable all the time.

In a chat room, I met "Bimrag," a comedian and Boston University student who was in a sketch comedy troupe called Welcome Wilma. He said I was wicked funny, funnier than some of the comics he knew. He told me I should come see him perform.

> **Bimrag:** You should come to the next Wilma gig. It's only an hour drive to Boston.
> **deadparrot3:** Yeah, I just can't drink the water.
> **Bimrag:** What are you talking about?
> **deadparrot3:** You know, Boston water is dirty! Love that dirty water!

Bimrag: Boston is really beautiful, actually. Have you ever been here? The Charles River is really amazing.
deadparrot3: I bet it's gross.
Bimrag: Well, that's your interpretation.

In the next room, Alan watched reruns of *The Young Ones* while I covertly tried to impress a real comedian by making it clear I was disproportionately afraid of Boston. I closed the door and told Bimrag that my favorite stand-up was Dana Gould, who I'd seen on television doing a joke about how Don Knotts can never make a crank call because everybody knows his voice.

deadparrot3: Do you know him? I think he's from Massachusetts!
Bimrag: Nah, I mean, I pretty much just perform at this one club called the Comedy Studio. If he's done a spot there, maybe I've seen him.
deadparrot3: He does this Don Knotts impression and says "I been lookin' at ya through the bedroom window!" and the other person yells "Is this Don Knotts?!"
Bimrag: Yeah, that sounds familiar.

I told Bimrag I would come see his show, even though I knew that was almost impossible. Boston was over an hour's drive away, and I'd never driven on the Mass Pike before. I knew there was no way I could figure out how to get there without Alan. I'd end up getting lost in Southie or, even worse, the Combat Zone, where my car would definitely be shot at by drugged-up, homeless hookers.

"I want to see a stand-up comedy show tomorrow," I told Alan. "I met a famous comedian online. The show is in Boston, though, so I need you to drive me."

"Come on. You're not going to Boston," Alan said, chuckling. "Anyway, it's a meeting night. There's a meeting."

"But I think it's just this onetime thing, you know? This comedian, he said he'd put me on some guest list or something."

"Don't worry about Boston," Alan said, dismissing the whole fanciful tale. "You're not going to some *comedy show*."

I could have insisted on driving myself, but I was scared to death at the thought of accidentally taking the wrong exit and finding myself lost on the hellishly gentrified streets of Back Bay. I quietly gave in, and spent the whole night drunkenly sulking that I'd missed the chance of a lifetime.

The next day, this e-mail exchange took place:

Dear Bimrag, I'm so so so sorry I missed your show. It wasn't my decision. My husband is a jerk.

I apologize, he replied, *but you're going to have to refresh my memory as a lot of people attend these shows. Who are you?*

My interest temporarily turned away from live comedy and toward live role-playing, however, when Alan offered to host "gaming night" in our kitchen. He invited three computer programmers from Rhode Island College—Eric, Mickey, and Big Bill—to bring their pockets full of 20-sided dice into our kitchen to play a card game called Illuminati. The gang had been holding their weekly game at Big Bill's place, until his wife got annoyed and put a stop to it.

Finally, Alan and I would have some kind of social life!

Mickey wore computer memory chips sewn into his long black trench coat for "extra memory." Eric spoke, periodically, in a fake British accent and carried wallet photos from stage shows of *Rocky Horror* where he played Dr. Frank-N-Furter. Big Bill had been in 'Nam.

They could quote entire Monty Python sketches, talked in computer code, and had favorite books all on their own—books that weren't put out by the Watchtower Society. I wanted so badly to impress them. I quickly tried to read the Schrödinger's Cat

Trilogy and learn all the steps to "The Time Warp." Mostly, they saw me as Alan's young wife who was a little dumb and kept the house really, really clean.

"You missed some dust on top of this doorway," Eric would say. "Nah, just kidding!"

Illuminati cards made fun of conspiracy theories I'd never heard of, like "Hitler's Brain," which I later found out was funny because some people thought his brain was being kept in a jar. The game was very worldly, but Alan still thought it was hysterical.

I got excited when the gang came over, even though I wasn't allowed to play with them. I made myself omnipresent around the kitchen, putting coasters under everybody's glasses and seeing if anybody needed a napkin or some home-baked bread.

When Alan wasn't plotting world domination with the Illuminati gang, he was plotting space domination with a hot anorexic boy from Emily's congregation named Ben.

Ben was fascinating to me. He wore British dandy–style suits and had blond hair that covered one eye. We had an anorexic in our congregation, too, but even though all her hair had fallen out, I didn't find her to be all that interesting. Ben's anorexia was more heroin-chic.

Sometimes Emily and Maya would invite Ben over for dinner, and we would all sit around a big bowl of spaghetti and collectively try to convince him to eat.

"Mmmm! This is SO good, Ben! You don't know what you're missing!"

"Oh, my goodness, Ben, you should really try this meatball! Don't worry, you won't get fat!"

Ben worked as a delivery boy for D'Angelino's sandwich shop, dropping off greasy BLTs and mayo-laden tuna pockets with all the irony of a nun mopping up at a X-rated theater. I saw him as the epitome of cool—everything Alan could never be.

Alan was a curmudgeonly, self-proclaimed beer aficionado who took smirking pride in being "the wacky guy" at any party.

He loved thinking of himself as some outrageous eccentric who was just way too smart to be held down. He refused to do anything that could possibly be construed as "normal." When I was a 16-year-old outcast, I found this to be charming. Now I just wanted him to die.

Ben was the exact opposite of Alan, which is why I was pleasantly surprised when he started appearing at my house every Tuesday night, carrying a box of *Star Wars* playing cards under his spindly arm. I didn't know why he'd want to spend time with someone as annoying as Alan, but I wasn't going to discourage him.

I was hoping this meant I'd get to hang out with him, too, but he and Alan were too engrossed in lining up their cards across the kitchen table to pay any attention to me. Sometimes I would try to make small talk, but there was no infiltrating the bond formed on Tatooine.

I saw Ben only on his way in and his way out. He was always going somewhere else after the game. He would drive a whole hour to Newbury Comics in Boston to pick up the midnight release of some UK import.

"Alan never takes me anywhere," I told him.

"If I had a wife as hot as you, I would take her out and show her off every night," Ben said.

I asked Alan if we could go to a concert with Ben one of these days, but Alan said he didn't like concerts. I asked if I could go to the concert with Ben alone, then.

"Probably not," he answered.

One night, after Alan went to bed and all the Mos Eisley cards were packed away, I mixed some vodka with chocolate milk and convinced Ben to hang out for a while. We lay on our backs on the scratchy faux-Persian rug, and I tried to explain that I wasn't really happy.

"I threw out all my music," I said. "Alan didn't like any of the music I had and I figured it wasn't very mature to keep it, so I threw it all away."

"If I had a wife as hot as you," Ben said, "I'd take her CD shopping every week."

By 5:30 in the morning, it was clear that we had done something naughty. My husband was sleeping and we'd stayed up all night to gossip. All bets were off. I wanted Ben to kiss me. I wanted him to be my boyfriend so we could go to concerts and I could stare at his great hair and I wouldn't be embarrassed by my creepy old husband in polyester dress pants whose favorite songs were comedic parodies about Star Trekin' played on Dr. Demento's radio show.

"Let's go get breakfast," I suggested.

"I should really go home," Ben said.

"But I have hypoglycemia and I need to eat and there's nothing to eat in the house," I said, trying my best to convince him. "I have to go get breakfast anyway. Please don't make me go alone!"

"I've never done this before," Ben said, giving in and putting on his jacket. "I've never stayed up all night talking to someone else's wife and then gone and gotten breakfast with her."

Having breakfast with Ben was exhilarating. I kept asking him about all the concerts he'd been to, trying to engage him in conversation so he'd stay out with me as long as possible. Unfortunately, there were only so many excuses one could make for needing to stay seated in a vinyl booth at Bickford's Pancake House. Eventually I ran out of reasons that he shouldn't drive me home.

When I returned, Alan was still asleep. I crawled into bed next to him, my heart rate flying from pancake syrup and the elation of being with a boy my own age.

Alan never knew I wasn't lying there all night long.

The next time Ben left our house, he was on his way to see British musician Robyn Hitchcock in Providence. I asked Alan if I could go too, and he said he didn't think I needed to see a concert and excused himself to use the bathroom.

"Ben, you saw that, you saw what he does. He keeps me in this house. Please, just tell him that I'm coming with you and he'll *have* to let me go."

"I can't do that," Ben said. "You're his wife. It's not my place to say that."

I begged Ben to let me meet him at a bank lobby across the street from the venue. It wasn't the smoothest pickup line in the world, but once we got through the initial awkwardness of whispered pleading and coercion, I was certain we'd have a lovely first date.

"It's totally fine," I assured him. "I always do this stuff. It's normal!"

Ben agreed to my plan in the span of three minutes, clutching his cards to his chest like a bulletproof vest against soul-sucking neediness.

When Alan emerged, I told him that I was going somewhere by myself. When he pressed me on where I was going, I told him it was none of his business and that he'd be bored and miserable all night, anyway.

"But if you must know, I'm going out with Emily, okay?"

Alan protested, but I refused to answer any of his questions. I threw on a short skirt and ran out the door. I knew he couldn't possibly believe that I was going out with Emily, but I wanted to punish him. This was what he got for not letting me divorce him.

Other than a Smithereens show, the only musical concert I'd ever been to was Victor Borge at the Warwick Musical Tent with my father. I was fearful. Who was this Robyn Hitchcock and what sort of bedlam would he sow among the crowd? What if I couldn't find Ben at the bank? So when I saw Ben waiting for me in the lobby just like we'd planned, I embraced him passionately. We hugged, then moved back to look at each other, holding hands and grinning like he'd just returned from the war.

"I love your skirt," he said. "You look just like that girl from Pulp!"

"Thanks! And you look so cute in that tie," I said, just as Alan walked in.

It took me a minute to register what had happened. Was that actually Alan—*here*? Had my husband followed me to this ATM or was Rick Moranis out of cash? I squinted. My sweaty husband was standing in front of me, grabbing at the wall, gasping for air like he'd just chased the man who stole his only bicycle through all of Italy.

"I knew it!" he said. "I knew you weren't going out with Emily!"

"What the hell are you doing following me?" I screamed.

"What am I doing? What are *you* doing? Running around behind my back?"

"I wanted to go to the concert and you hate concerts, so I came with Ben!"

I couldn't believe that I'd let him follow me. In my excitement at seeing the concert, I hadn't thought about any ramifications. I knew that Alan would be pissed off at me when I got back home, but I never thought he'd be *here*, pissed off in this bank lobby.

"You two are having an affair!"

"Oh, please!" I yelled. "We are seeing a cool concert and you have no right to follow me. Go home, asshole!"

"You planned this from the beginning! You even tried to trick me by saying 'I doubt you'd be interested in this,' when you told me about it."

This was true. So true that I had to immediately deny it. "Fuck off. You're lying!"

Ben looked like he was about to bolt, so I put my hand on the sleeve of his shiny suit jacket and whispered, "I'll handle this."

"Go fuck yourself," I told Alan.

"Come home right now!" he insisted.

"Um, guys," Ben said. "I don't really want to be in the mid—"

"I am a grown-up, Alan! You can't tell me what to do!"

I tugged on Ben's sleeve and pulled him right past Alan, out the door.

"Go home, asshole," I yelled. "Leave us alone."

"Well . . . you'd just . . . you'd better be home by eleven," Alan sputtered. "Or else I'm telling the elders."

I tried to play it cool, like, Whatever, so my husband caught me sneaking out to meet you in a bank lobby to go to a concert. I mean, how else am I supposed to hang out with my friends?

Despite my reassurances, Ben seemed a bit preoccupied. "I really don't feel comfortable with this," he said when we got inside the club. "I play cards with the guy every week. Now he thinks I'm having an affair with his wife. And he's going to tell the elders."

"Oh, please! He won't tell anyone anything," I reassured him. "And anyway, you and I know that we're not having an affair!"

"Kyria, do you realize that I've never had sex?" he said. "I'm a virgin!"

"Well, maybe you'll meet someone at an assembly and get married soon. You never know!"

"I do know. The thing is, I have this regret. I was at a concert one night and this girl came up to me. She said, 'I always see you at these things by yourself and you look so interesting, but you always leave alone.' And then I told her that I couldn't go home with her. I could have had sex that night but I didn't! Why?"

"Duh, she's not a Jehovah's Witness, so you couldn't have sex with her," I answered glibly. I really didn't understand what his point was. What, was he in love with this worldly girl or something?

"But have you ever actually thought about why we're Jehovah's Witnesses?"

"No!" I said, incredulously. "It's the *truth*!"

I couldn't believe Ben was asking me this. Of *course* I'd never thought about why we were Jehovah's Witnesses. I wanted to live forever, and you didn't earn eternal life by sowing seeds of doubt in your mind. We didn't read apostate literature or do anything that could make us lose our faith.

"Well, I've thought about it," he said. "I've thought about it a *lot*. And I don't have an answer."

"Okay, well then, if you want an answer . . . We're Jehovah's Witnesses because . . . what if it's the one true religion and we leave?"

"But what if it isn't?"

"But what if it *is*? Do you want to lose eternal life?"

"Kyria, I could have had sex by now. I'm twenty-two and I'm never going to have sex." He put his head in his hands.

"Oh, come on. Of course you'll have sex! Just try to meet somebody at an assembly or something! You can get married!"

Ben was getting worked up over absolutely nothing. What, he didn't go home with some strange girl in a club and now he was having a nervous breakdown over it? I was, like, a million times better than whoever this mystery girl was anyway. If he cared so much about coming, I knew how to make that happen.

"Do you want a hand job?" I offered.

Ben burst into tears. "No, I don't want a hand job," he said. "I mean, I do, but I don't! No!"

"Come on, let's go back to your apartment and I'll give you a hand job," I cajoled. "It's not sex—it's just my hand. It's okay."

"No. It's not about that. You don't understand what I'm getting at."

There was nothing I hated more than having people tell me I didn't understand something, so I grabbed his face and stuck my tongue down his throat. After all, *he* was the virgin.

Ben kissed me gently, deeply, passionately. Then he pushed me away.

"I got in trouble with the elders last month because Maya and I were fooling around and I don't know, like, I really like you, Kyria. I wish you were my wife and I'd take you out every weekend. But Maya . . ."

I was shocked. I knew Emily and Maya invited him over for dinner a lot, but I thought that was because he was anorexic and we were trying to convince him to eat.

"I had no idea that you two were going out," I said.

"We're not going out! She just knows stuff about me that no one else knows. She understands why I'm, like, you know, why I won't eat and stuff."

I was married to someone else, but I felt like Ben was breaking up with me.

"Okay, great. Well, why won't you eat?"

"I can't tell you."

Fuck. Maya and Ben had some impenetrable bond now? How was that even possible? She listened to shit like Aerosmith! Then again, Maya *was* really skinny. Too skinny, come to think of it. What, was she, like, bulimic or something? Is that how they connected? This was *so* not fair! I was a drunk and a cutter and I had OCD. Did I have to come up with an eating disorder now too?

"So, what, you had sex with her or something?"

"No! We didn't have sex or really do anything sinful, but the elders *thought* we had sex. I've been reprimanded, and if one more thing like that happens, I'm going to be disfellowshipped."

"Can't you just tell them that you didn't have sex?"

"I did. They didn't believe me."

I couldn't believe that Ben wouldn't let me give him a hand job. He'd already gotten in trouble for something he didn't even do. He might as well enjoy life a little in exchange for his punishment.

A few weeks later, I found myself lost in Somerville. I'd taken the wrong exit off the highway, just like I knew would happen as soon as I left Rhode Island.

"I am *so lonely*," I had said to Frank earlier in the day as we sat on the phone moaning at each other.

"I want to meet you," Frank said. "I want to kiss you. Come to my house."

"You know, no one has ever said they wanted to kiss me before," I told him.

"What are you talking about? Aren't you married? Doesn't your husband tell you these things?"

"Yeah. I mean. We don't talk like that. I don't know. I dress up and stuff, though. I like sexy underwear."

"Oh, my God. I think I'm getting an erection. You need to come over right now."

I laughed. Why would someone say that? I scribbled down directions to Somerville and told Alan that I was going to the mall. Frank said it was about a 45-minute drive to his place.

I'd never driven on the Mass Pike before and had trouble reading directions at 60 m.p.h. One of the signs said "To New York" and I knew I didn't want to end up in New York, carjacked and mugged, so I got off the highway. After about an hour, I stopped at Somerville Lumber because I'd heard their advertisements on the radio and knew it must be safe. I called Frank from a pay phone there, began whining into the phone like getting to his house was my math homework and I *just couldn't do it*!

It took me three hours to get to Frank's house, to the friend's basement where he slept on a mattress on the floor. The friend didn't seem happy to meet me, which was funny, because I figured Frank must have told him all about this beautiful girl he was in love with and even wanted to kiss.

Frank was tall and gaunt, and wore a baseball cap. He had a very "down home" look, like he should be in overalls, gliding on his back underneath a car. He pulled me onto the mattress on the floor and we made out. His hair was all messed up from the cap, and I began to smooth it. He pulled my hand away from his head and put it on his erection. I grabbed at his crotch to show him that I knew what I was doing, I knew what an erection was.

He wanted me to put his penis in my mouth, which was not something I was going to do. He asked me to make love to him, which I hadn't expected. I thought he just wanted to kiss me. Nobody said anything about sex.

"I can't have sex with you," I said.

"You drove three hours to get here! Why can't you?"

"Because I want to," I said. This sounded right. Some dramatic dialogue written for star-crossed lovers, like we were in a movie where Frank had a baboon heart.

"That makes no sense," he said.

"I mean, I can't because I *want* to."

"What the fuck are you talking about? If you want to fuck me, then you should," he said.

"No, you don't understand. I can't because I want to." I kept repeating that I *wanted* to, realizing that it wasn't true. "I'm hypoglycemic and I am supposed to eat something every two hours," I told him. "Wanna grab dinner?"

Frank suggested Applebee's, but I told him I didn't like chain restaurants. "They're so plebeian, you know?"

"Fine, whatever," he said. "I don't know what your problem is."

We drove to a mom-and-pop bar that served fried seafood on an outside deck with plastic sheets for windows. Frank put his chin in his hands and watched as I ate a fried clam roll. After two hours of not having sex in a basement, I was famished. Frank didn't eat anything, saying he was broke and a little angry.

"Angry about what?"

"Never mind."

"Want a clam strip?"

"No. That's not what I want."

"Oh, do you want a burger or something?"

"Are you almost done or what?"

I drove Frank back to his friend's basement, and I told him I loved him.

"I love you too," he said. "Why don't you just come in and let me make love to you?"

"No. Just tell me how to get home."

I wound my car through the one-way streets of the suburban housing development where Frank's friend lived. I had driven three hours to make out with a stranger I wasn't really attracted to for no reason except that I hated my husband. I was trapped and this was as good as my life was ever going to get. I didn't even know how to get home. I didn't know anything. As I pulled onto the highway, I decided that the best thing for everyone would be for me to stop living.

I want to die, I thought. This time, for real. No high school–ish, Sylvia Plath–esque suicide where I'd impulsively swallow a bottle of cold medicine. No cry for help where you wait until you hear the key in the front door to stick your head in the oven and feign sleep. Rather, not existing. The kind of selfish suicide where other people die along with you.

Dead. For real *dead*. Can't come back *dead*. Fucking *dead*. Was I prepared to do this, and not have the option to change my mind?

I decided, as a compromise, to drive without looking at the road. Tears the size of biblical hailstones were pouring off my face, making my hands all snotty and slippery. I remembered something my father had said about the blizzard of 1978, how he knew this particular storm was different because the snowflakes were huge. "Nobody else believed me," he once said. "But I knew when I saw those giant snowflakes that it was going to be bad."

I drove while hunched over the steering wheel, looking up through the dark, tinted strip of windshield. I didn't see the road, only a line of trees leaning their green shoulders on electric wires. Sometimes I would swerve onto the other side of the road. I wasn't *trying* to drive headfirst into an oncoming truck, but if it happened, thems were the breaks.

I realized that if I got home safely, it would be an accident.

Frank was still sleeping when I called him at 9:00 AM the next day.

"I want to be with you, but I can't," I told him, even though I didn't feel anything about him one way or the other. "I think I'm going to tell my husband everything."

"Jesus Christ! What? No! Is he going to come and find me?"

"No, he's not like that," I said. "We're Jehovah's Witnesses."

"Please, I'm begging you not to tell your husband about this."

Poor Frank couldn't understand why I was going to tell Alan what had happened. It wasn't because I loved my husband and wanted to confess. It was because this was part of Alan's punishment for not letting me divorce him. If my husband refused to cheat on me, then I was going to do whatever I could to make him crazy.

I told Frank I loved him and hung up the phone.

When Alan got home from work, I met him at the front door. I explained that I had driven to Massachusetts all by myself, that I had done this because he couldn't give me an orgasm and I didn't love him.

"Massachusetts? Where did you go?"

"I just drove around," I lied. "I met some guy and we made out, but we didn't have sex."

"I thought you were going to the mall."

"Uh, I started to, but I got bored."

"I'm calling the elders," he said. "You can't go wasting gas like that on me."

It was not unusual for elders to visit newlyweds—many young couples required a visit of encouragement here and there. The elders said a brief prayer and read some scriptures about idleness and showing obedience to your husband. They also recommended that perhaps Alan might want to allow me to get a job, something to keep me occupied during the day.

So I called my father to get me in at Worldwide Construction Equipment, the office where he worked as a bookkeeper. The owners already knew me because I helped Dad clean their showroom on Saturday morning. Immediately, I was promoted to secretary.

CHAPTER 20

Continue Growing Older as God's Promised Paradise Approaches

One Saturday afternoon, my mother picked me up in her red Dodge, citing some vague reason why I should accompany her to Lincoln Mall. She went to the mall at least once a week, preferring to pay her credit card bills there in person, as paying by check did not afford one the opportunity to buy a sun catcher or stop at Newport Creamery for a grilled cheese with tomato. On the way, we stopped at Dunkin' Donuts, which was not unusual. However, we sat in the car for 15 minutes and drank our coffee, which was noticeably odd. You don't have to sit still to drink coffee when you're on your way to the mall; that's why someone made millions after inventing sippy lids.

Mom said she wanted to "be still for a bit," and I took the opportunity to stare at our reflection in the windshield, unmoving save for the flash of pink lettering as the Styrofoam cup moved up and down. We were relaxing, taking siesta. Which is why I was nonplussed when Mom rolled down the window and began talking to a man in mirrored sunglasses who had just parked next to us in a pickup truck.

"Kyria, this is Michael. I used to work with him at the law office, but now he works as a firefighter."

"Hey, I'm Mikey," he said, reaching across my mother to shake my hand. "I'm over in the Nort' Providence station, right near Cappellini's Pizza and that fancy place, Palazzo. You know it?"

"Sure. Palazzo, I love that place. Nice to meet you," I said.

Mikey looked to be in his late forties, with a dark broom of a mustache and a tiny stomach forming above his pleated acid-washed jeans.

"Nice ta finally meetcha," he said. "Ya got a great mudda."

"Yeah," I said. "Sure do." This guy was now officially way too friendly.

He looked at my mother and nodded his head. Mom nodded her head back at him, and her eyes began to tear up. I was baffled. Was I about to be kidnapped?

"You know what I tell your mudda? Right? You know what I tell her? She looks like Twiggy! You know the model Twiggy?"

"Yes, I know Twiggy," I said. He clearly wasn't looking for another answer.

"She looks just like Twiggy!" he said, screaming with laughter.

My mother squealed and punched his forearm through the window.

"Oh, Michael, I do *not* look like Twiggy!" she protested. Then she got out of the car, and they hugged, walking together to the back of his truck. She was still wiping away tears when she got back into the car.

"What the hell is going on, Mom?"

"Language!"

"What the *heck* is going on, Mom?"

"Michael is my friend," she said.

"Okay . . . ?"

"No, he's my *friend*, Kyria!"

Holy shit. Mom was actually having an *extramarital affair*! I couldn't believe my mother had the *cojones* to risk getting disfellowshipped by having an affair, something that I couldn't even bring myself to do.

Now Mom would have to call the elders and admit her transgression. If she admitted it herself, she'd have a better chance at being forgiven. Jehovah already knew anyway, so even if she tried to hide it, the information would eventually come out. Jehovah knew everything. He even knew what was truly in our hearts.

The elders would then hold a closed hearing at the Kingdom Hall, where they would ask her to divulge all the details of her sin so they could accurately and prayerfully consider whether or not she deserved to be forgiven. The main problem was that apologizing wasn't enough. Some people—wicked, evil people—often tried to try to sneak into paradise without following the rules.

Mom put her head on the steering wheel and started bawling.

"He wanted to meet you because I've told him so much about you. I'm so sorry. I didn't mean to hurt you or your brother," she sobbed.

"It's okay, Mom. No one got hurt," I said. I didn't know how to deal with this. I'd always thought of my mother as having kind of a lizard brain, functioning solely on fight-or-flight and the need to have her children take out the trash. For the first time, I realized Mom was capable of having conflicting, complex feelings. My mind was officially blown.

"No, it isn't okay, Kyria. It isn't." Mom was crying. "What am I going to do now? What is Jehovah going to think?"

She told me how Mikey told her she was beautiful and smart. Because she loved Jehovah and her children, she resisted for as long as she could, but he just "wouldn't let up with the compliments." He brought her flowers on Secretaries' Day, when my father wouldn't even acknowledge that she existed. Eventually he gave her the bouquet that broke the camel's back and they got together.

"Your father and I are getting divorced," Mom said. She was weeping and hysterical, but this was the best news I'd heard in years. I knew she'd probably be disfellowshipped, but much like at my own baptism, I didn't feel what I knew I was supposed to be feeling inside.

"Thank God!" I said. "It's about time."

I don't think my mother heard me say this, though. She just kept telling me how sorry she was, as if I still lived at home and depended on her. If anything, I was only concerned for my father, who really *did* depend on her. How would he get access to clean laundry and leftovers? Who would he hide in the basement from? As it stood, the only social life he currently had was coming over to my apartment to watch television because Alan and I had recently bought a pizza stone and a bread maker.

At least once a week, my father would come by and we'd fill him with pizza and force him to get drunk on rusty nails—Scotch and Drambuie with a twist of lemon.

This proclivity for bartending started during our wedding. The new son-in-law had politely asked the new father-in-law what his drink of choice might be. Dad was used to drinking a single can of Genesee Cream Ale alone in the basement, hiding from my mother, who would scream, "My *father* was an alcoholic!" so he wasn't used to someone *asking* him to drink.

Nervousness and a lack of experience with this question caused him to blurt out the first Chinese place-mat-menu item that came to mind: a rusty nail. And thus, a not-so-favorite "favorite" drink was born.

Once Alan and I figured out how to make a rusty nail, we kept them coming. Our home bar was like the cartoon conveyor belt that keeps cramming cigarettes into your mouth until you've had so much you have no choice but to learn they're bad for you.

"Oh, no, please stop," Dad would say as we forcefully closed his fingers around a refilled highball glass. "Guys, seriously. Guys, what are you trying to do to me?" Then, "Hey, do I smell pizza?"

We lingered over our homemade gourmet pizzas, and took turns picking burned bits of cheese and sausage off the pan on the counter. Alan's pizza was a *man's* pizza, coated in onions and every type of meat you could possible pull out of an animal. This pizza was so virile you had to eat it off power tools. We poured fingers of Yukon Jack whiskey over ice, and I'd drizzle the sickly-sweet liqueur against the sides of my tongue like flaming, liquid gummy bears. Then we'd hand Dad another rusty nail and sit on the couch, filled with burned cheese and onion-pepperoni bits.

"You guys are going to kill me," Dad would moan, leaning back and clutching his stomach before breaking into an impression of *Monty Python*'s Mr. Creosote.

Alan would pound on the piano like a workbench, until I got jealous and booted him. I'd play whatever Dad wanted to hear. "Be My Little Baby Bumblebee," followed by "Take My Breath Away."

He'd still be holding his stomach and groaning when he left, gleefully pretending he hated us for everything because we were surely trying to put him in his grave.

If my mother left him, how could he go on visiting us? Who would he need to get away from?

I had two major duties at my new job: putting people on hold and separating colored pieces of paper.

"Worldwide Construction Equipment. Please hold," I'd say, while placing colored pieces of paper into neat little piles. I arranged things both alphabetically *and* numerically. I even rolled backward in a chair with wheels on it.

My father sat in the office diagonally across from me, where he balanced the company's books on an electric adding machine and sang along to golden oldies. Real songs, made-up songs, Dad was the guy who sang all day at work. It was endearing, usually.

On Friday evening he'd sing, "It's a five-o'clock world," and on Monday morning he'd sing, "Monday, Monday," or, "Can't trust that day." He'd often burst into "School's out for summer!" for no discernible reason. Sometimes he'd even let loose with a Tourette-ish "You're So Vain" while on hold during a particularly annoying accounts-payable call.

The day after my mother left him, he stopped singing. He walked up behind me while I was seated at my desk separating colored papers. He put both palms on my shoulders, startling me.

"I'm going to kill your mother," he said. "That whore. She cheated on me. I'm going to strangle her in her sleep."

"Okay, Dad," I said, and hoped the phone would ring.

Later in the day he put his hands on my shoulders again. This time, he said wistfully, "I bought her a leather coat."

Mom called me at home that evening. "You've got to come over," she said. "I don't know what to do. Your father is trying to give me a leather coat."

My mother had someone better, and it was at this inopportune juncture that my father suddenly discovered a reason to want her to stay. It occurred to me, then, that as much as Dad hid in the basement, bitched about her raw spaghetti, and tripped over her throw rugs, he had also taken for granted that she would always be there. Not just that she would be there to make him dinner and keep the bathroom clean, but to *be there*. Every night at eleven she would be sitting on the couch with a detached dresser drawer full of hair curlers, drinking a rum and Coke and humming along to the Nashville Network. She would fall asleep in front of the television, and hours later my father would sneak downstairs and shake her gently and whisper, "Hey, Minnie Pearl, let's go to bed."

He, like the rest of us, figured that would never change.

Now, faced with the stark reality of living alone, Dad was buying coats. I had never seen this side of my father, the kind that fills the kitchen table with roses and buys leather goods. It must have been the side my mother saw when they were first married. Dad couldn't have been more charming and earnest if he'd been wearing short pants and given Mom a macaroni necklace.

"I don't know, Kyria. He's *trying*," my mother said while preparing beef Stroganoff. "I just don't know what to do."

The jacket was purple with matching leather-covered buttons. It fell just below the hips and fit her perfectly. For about a week, I think Mom honestly thought about staying. You could see her turning "purple leather" into a metaphor for the direction of their relationship, wondering if somehow the past 25 years had been a fluke. Maybe her husband had finally become the Julio Iglesias she'd always wanted him to be. Maybe they had become the loving couple I'd always dreamed of having as parents. Maybe they would surprise us all and record a duet of "Always on My Mind."

They didn't. My mother left, and the elders announced her disfellowshipping about two weeks later. She had committed adultery, was filing for divorce, and was supposedly unrepentant.

Procedurally, the announcement came at the end of our meeting, just before we sang the final song. A brother would announce that so-and-so had been disfellowshipped and was no longer an accepted member of the Jehovah's Witness organization. Then we'd open our book of Kingdom Melodies and sing, "Joyful go! Fearlessly go! Onward let us go!"

I knew the disfellowshipping announcement was coming, because my mother had called to tell me in case I felt uncomfortable and wanted to skip a few meetings. But I had no intention of skipping such a climactic, life-changing moment. Unless she repented, my mother was going to die at Armageddon. And I was going to be there.

One of my greatest fears as a child had been accidentally touching an apostate. They picketed our assemblies and always blocked the entrance to the Civic Center by standing in front of the snow cone vendors. Apostates had crazed eyes and yelled things like "J-Dubs lied about the end of the world, 1974!" I wouldn't read their signs for fear of being possessed. I ran past them with my eyes closed and my fingers in my ears. I ran past them because my parents told me *never* to talk to an apostate.

Talking to an apostate—someone who used to be a Jehovah's Witness and was now disfellowshipped—was seen as a disfellowshipping offense in itself. This, we were told, is like *letting a demon enter your mind.* We were not allowed to be in contact with any person who might offer counterarguments against the Jehovah's Witnesses, unless we were going door-to-door and proselytizing them, in which case, we were protected by the Holy Spirit.

If I were ten years old, I would have been afraid of my mom, but now that I was 20, she was just my mother. Maybe all the *other* apostates were demon-possessed, I figured, but obviously, my own mother was just a woman who made a mistake in the eyes of Jehovah. I knew apostates were evil, but I also knew my mother wasn't.

I tried not to think about it too much. Mostly, I was just jealous that she'd escaped her unhappy marriage while I was still locked deep into mine.

After her disfellowshipping was announced at the Kingdom Hall, I stood holding my songbook and forced myself to look like I was forcing myself not to cry. I felt nothing except what I usually felt in situations like this: extreme guilt over my lack of feeling. My father didn't even come. I'm sure he was sitting in the basement mindlessly underlining the same passage in the same *Watchtower* over and over again.

During the prayer, I let out a small contrived sob or two. The congregation's eyes were closed, all heads pointed at sensible shoes. No one would know my noises were not accompanied by tears.

At the toll of our *"Amen,"* I expected a rush of sympathy from my congregation. My mother's oldest friends would throw their arms around me, crying, "Only Jehovah knows what is truly in our hearts!" No one seemed particularly moved, however. They packed their *Watchtowers* into their briefcases, wiped their children's sticky hands with Wet Naps, made lunch plans. Nothing had happened to change *their* lives.

"I'm just . . . devastated," I said when one sister asked how I was holding up.

"Well, aren't we all?" she said, and walked away.

It was almost as if everyone knew I hadn't really lost her, that I had no intention of shunning her. That I, too, was an apostate. After my grandmother stopped talking to her, Mom promised that she was going to get reinstated and gain back favor with God's organization. After a year or two, the elders would be guided by the Holy Spirit to decide whether or not she had truly repented. In the meantime, she'd have to come to every meeting and sit in the back row of the Kingdom Hall. She wouldn't be allowed to speak or look at anyone, nor would anyone acknowledge that she was there. It was like a fundamentalist hazing. Mom was as good as already drowned in molten lava at the Great War of Armageddon. If old friends saw her in the supermarket, they would look away. There was nothing there but a dead woman.

I could count on my right hand the number of people I'd known who had been disfellowshipped from my congregation. I added my left thumb: *mother, apostate.* I knew she was going to die, but why didn't I really feel it, deep inside?

Mom moved out of the house we grew up in and into a modern condo, nicer than any apartment I'd ever seen in my life. Now that she was an adulteress, she had a garbage disposal, a dishwasher, and a reserved parking space. While I got the feeling that her boyfriend was helping out, she was still working two jobs, one of which was second shift at a pancake house, in order to pay off her credit card debt. Although I couldn't verify it, I was pretty sure that my mother hadn't been sleeping at night.

A week later, while I was drinking alone at home, my uncle called from Tennessee. My father's siblings all lived down South, and it was always a bit of a culture shock for my New England ears to hear my visiting cousins ask for a bottle of "sody pop."

"Kurria? This here's Uncle Ronny, Daddy's brother," a voice said in a comforting Southern drawl. This was the kind of extended family we had—the kind where relatives always had to remind you of how you were related to them.

"I'm givin' you a ring cuz I think you should know I just talked to your momma on the phone and she's very upset, Kurria. I don't mean to alarm you, but she offhandedly mentioned that she might, well, she might go on an' kill herself."

As usual, I was drunk and not even sure how my uncle had gotten my phone number. "So, uh, should I do something?"

"Well now, Kurria. If I were you, I reckon I'd get there 'bout as fast as I could, yes."

I was so shnockered on apricot brandy that I had to hold on to a fence for support while walking to the car. I should not have been allowed to brush my own teeth at this moment, let alone operate a motor vehicle. Yet I was going to drive to my mother's house because I had no other choice.

Miraculously, I didn't mortally crash headfirst into an unsuspecting church youth group's picnic bus. Given a wide berth, I was even able to park in the lot of my mother's enviable condominium. She answered her door half-dressed and looking like a sheepish child.

"What the fuck, Mommy? Uncle Ronny called. Are you gonna kill yourself or something?"

"I'm not going to kill myself, Kyria," she said, closing her bathrobe around her bra and nude control-top panty hose.

"You've been drinking," I slurred. "Why are you calling Dad's brother and threatening to kill yourself? Don't fucking kill yourself! And don't call long-distance to Tennessee!"

"I'm not going to kill myself! Look, do you want something to eat? I have leftover pea soup. I can heat it up in the micro."

Mom didn't make it to the microwave. A few minutes after I showed up, she passed out in our old green rocker, a chair that had sat in the corner of our kitchen since I was born. It was out of place and didn't quite match the new furnishings. Both my mother and the old chair looked woefully alone. I curled up on her new couch and went to sleep myself.

CHAPTER 21

Making Room for Jehovah in Our Marriage Bed

Big Bill didn't drive a car, because he'd been in Vietnam. As a combat veteran, he'd earned the right to have quirks.

"Oh, I have my license. I just won't drive," was all he'd say. When you asked him to elaborate, he'd toss dice around in his pocket and smile maniacally. No one pressed the issue too much, fearing the answer might be, "I once strangled a baby to make it stop crying."

"Eh, my parents were killed in a car accident," Big Bill once confided in me. "And, if you're wondering, I didn't kill them."

Big Bill bragged that he knew how to fold a single square of toilet paper in such a way that you could use it in the jungle even if you had serious shits. He liked D&D and *Star Trek*, both generations. Except for the refusal to work or drive a car, he was your typical, sci-fi-loving, 12-sided-dice-owning nerd, and he made a seamless addition to the rest of the geeks that graced our kitchen table on gaming night.

Big Bill also had a creative side, however, and his latest obsession was with something called "poetry slams," an Olympic-style competition where audience members graded the performers on a scale of 1 to 10, decimals included.

He asked me to drive him to a poetry reading in the attic of a coffee shop called Beans and Bags, located on the hip, gourmet-pizza side of Providence. It wasn't a slam, and I wouldn't have to perform. The only caveat was that I would be driving.

In the artsy attic, poets read sob-inducing epics about their abortions, fathers that didn't love them, the situation in Kosovo, and the plight of their peoples. Someone ranted about the god-damn police busting up their rave. Someone else was introduced as a "stand-up poet" and read a list of the top ten things a cat thinks when it runs from one room to the next. That was a big hit.

Alan and Big Bill's wife came with us to the first reading. They spent the night rolling their eyes and stifling inappropriate laughs by coughing. Big Bill himself even apologized a lot, and said the reading had been better the last time.

"Actually, I think I want to do this," I said.

Big Bill's wife laughed first. She was intimidating to me because she was a high school drama teacher.

"You?" she said. "Really? You?"

"Yeah, I'm serious. Next time, I'm really gonna do this."

"We'll see," Alan said. "I don't think you will."

When we got home, I asked Alan if he thought my poetry was great, or just really good.

"It's not good at all," he said. "I don't like it."

"You're wrong," I told him. I knew how to evoke emotion. I knew how to turn a metaphor. My poems about being in love were some of the more moving poems about being in love that had ever been penned, ever!

"I'm a great writer! I know I am! And one day, Alan, you'll know it too."

"That's nice. I'm just telling you it sucks."

The New England poets had a name for their scene: the poetry triangle. It consisted of every reading in the cities of Worcester,

Providence, and Boston, all located within an easy, one-hour drive from one another. For the most part, the same poets were at every reading. My lack of a social life, coupled with my ability to borrow the car, ensured that Big Bill and I would always be two of them.

Most of the readings took place in bookstore basements where hippies sat cross-legged on milk crates and teenage goths gave each other back rubs. Old warhorse poets guzzled coffee and told outlandish tales about performing poetry in the back of pickup trucks after arriving at their weekly venue, only to discover that the bookstore/café/diner had been closed down/burned down/moved. These poets held their readings for five people crammed into a hatchback in the rain—these were true lovers of the spoken word.

In Boston, performers tended to be slicker, more cosmopolitan. The reading was hosted by Patricia Smith, a journalist for *The Boston Globe,* and we all clamored to impress this beautiful anomaly who actually got *paid to write.* The poetry slammers here were real, live rock stars. Some of them had been on a prizewinning National Slam team the year before, which was subsequently profiled in a documentary called *Slam and Deliver.* They moved their hands when they read their poetry, they closed their eyes, they *whispered.* When they finished, they put their heads down in dramatic silence.

I was overwhelmed with the need to interact with these people. I wanted to be them and I wanted to make out with them, possibly both at the same time. On top of this, they seemed like they wanted to know me too. Boys here talked to me, they complimented my "work." And unlike my husband, these guys were actually my own age.

The first competitive slam I drove Big Bill to was in the Rhode Island College student union, a "pass the hat" reading called Words Out Loud. The host was a 30-something poet named Ted, who wore a black beret and a tie-dyed shirt with a wolf airbrushed onto it. With free entertainment in an air-conditioned room, Bill said he figured the night paid for itself.

"It's someplace to go," he told me. "Plus cute *college girls*."

I told Ted that I wanted to read a poem about the house my grandmother lived in. He said I could read whatever I wanted to as long as I didn't go over four minutes, and handed me a sheet of paper with Bic pen lines drawn on it. I wrote my name somewhere in the middle, around number eight, right after "Daddy Turtledove."

My poetry debut, and I knew this for certain, was about to blow this room away. The childhood magic of treading water on a shimmering lake was so beautiful and poignant that I expected it would receive a standing ovation before I even reached the second stanza. What I didn't expect was that I would end up shaking so hard I was barely able to keep myself standing upright. I was completely incapable of speaking, but otherwise, I rocked the mike.

Between the open and the feature, there was a short cigarette break. I looked up to see Ted and his wolf shirt swiftly approaching my table. "Thanks for sharin' your poetry tonight, Kerrier. If you want, next time I can show you how to adjust the mike, 'cause no one could hear you." Then he handed me a Xeroxed sheet of paper that said "You've lost your virginity! Words Out Loud!" Below the sketch of a naked woman jumping into the air, Ted had signed his name.

The main event for the night was Seth Gideon. His poetry involved a lot of jumping. He was surreal, bombastic, and probably extremely deep. He jumped up on the block-shaped tables and bounced on the couches. Because of this, he managed to hold the attention of ten people for almost an hour. I was too starstruck to say anything, but the very next time I saw him at a reading, I had an excuse to introduce myself.

"I really loved your feature at Rhode Island College," I said. "Are you, you know, signing up for the open mike tonight?"

"I probably won't read anything tonight, you know. I don't have anything new and I think *some people* are starting to grumble about it."

"Oh, but *I'm* new," I insisted. "So you should read old pieces anyway!"

"Well, I'll go through my work. I'll see what I have with me."

I'd been given a glimpse into the inner world of open-mike-night personalities. I loved that people cared enough to be annoyed at Seth. An hour later, the redheaded wunderkind jumped onstage and said, "This is an oldie, by *request*." He put his head down for a moment, found his motivation, and began to shout:

Truicide! The truth hurts because it is strangling itself on an umbilical cord made from AM talk radio! Truicide! The space between what exists and what just wants to take your tax dollars! Truicide! It is waiting under your bed, Uncle Sam. It is waiting up in Washington!

He bowed deeply to a shallow smattering of applause. I was, to put it mildly, completely enraptured.

I was starting to get the hang of the confessional poetry thing, so the next week I read a piece about how my lover couldn't satisfy me sexually. Written confession, baring your soul, capturing the moment of pain and turning it into *art*. This was how the big guns rolled.

"It makes me sad to hear you read things like that," Big Bill whispered when I got offstage. "You know, my wife may not love me, but one thing she's never complained about is my Tantric sexual technique. That's when the woman is satisfied before the man is."

After the reading, Seth walked me out to the parking lot.

"I liked that piece a lot," he said. "It was so sensual. It reminded me of Patricia Smith's work."

"Thanks, that means a lot coming from you!"

Instinctively, I let my wedding ring slide off my finger and into the pocket of my baggy, rolled-up jeans. Seth's mouth was on mine. His hands were grabbing my ass. I was telling him how much I wanted to *do it*. But not at my place, I said. Somewhere else.

I went back inside and told Bill to find himself a ride home because I was going to hang out and get coffee with the other poets. Then Seth and I drove to a Motel 6.

Having sex at a motel didn't strike me as strange or unusual at all. I knew that getting a hotel room was how worldly people always had sex. I had seen it in movies from the '60s.

I didn't care anyway. I was overflowing with excitement. I just couldn't wait until we were done committing adultery! Then I could go home and tell Alan that I'd finally had an affair and he'd get angry and scream and tell me to get the fuck out. Alan would divorce me and I'd finally be free!

My clothes were off by the time Seth shut the fireproof door. He put his mouth on me, *down there*. His tongue felt floppy and gross, like a goldfish in your wet swimsuit. I had no idea that a man might actually want to put his face in a vagina. Wasn't that dirty? Gross? He pulled himself up from my crotch to kiss me. His mouth tasted sharp, but I figured I'd play it cool and not say anything.

Then, we *did it*.

"Was it good for you?" I asked. Seth looked at me strangely and laughed.

There was always the possibility that I wouldn't actually get disfellowshipped for this, but I wasn't even thinking that far ahead. I'd deal with Jehovah later. Right now, I was giddy with the thought of Alan screaming at me. What a great poem this would make.

"I'd better get home," I told Seth. Maintaining an air of mystery, I added, "I've gotta go, but I can't tell you why."

Twenty minutes later, I arrived home to find Alan snoring on the couch. I tried to wake him, but he was sound asleep.

"I had an affair," I said loudly. "Did you hear me? I had an affair?"

"What?" he asked, rolling over into a brocaded, decorative pillow that I'd told him was not for use. "Where?"

"Wake up. I had an affair. I just got home. I cheated on you."

Alan sat up a little. "An affair? With who?"

"Look, you don't know him. I had an affair. I'm in love with him. He's a poet. He likes my poetry. It's over."

Alan seemed confused. He wasn't getting as angry as I needed him to get. Maybe it was because I'd just woken him up, but he had a docile expression on his face, like a puppy. And not even a sad one.

"I understand if you want to kick me out," I said. "I'll start packing right away."

"I know what you're trying to do," he said. "It won't work."

"Oh, yeah? You don't know anything! What do you think you know?"

"I'm not going to kick you out, Kyria. See, I want to *forgive* you."

I walked to the kitchen, grabbed a bottle of whiskey, and brought it back to the couch. Alan was calling my bluff, showing passive-aggressive Christian mercy when he was supposed to be meting out vehement Christian justice. Forgiveness. This had not been part of the plan. Having him hate me, then getting thrown on my ass on the sidewalk—that had been the plan. Not forgiveness. Not keeping things the same. Anything but the same.

"I think we can work this out," Alan said. "I'll call the elders tomorrow and we'll work this out. You'll stay here with me."

"Actually, I think I'd like to leave," I said.

"You're not leaving me," he threatened. "If you do, I'll absolutely refuse to forgive you. I'll make *sure* you're disfellowshipped."

Why the hell couldn't I get a divorce? I was starting to resent Jehovah as much as Alan for keeping me in it. It was like God was a crooked lawyer, trying to catch me in a technicality. *You signed the papers*, he seemed to be saying as he thumbed his holy suspenders and puffed on a cigar. *Now the old farm belongs to me! Forever!*

Alan grabbed my wrists and pulled them up to my chin. "If you dare walk out that door," he said, "I'm calling your parents."

Keeping me out of God's promised paradise and sentencing me to eternal death was one thing, but calling my parents was over the line. After all the time and money they'd invested in my wedding, I knew they'd have my head on a spit if I tried to leave Alan.

"That's not fair!" I screamed. "You can't do that!"

"Yup. I'm calling your parents right now and telling them that you're trying to leave me. That's what I'm doing!"

"You can't! You *can't* call my parents! You have to let me leave! I'll *kill myself* if you don't let me leave!!"

"I won't let you leave," he said. "Guess you'll just have to kill yourself."

The next day, I was in the bathroom, squirting shampoo into travel bottles, when the doorbell rang. Alan poked his head into the room and tapped his fingers against the door frame.

"I know who *tha-aat* is," he sang, smirking. "Nobody important, though. Just your *parents*."

I dropped the Pert Plus and ran out the back door, making it safely past the angry rooster and the Highland cattle, only to be intercepted in the front yard. I felt a tap on my shoulder, then Alan grabbed me by the collar, jerking my neck back as I ran downhill. My father's car was at the bottom of that hill. I was pushed into the backseat, with someone's hand on top of my head, cops-in-

Miami style. My father put his palm over the lock and my mother sat in the front seat and turned around to glare at me. This was officially an intervention.

"What the hell are you trying to do?" my father yelled. "Are you trying to be your mother, is that what you're trying to do? Oh, your mother had an affair, so now you have to copy her? Are you trying to be a whore just like your mother?"

My mother put her head down. "Gerald, please!"

"You want to be a whore just like your mother?"

"Do you want to get disfellowshipped like me, Kyria?" my mother asked. "Because believe me, it's not fun! I want to save you from my pain."

"I don't want your pain," I said. "I just want to get a divorce."

"Oh, you're bored now, is that it?" Dad said. "You said you wanted to get married and we paid big bucks for the wedding and now you're bored? I don't think so."

My mother nodded her head in agreement. My parents were like a tumultuous rock band who had put aside their differences to reunite for one final benefit concert. *One night only, don't miss this final chance to see your parents as they Rock Against Divorce!*

"I don't love him anymore," I spat.

"You should have thought of that before we paid for that wedding," my father said.

"I swear I thought I loved him when I married him."

"Everybody told you that you were too young to get married, and you ignored us all. You told us all that you loved him, and we believed you!"

"Don't leave him, Kyria," my mother pleaded. "We're not taking you back if you do. We're not supporting you this time."

My mother had put up with my father for decades, and here I couldn't even stick it out with Alan for five years. She had not raised her daughter to have an easier life than she had. My leaving Alan was not fair.

Alan was off to the side of the driveway, peering into the car and watching my parents make me stay with him. He stood with his arms folded, smirking like his little sister was getting punished.

Meanwhile, my parents barraged me with more threats and Bible verses as if co-writing an advice column for a fundamentalist *Redbook*. (*Ladies, are you stuck in a rut of boring breakups? Try adding a little spice to your divorce by leaving that special someone while your parents scream at you in the driveway and tell you that you're going to die at Armageddon.*)

"Look, Kyria, what's it gonna be? You gonna go back in that house and stay there? Or are you gonna be a whore like your mother?"

"If you leave, Kyria, we're going to have to call the elders. You'll be disfellowshipped and I'm telling you, you don't want that."

"Are you gonna go back in that house, Kyria? Are you?"

"Yes," I said, defeated. "I'm going back in the house. I'm sorry. I promise I'm going to stay with Alan."

I got out of the car, and Alan put his arm around my shoulder.

"You see?" my husband said sweetly. "I told you. You can't leave me."

Several hours later, I was leaving again. Not only was I drunk and walking in the middle of the street, but I was very self-aware about it. It was more poetic to walk in the middle of the street. A yellow cab drove slowly alongside me.

"You okay, girl? Why don't you walk on the side of the road?"

"No, thanks."

"You gonna get hit by a car that way."

"Yep. That's the idea."

"You should get in the cab. Come on, get in my cab, girl."

I decided to move to the sidewalk so as to avoid the well-meaning advice of annoying, lecherous cabdrivers. I wanted to get hit by a car in peace.

After walking for maybe 90 minutes, I arrived at Ben's apartment. But he wouldn't let me inside.

"The elders are still after me for that thing I told you happened with Maya," he said. "Anyway, the last time I saw you. I was too tempted to commit a sin."

"Nothing will happen! Just let me in. Let me sleep on your floor."

"Kyria, I can't risk getting disassociated. This congregation is my whole life. I deliver sandwiches for a living. If I lose this, I have nothing."

"Ben, nothing will happen. I promise to tell your elders that nothing happened."

He thought for a minute, shaking his head as if the elders were in his house, as if they could see every impure thought through a telescreen.

"I can give you money for a hotel," he countered. "I'll give you fifty dollars if you leave."

"Fuck you, Ben."

"Hey, I'm offering you money here, no questions asked! I'm the good guy, okay?"

"I don't want your money. I want you to let me stay here tonight."

Ben began to close the door. "I'm not trying to be mean, Kyria, but you have to find somewhere else to go."

"I'm not going anywhere! I'm staying on your front porch! You'll wake up and have to step over me!"

"It's not my choice," he said. "It's the elders." The lock snapped shut.

I sat down on his front steps and curled up in a ball on the concrete. Tomorrow, I would bring back all his tapes and CDs. Tonight, I was going to scream and cry and sleep and stay there. I'd make Ben walk on me in the morning. I'd be a mess. On his way to deliver turkey pockets, he'd see exactly what he had done.

Twenty minutes later, a car flashed its headlights at me, and my dad pulled into the driveway and rolled down his window.

"Get in the goddamn car," he yelled. "Right now."

CHAPTER 22

Closing Our Minds to the Ideas of Unbelievers

I woke up on my couch and vomited into my shoes. Alan was still sleeping. I walked into the kitchen and parted the curtains above the sink. I was greeted by a full fan of peacock feathers from my landlord's incongruous urban pet.

I pulled the phone into the back stairway, stretching the cord into a line so taut you could teach geometry by it. I leaned back on the steps and called the poet I'd had an affair with. I was begging him to save me.

"Seth, I told my husband about us and I need to come live with you, okay?"

Alan was listening through the door now, breathing and tapping his foot loudly, making no attempts to hide the fact that he could hear everything I was saying.

"Your . . . husband?" Seth sputtered on the other end of the line.

"I told him about us and now we're getting divorced. Well, he didn't want to divorce me, he wanted to forgive me, but I'm leaving anyway and I have nowhere to go."

"Wait. You're married?"

"He won't let me leave. Please, please let me come stay with you. I'm going to get disfellowshipped and they're going to kick me out and no one else will take me in."

"Kyria . . . back up, okay? I can't understand you."

"Okay. I'm a Jehovah's Witness and I'm going to be kicked out because we had sex. My parents don't want me to leave my husband and my friends won't help and I tried to walk to my friend's house but he wouldn't let me in. So I need to leave now and I need you to come pick me up and let me live with you!"

"Oh, my God."

"Will you come get me?"

"I'm so sorry. I had no idea."

"That's okay, I never told you! So will you come help me? Please help me," I begged.

"I'm so sorry. I really am. But I . . . can't. You can't come live with me."

Why hadn't he said yes already? Why weren't two fancy mice leading me up a carpeted ramp into Cinderella's coach?

"Seth, you have to, or I'm going to kill myself."

"Listen to me. Do not kill yourself! You have to talk to someone."

"I'm going to kill myself if you don't come! Please, please come and get me!"

"I'm so sorry, Kyria. I didn't know any of this! I didn't know this would happen and I didn't know you were married! I'm sorry, but I can't let you live with me. I just can't."

"But you *have* to!"

"Kyria, I am not qualified for this. I have to go. Okay? You have to call someone else. A hotline. I'm sorry, I'm so sorry. I have to go now."

"Seth," I said. "Please save me."

He whispered, *"No, I can't,"* and hung up. I realized we weren't on the phone anymore.

Alan opened the door and followed the phone cord downstairs like a rock climber follows rope. I snorted and choked on the snot idling in the back of my throat.

"So, looks like your boyfriend abandoned you, huh?"

Alan was standing over me with his hands on his hips. He *tsked* his mouth at me. *For shame.*

"I guess he doesn't love you after all. Well, what did you expect would happen with a worldly boy?"

"Fuck you! I fucking hate you!"

"You hate me? Whatever. You're the one that just got abandoned. But I'm still here. I'm still taking care of you!"

"Leave me alone! I'm going to kill myself! I hate you!"

"You don't hate me. You love me! And you wouldn't dare kill yourself."

I stood up and I pushed him. I pushed him because that's what I'd seen look good in the movies. For the same reason, Alan pushed me back.

"I'm not letting you leave me," he said.

He'd pushed me. That was domestic abuse, right? Another excuse to leave him, I noted happily. I pulled away from him and ran through the house like a spurned wife in *The Godfather*, throwing dishes and clearing whole shelves with my forearm while Alan wondered what was happening to his life. Once, I'd been a pretty 18-year-old, smiling my bucktooth smile through the oval cutout of a puffy wedding album cover. Now I was a housewife *on the verge* screaming, *"I hate you,"* shrieking, *"I'm leaving you."* I broke my favorite dishes. It didn't matter—except for the expensive Noritake wedding china, which I was careful not to disturb.

My pet lizard, Timothy, sat on his heat rock and sunned himself under a clip-on sunlamp. His belly was full of pet-store crickets and a tiny tree frog that had once been named Nathan, until the day I put Nathan and Timothy in the same tank together.

I put my hands on the tank. If this didn't prove that I couldn't give a *goddamn fucking shit* what happened today or tomorrow or ever again, *well*. I pushed the tank off the table. The tank didn't shatter—it buckled, like the hood of a car. Glass shards pointed up and out, the wreckage from a gale-force tantrum.

"You didn't just do that," Alan said.

"He's dead," I said. "Is he dead?"

I felt like I'd been playing with a gun I found in a shoe box, and suddenly the neighbor's kid wasn't moving.

"Yeah, I'd say he's probably dead! What the hell did you think you were doing? You are going to clean this up!"

"I won't clean it up and you can't make me!"

Unchained crickets hopped to freedom through pieces of broken glass. Timothy was under there somewhere, settling below a layer of aquarium rocks. I heard crickets chirping from new parts of the house. A cricket in the bathroom, the kitchen. A cricket in every pot.

I decided, immediately, again, to kill myself. So I called my mother. The irony of using someone as a suicide hotline who had once left me half-dead on a bathroom floor with a tub of yogurt was lost on me at that moment.

"Mom, I'm going to kill myself. I killed Timothy and I'm going to kill myself."

"What? Who's Timothy? Who did you kill, Kyria?"

"Timothy, my lizard! I killed him!"

"Okay, okay. Timothy the *lizard*. Okay. Your lizard, right."

Mom sighed into the phone, repeating, "Okay, the lizard. Just the lizard."

"I'm going to commit suicide, Mommy."

If I'd never needed my mother before, I needed her now. Alan was nothing but a blur to me. I couldn't even talk to him. I wasn't even aware if he was in the same room with me.

"All right, sweetie, okay," my mother said, urging me to calm down. "What do you need? Do you need me to take you to the hospital?"

"I don't know. Maybe."

When I was three, I grabbed my mother's old-fashioned safety razor, the kind with a real, replaceable razor blade, and sat in the bathtub to "shave like Mommy." I think I wanted to impress her. My mother took one look at my little white legs streaked with blood and I barely even knew that I had hurt myself, that's how calm she was while she stopped the bleeding and drove me to the hospital. That's what I needed again.

And that's what I got. Only this time, Mom took me to a different wing of the building.

My main regret about having a mental breakdown is that I didn't get to stay in a cool, Hollywood mental hospital with sexy schizophrenics and eccentric millionaires. I had no hot, introspective roommate who was just "meant for a different time." I never found love. I never located the doctor with a controversial psychiatric method to successfully test on me.

Beyond the 45 seconds they spent interviewing me each morning, none of the doctors seemed interested in talking to me at all.

"Are you still going to kill yourself?" someone would ask.

"Um, I guess so?"

At this, the doctor would scribble something on a clipboard.

"Do you feel unsafe being alone?"

"Well, I mean, I am going to kill myself, so I guess that's not safe."

"Do you still need to stay here to be safe?"

"I don't know."

"Do you feel like you'll harm yourself if you go home tonight?"

"I don't know. I guess so?"

The doctor would again scribble on a clipboard.

"Thank you, Kara . . . er, Kyria."

The hospital would have been more rehabilitating if I'd spent my time sitting in the waiting room. I couldn't even get good drugs. When I asked for something to help me sleep, they gave me Dimetapp in a paper cup, then scribbled something on a clipboard.

At least my nasal passages were perfectly clear.

I sat in a shared room and listened to Depeche Mode on a bright yellow Sports Walkman. I wondered if any of the apathetic staff would notice if I suddenly garnered access to an X-Acto knife and started going to town on my arm. I bet I could cut my way through the first verse of "Waiting for the Night" before a clipboard-toting nurse-practitioner asked, "Do you feel like you might hurt yourself?"

I also met with a therapist who projected a radiant beam of annoyance upon every word I said. She couldn't have been more disinterested in my problems if I'd been an heiress complaining about how much I hated my new jewel-encrusted yacht.

"Are you going to kill yourself today?" she said, yawning.

"I don't think so. I think I'm feeling better."

"Well, that's *good*, isn't it?"

"I . . . guess so?"

Once the therapist realized I wasn't going to kill myself, the tone of our meetings changed dramatically. Now that I was no longer suicidal, I had approximately ten minutes to figure out what I wanted out of life.

"So are you going to leave your husband?" she asked snottily.

"I don't even think I can."

"Okay. Let me phrase it this way: What do you *want* to do?"

What did I want? Well, I wanted to believe that Jehovah's Witnesses were the one, true religion. I wanted what I'd been promised since I was old enough to understand English, which was to survive Armageddon and live in a perfect paradise on earth, forever—never dying, never growing sick or old.

At the same time, I also wanted to be free to watch R-rated

movies like *Taxi Driver* and not have to hide them under the couch. I wanted to eat Halloween cupcakes, to cook a Thanksgiving turkey without calling it an "Autumn Dinner." I wanted a new job and a high school diploma and a husband that didn't call my parents to help kidnap me. I wanted to leave Alan and get paid to be a poet, and most of all, I wanted all of this to be okay with Jehovah.

"I don't know what I want," I told her.

She fell back in her chair and glanced at her watch like she was missing her favorite soap opera, on which one of the characters was suicidal and trying to leave an unhappy marriage.

"Well, look, you need to make a decision. I can't make that decision for you. Tell me this much, do you think you can stick it out with your husband?"

"I don't know. I mean, I don't love him but if I get a divorce then I'll be disfellowshipped and, I don't know, maybe I *do* love him and I just don't know it but he doesn't like any of my poetry and I want to go to concerts. I just don't want to die at Armageddon, but I don't feel like the Jehovah's Witnesses are bad people, you know?"

"Okay, slow down. I can't follow you. Do you want to leave him or not? You have to help me out here, okay? What are you going to do?"

I knew I'd better decide something soon or she'd punch me in the kidneys.

"I don't know. Leave him? Stay?"

"Leave him? Okay. You think about it and you let me know. We can't keep going around in circles like this. You need to make a decision."

The next day, I told the therapist I wanted to leave my husband.

"Oh, um. Okay! Well, great, then!" she said, slapping the side of her chair. She seemed surprised that I'd made a decision that fast, which made me wish I'd taken more time to think. Under pressure to get out of the hospital, I hadn't made a decision—I'd made a random choice.

The hospital bills were stacking up. We didn't have insurance, because Alan didn't have a full-time teaching job anywhere. I didn't know if I wanted to leave the Jehovah's Witnesses, but I knew for certain that I wanted to leave my husband, and that involved leaving the Jehovah's Witnesses.

I also knew I'd never have another opportunity to leave. If you can't announce major life changes the day you come home from the mental hospital, then you have officially missed your chance. This would be like telling people that I was under doctor's orders to leave Alan. I had to start my life over and call her in the morning.

The only problem with deciding to leave my husband was that I *lived* with my husband. I was dependent on him for rent, cable, pizza dough, and AOL. All my credit cards were in his name. In a most unfortunate turn of nepotism, I also worked at the same company with Alan, who had been delivering construction equipment for Worldwide in order to supplement his part-time teaching career.

Worse yet, my mother-in-law, Barbara, had recently taken a break from gluing googly-eyes onto ceramic ducks and was now answering phones four feet away from me. She had been an excellent coworker, despite the fact that once each week she had a petit mal seizure and needed to be taken to the hospital.

My options were limited. Sarah had been away at college, and not only that, it was a Christian college. Now she was spending her summer in China teaching English, spreading the news of Christ and peeing in a communal trough. Considering her mother had already kicked me out once, asking to recover from my adultery-fueled nervous breakdown in her daughter's empty bedroom seemed like an awkward request.

Emily and Lisa would be preparing to shun me, busy fashioning blinders from the pages of *You Can Live Forever in Paradise on Earth*. I wasn't disfellowshipped yet, but I was on the fast track.

I called every poet I had a phone number for, except for Big Bill, who retained loyalties to his friend and Dungeon Master, and Seth, who claimed he somehow couldn't let me live with him forever, even after he'd gone and had sex with me once.

Poets were used to having homeless, mentally unstable bohemians sleeping on their couches, so it didn't take long to find someone who could help me, a local scenester named James "Penn" O'Leary. His parents were in the process of moving to Michigan and I had a place to stay until they sold their house in Lincoln, Rhode Island, around the corner from where I lived with Alan. Within a week, I also had a new boyfriend: Penn.

CHAPTER 23

God's House Is Always Open for

Those Who Work There

Penn held both of my shoulders firmly and turned my whole body to face him. We were sitting in the basement, behind the sheet draped over a clothesline that separated his bedroom from the washer/dryer set.

"Kyria," he said, pausing to breathe out through his nose, "I love you, but I can't hide you."

He said this to me with great intensity. He said everything with great intensity. *Kyria, I need you to enjoy eating this buttered toast as a delectable breakfast addition . . . you can't afford not to.*

"I think you should call your husband and let him know where you are. And then we should get your stuff."

Alan had filed for divorce and I was served papers. I was aware that I must have moved in with Penn, but I didn't remember it happening.

"No one cares about me anyway," I whined, a 22-year-old re-peating the party line of 16-year-olds everywhere.

"If you don't want to let them know where you are, I respect that," he said. "But you still need to get your clothes."

Being *respected* for my wishes was a new experience. It made me feel like I could get away with anything.

"Can't we just leave everything there? I don't care about my stuff," I said.

I loved my convertible couch, but I had inexplicably acquired the romantic, Merchant-Ivory ideal that I was starting over—a neo-Victorian naiveté to match my tacky collection of musical dolls. I fancied myself an unencumbered hobo, traveling the rails with only a cute purse and a rusty, bloodstained knife.

I was superstitious. I believed that everything I brought with me would be tainted, possessed, sticky with unhappiness. I wasn't only burning bridges, I was burning love notes, diaries, and wedding photos. It would become a weekly ritual, watching the ashes of composition paper fly up out of the sink like reverse snowflakes.

Thankfully, Penn realized that I would not be as idealistic when I had to replace all my demi-cup brassieres. "Kyria, it's your stuff and you deserve it!" he said, squinting as if it were sunny in his basement-bedroom. "You can't let him do this to you! You have to stand and fight."

Penn O'Leary was a born fighter. He had seen corruption in this town and he was about to shake it down. He was even writing a book. He couldn't tell me what the book was about, unfortunately, or I would be in danger. But when his reporting was finished, it was going to implicate the whole Providence Police Department all the way to the mayor. It started when the pigs shut down a rave in the Thayer Street Tunnel.

"But, it was in the bus tunnel, right?" I asked. I wanted to make sure I hadn't misunderstood him. "There was no permit or anything? Maybe it was illegal?"

Penn skillfully opted to answer a different question, one that I hadn't asked. "The cops, man. The way they just busted in there! We were just dancing. It's illegal? *They're* illegal!"

The mayor of Providence, Buddy Cianci, had once hit a man over the head with a fireplace poker, and now he had his own line of marinara sauce. But I was having a hard time figuring out how shutting down an illegal rave in a public bus tunnel was the genesis of "unparalleled corruption that rocks the very foundations of our state." Poor Penn was so scarred by the experience, he could barely articulate how his human rights had been violated.

On our way to a poetry reading at a performance space in Providence called AS220, Penn suddenly stopped walking. He pulled me off the sidewalk and underneath a tree. "Listen, I have to tell you something, and I don't want you to get scared."

I have to leave. His mother wants me out of the house.

"When my book comes out, things are gonna get pretty hot," he was whispering. "I may have to go underground for a while."

I had absolutely no response to this. What things? What hot?

"Oh. Okay, Penn. That's . . . great. I mean, bad. For you. Okay."

"You know, because I have this 'record,' the pigs are really on me. You know that parking ticket I got last week? That was a setup—there was no sign! They think they can fuck with me, but I'm fighting that ticket. I will not pay into their corruption! I'm taking a chance on this book. I have to tell the truth, Kyria. I'm the only one who can."

I smiled, breathing in through exposed teeth. "I respect that," I told him.

I should have spent the rest of the night wondering what was going on inside his brain that made him think the police were giving him parking tickets because of a book that he hadn't actually started writing yet (even Winston Smith in *1984* had to put his thoughts down in an actual diary before they put rats on his face). Instead, we went to the poetry slam at AS220. Short for Art Space 220, the venue had a café and a stage and a constant stream of painters and puppeteers who lived and worked in the collective "space." There seemed to be an inordinate amount of papier-mâché behind the stage. This may be why Penn suddenly took on the appearance of a stable boyfriend to me. The only people *he* shared a bathroom with were his parents.

I'd never had an abortion, so my poetry topics were limited. I could write a poem about my difficulties living life as a person of mixed race, which would be Scottish and Jewy. Did having a grandmother who prepared matzo brie count as a nationality? I could write about politics, but considering my family only watched the news during a presidential address so that my father could look for signs in Revelation ("Look at him! He even *looks* possessed by Satan! Oh, peace and security, they'll cry, and then the end will come!"), I didn't have much of a political slant. I was qualified to write about the Jehovah's Witnesses, but that didn't seem very "cool." I could write about the "revolution," but that seemed played. Or I could write about being in love. Now, that was something I knew.

I had a crush on Penn, so I wrote a poem called, aptly, "Crush." It kicked off with the lines "It's Junior High Love, baby/it's 7th grade passion!" And ended with "I feel so sexy/I think I'm gonna buy a training bra!"

It was moderately humorous.

I shook while I put my name in a hat, and I shook while the emcee pulled the names back out to announce the lineup. I shook when I found out when I was performing, and I shook while I read the poem. I performed eagerly, which is another way of saying I continued shaking. The audience—filled with lovely, non-judgmental, very *high* poets—laughed. This time, I *wanted* them to laugh.

Penn performed a piece about his friend getting really fucked-up at a rave and subsequently dying in a fiery car crash. He imitated the flames with wiggling fingers and screamed, "Look out, Keith, look out!" For all his good intentions, it had all the subtlety of a 1950s teenage death ballad. But Penn knew how to emote, and by the time the poem was through, everyone understood firsthand what it felt like to be trapped in a burning car.

Even with the smokeys hot on his tail, *breaker-breaker*, Penn was adamant that I should call my husband to arrange to take what was rightfully mine. He made no distinction between relinquishing a bag of socks and relinquishing the rights of women to vote. He was ready to stick it to the man, and we weren't about to reverse all the progress of the suffrage movement by leaving stuffed animals like Brown Bear and Turtle in the basement of a man I didn't love.

I called my husband that night and got a mumbled "Whaddya want?" followed by a threat to throw everything I owned in a pile on the sidewalk.

"You have one day to get here. If you're not here by tomorrow, your stuff is gone." He was playing the part of the spurned lover, and it was wonderfully dramatic.

"You can't do that," I said.

"You cheated on me," Alan sniffed. "Why should I let you get anything at all? Everyone is telling me to throw it out. You're lucky I'm not!" He hung up the phone.

This was exciting, and not just in an "imminent prizewinning slam poem" kind of way. I imagined the attention I would garner when I unveiled my yet-unwritten poem: "A Sestina upon the Eve of Learning That You Wanted to Throw All My Belongings on the Sidewalk."

It never occurred to me that his behavior was, say, inappropriate or unacceptable. Nor did it occur to me that people have the right to end a relationship they no longer wanted to be in. I had cheated on him, I was leaving him; therefore, he deserved the right to break everything I owned. This was what people did when they broke up. Like how women go to the bathroom in pairs, and how sometimes they deserve to get knocked around.

When I told Penn about the threat, he immediately went into fight-or-flight mode, pacing back and forth and flapping his sheet-walls.

"We're going to do this, okay? We're going to rescue your clothes!"

I knew that Alan probably wouldn't throw anything away, but I was suddenly getting so much attention. The fact that Penn believed it made me believe it too. "I don't know, Penn. I don't even know how we'd get everything! Anyway, he's probably thrown all my crap on the curb by now!"

Penn wasn't listening to me. He was plotting, mentally writing his next exposé of corruption among Jehovah's Witnesses and his totally unfair parking tickets.

"The only thing is, I don't know if we can use my mom's car. She might have to go to work," he said. He paused to think, and it was successful. "I'm calling Aidan and Stacey! We're going in!"

Penn had gotten tight with Aidan after they'd performed together on a championship poetry slam team. They were both superstars, but Aidan was even more super. He ran what was arguably the most popular poetry reading in New England—Wordplay—at the Midnight Diner in Worcester, Massachusetts. On any given Sunday night, the room was filled with poets who'd carpooled for over an hour from Rhode Island.

Aidan's wife, Stacey, was a punk-rock goddess. In college, she was a Russian lit major. After her indie label–signed band Kitty Cosmonaut broke up, she and Aidan formed a powerhouse poetry couple in the unlikely slam stronghold of Worcester, home of Abbie Hoffman and abandoned factories. They read love poems to each other from the stage and they drove a Saturn—*stick shift*.

Aidan and Stacey agreed to lend us their time and their car. Without asking for compensation, they would trek an hour from Worcester to Lincoln to help carry the belongings of a girl they'd just met into the garage of the parents of a guy *she'd* just met. Penn and I rendezvoused in the basement and drew up a plan.

If Alan tried to block the doors or flush my socks, we'd firmly explain that we were taking these things because they no longer belonged to him. That's what Aidan said we should say. Penn said Alan deserved to be cleaned out, that we should take *his* things and throw *them* on the sidewalk and see how *he* liked it. Either way, I had two large men and a punk-rock Betty ready to defend me against the wrath of a spurned fundamentalist math teacher.

I would have been incapable of walking back into my apartment and demanding my stuff if I had been alone. Instead, I sauntered in with three rock stars by my side and an expression on my face that said, Look who already has three new best friends.

I didn't say "I'm here," or ask, "Where's my stuff?" I entered the house silently and started taking things. I knew that people who are divorcing don't speak to each other, and if you do speak, it's only to scream, "You ruined my whole life!" as you hurl a wineglass against a wall. I turned him invisible.

If Alan tried to pull anything sleazy, I was certain my new punk-rock friends would go ballistic on him. They'd stomp into the kitchen in their combat boots and black jeans, screaming, "You fucker! You motherfucker! We're taking this end table and you can't stop us! Oh, you're giving us that blender all right. Now put up or shut up!"

But Alan had only thrown away a couple of my things, acting like an enormous asshole by depriving me of the ability to say he threw out *all* of my things. Or even the important ones. When asked what items he'd viciously wrenched from me, I could only answer, "An unfinished dollhouse and about five pairs of plastic legs that I bought at a sock store that was going out of business."

He'd known how much I'd wanted those plastic legs. Cut off just below the knee, the toes were weighted and in a constant ballerina state of *en pointe*. He knew that no one else would be able to sympathize with my loss, so I would forever look like an idiot complaining about "my poor, lost plastic legs, the ones I was totally hoping to make an art project out of someday." Therefore, I would have to keep it all inside. Checkmate.

Aidan and Stacey never got the chance to gore my husband's temple while defending my right to take place mats, and not only because they weren't wearing any studded wristbands. Instead of standing in the doorway with his hands on his hips, booming, "None shall pass!" Alan quietly retreated to the bedroom. He spent most of his time there, occasionally poking his head out to sneer and cry simultaneously.

As I was shoveling my grandmother's flatware into a plastic Shaw's grocery bag, Alan stuck his head and the tips of his fingers through the bedroom door. "He's even fatter than me," he said, nodding his chin in the direction of the room my new superstar boyfriend was in.

"Please. He is not!" I retorted. "You're fatter!"

But it was true. In my quest to find a place to live and someone new to love me, I hadn't had time to notice that Penn was, in fact, obese. Well, whatever! He was a freedom fighter bent on uncovering corruption in bus tunnels and he had read tons of books about legalizing marijuana. Okay, so maybe he wasn't in the best of shape and his flowing pirate blouses resembled something out of a Meat Loaf video. He knew tons of famous poets, and more important, they knew him back.

We carried a few boxes up from the basement. They would have seemed heavy if I wasn't so excited by the first new friends I'd made in years. I was like a five-year-old at a birthday party, sugared-up and swinging wide-eyed at the Elmo piñata.

No one talked much. Stacey did note that my house was "incredibly clean," that I was "incredibly organized," and she liked my kitchen. True, the place was tidy. Even after I'd spent a week in the hospital followed by another week at the O'Leary Retreat for Socially Maladjusted Divorcées, my home remained neat. This was because all I'd done for the past three years was drink vodka and cut myself, then organize my closets and vacuum the walls.

I took mostly clothing and the few books and CDs I owned at the time: Woody Allen's *Without Feathers*, my monogrammed Bible. I took a faux-antique pencil drawing of dead butterflies that I'd bought at the Bombay Company. I took my grandmother's wedding ring, which my mother was certain I meant to hock and which I never once thought of selling.

There was no way to prove that I wasn't leaving because I was secretly an evil, God-hating, nihilistic whore who wanted to sell all their jewelry. They saw me as reptilian and cold, leaving my husband like an alligator eats a dog.

I left everything else—my insulated draperies, my bread maker, my fabulous butcher-block kitchen table, the heft of which I would never be blessed to eat oatmeal off again. I left the musical porcelain doll that played "Try to Remember" with feathers falling off her velvet hat. The bath mat, the Roman shades, my favorite bowl. The tinny console piano. The only computer I knew of that had AOL access. The wood-cased color television that my father had bought from my uncle when I was ten years old. I left so many large and heavy things.

My clothes had been shoved into black trash bags meant for wet and moldy oak leaves. The bags would become increasingly thin and veiny over the upcoming weeks while I used them as interim dresser drawers in my interim bedroom. In the meantime, they were my handle-tie furniture.

My favorite room in the house was the room I left through. It was an enclosed porch where the interior wall was actually the old exterior wall. The brick had been painted white, something I'd previously seen only in restaurants. The right side of the room was maxed out with five long, wooden windows that rattled and let pins of cold air tickle your fingertips when you felt for a draft. When I was drunk in the middle of the day, I used to sit on my wicker love seat and sing unfortunate choices of

Natalie Merchant songs to the outside/inside bricks until I felt happy being sad.

I must be one of the wonders of God's own creation.

I walked out without a word, leaving Alan holed up and crying in the bedroom. I didn't say, *"Thank you"* or *"Fuck off"* or *"See ya later."* I didn't know how to leave anyone. I couldn't tell if this was normal, or mean. Aidan and Penn carried my bags and liquor store boxes down the stairs and deposited them in the Saturn.

"You should take more stuff," Penn said. But what kind of stuff? Another frying pan or a bath mat? I didn't have the energy to selectively choose parts of the past four years. I didn't know what I'd need two months from now, what I'd regret and what I'd be glad not to own. *Let's see, I need that Tupperware deviled-egg container and that crepe pan and this olive fork, but I guess I don't really need a lemon zester unless I'm making crepes. . . . Oh, what the hell, grab the zester!*

"We can make a second trip. We can get your piano," Penn said, plotting again. "You keep the keys and we'll come back with a truck in the night. The bastard owes you that much!"

I had just eaten a man's beating heart because the only way to leave my marriage was to get freaky with a slam poet. As much as I wanted to get my propers, I barely had the gumption to take my own socks out of the house, let alone schedule a caper to steal his mother's piano.

"It's not that kind of breakup," I told him. "I'll get my own piano someday."

"Christ! You let him walk all over you! Someday, Kyria. Someday, I'm going to buy you a piano!"

He promised me this piano in all earnestness, as if we weren't about to take things from my ex-husband's apartment and move them into his parents' garage. Unlike Penn, who was a full-time poet, I actually got *paid* at my job. So if anyone was going to be buying anyone else a piano, it probably wasn't going to be the live-at-home bus tunnel raver.

"I can't wait for that piano," I told him.

We checked the trunk of the car, making sure it wouldn't pop open and spew my whole life across River Road, and just like that, I didn't live at home anymore.

The O'Learys' garage was filled with the things families keep outside—cans of WD-40, a box overflowing with Christmas ornaments, and, of course, the belongings of a homeless Jehovah's Witness trying to escape a loveless marriage.

My clothes were dropped on the bed in Penn's sister's room. I would no longer be sharing Penn's twin bed and apple-bong in the basement. I had my own room now, courtesy of his sister, off at college. I thanked Aidan and Stacey for their help with the same amount of awareness that a ten-year-old has when writing a thank-you card to Aunt Bertha for the new schoolbag. Then I shut the door to my new home.

I sat on the scratchy quilted bedspread and leaned back on bags of clothing to get a good look at the room.

My first emotion was that I needed a drink. I wanted to jump into my car and head to the packie for a bottle of potato vodka. I'd even thrown a few whiskey bottle–shaped chocolates in the bag too; they'd kept them in a bowl on the counter lately. Then I'd sit on my wicker love seat and warmly listen to the glass in my windows quiver along with "Like the Weather."

My second thought was, What items are in the drawers of this nightstand? The room was unsettlingly sterile. The dresser could easily have contained a hotel notepad, a list of pay channels, and a room service menu. Either this girl had no interests outside of pencil erasers, or she had managed to take every hint of her personality and bring it to college with her.

White walls, white replacement windows, and white baseboard heating. I knelt on the off-white carpet and put my elbows on the windowsill. My view was of a backyard—a flat, strange plot of grass distinctly lacking my former landlord's chicken coop or any peacocks on the lam.

My third thought was that I still needed a drink. I headed to Penn's basement abode and requested immediate alcohol. But his mother was home and therefore we could not raid her liquor cabinet. We also could not go to the liquor store because she had the car keys in her purse. Unsurprisingly, Penn suggested we smoke a little weed instead. Then he declared that he was going to make me a Greek omelet.

"The secret," he told me, "is not to peel the skin off the ginger. That's the best part. You'll see!"

Before I'd ever smoked pot, I was under the impression that the effect of the drug would be somewhere between heroin and peyote. That we would be able to cook an omelet after injecting the Mary Jane was unthinkable to me. Wouldn't we be busy thinking we could fly or lying headfirst in a dirty litter box? Now I knew the main difference between being high and being sober: You make poor decisions involving ginger.

In the kitchen, Mrs. O'Leary was talking to me. There was a soft, diffused light on, and this made me jealous. Recessed lighting has always aroused feelings of envy in me. It was something that people with money had, something for people who actually owned the houses they live in. Growing up, we illuminated our kitchen with a round fluorescent *creature* they dared to call a "lightbulb." It cast a green, Automat glow on the whole room, turning us into a family of pallid, Jell-O–filled dessert cups.

Anyone else might have felt off-put having a socially inept, emotionally damaged cult member sleeping in their daughter's bed (and, alternately, with their son). But Mrs. O'Leary was a nurse and a feminist. She worked with troubled people. She told me that I was a strong, independent woman, and I could do this. I was strong but I just had to put my mind to it.

"People never know how strong they are until they're in a situation where they have to use that strength," she said.

Okay, *whatever*, I thought. When someone's mother talked, it could immediately be discounted. I longed for Penn to hurry with his inedible ginger eggs. He was sashaying across the kitchen with a feta cheese–smudged apron barely staying tied beneath his breezy pirate blouse.

He leaned in and whispered to me, "One of the most important parts of smoking pot is learning to act like you're not high."

Penn's mother said, "Can you please convince him to peel the skin off the ginger? He doesn't listen to us."

Even though I continued living in her house, this was pretty much the last time we spoke. Because she was a mother, I automatically saw her as the enemy. She'd saved my life, but I wasn't in a position to thank her properly, and wouldn't be for many years.

I awoke to an alarm beep that I'd never heard before. I turned on some recessed lighting and fiddled with a strange shower knob in Mrs. O'Leary's master bath. I'd never known anyone who had a bathroom connected to their bedroom before. If Penn and I get married, maybe they'll give us the house as a wedding present, I thought. I could have a master bath forever!

I dragged several leaf bags out of the closet and dumped a pile of underwear on the floor.

After rooting around for a minute, I found two matching items—a modest 100 percent polyester blouse and a knee-length wool-blend skirt, both of which had previously belonged to my mother. All of my work clothes were hand-me-downs, purchased at a local Pawtucket department store called Apex, a favorite destination of the fashionably modest sisters in our congregation. The anachronistic outfits hung on my body like an old suit on an old man. I dressed myself like a 55-year-old legal secretary, minus two graciously removable shoulder pads.

I shoveled my entire wardrobe back into the trash bags, which, in turn, I shoved back into the closet because the real estate agent was bringing people to look at the house and did not wish for the nice couple to be greeted by rhinestone epaulets and Velcro shoulder-enhancers strewn across the floor of their future sewing room.

I felt inside my purse for the comforting medicine-bottle shape of Absolut Citron. I fingered my wallet to make sure I hadn't forgotten my razor blades. I felt for my car keys. I was ready for work.

I drove Penn's new car (his mother's old station wagon, actually, which she had finally relinquished to him) to the office of Worldwide Construction Equipment, where, despite my lack of a high school degree, they still let me answer the phones and add long numbers on cardboard balance sheets. The only entity I had recently wronged who didn't work there was the evil ghost of my murdered lizard, Timothy, haunting me from behind the industrial coffee machine. Alan, my father, Alan's mother—they were all here. It was very convenient for everyone who hated me and claimed I had ruined their lives to know exactly where I was at all points in time between 9:00 and 5:30.

If I wanted to ram myself into a wall, this was also the one opportunity during the day where I was alone with a 1994 station wagon and vodka.

I drove into Cumberland, toward the office of Worldwide. I drove past my old brick duplex, poetically hoping for boarded-up windows, or my landlord's peacock impaled on a stick. I stopped at every yellow light, doing my best to stretch the ten-minute drive into twelve minutes, or even fifteen.

I parked on the other side of the lot, away from the fleet of white Worldwide vans. I walked into the open garage, past the shelves of industrial fasteners, past the padlocked case of diamond-tipped drill bits and past the manager, Leo, who was wearing protective eyewear and sawing metal rods in half. He had orange sparks coming out of his head.

Even with the garage wide open, the smell of burning steel wafted into the office and seeped into the rugs. The air was smoky with metal dust waiting to alight on our filing cabinets in a non-OSHA-compliant layer. Through a Plexiglas window, I could just make out my soon to be ex-mother-in-law, Barbara, swiveling back and forth in front of the typewriter at our very cramped, very shared desk. As usual, she had gotten there early and taken my favorite chair.

I hung my sweater over the back of my swiveling task chair. As I sat, I wondered if I should say "Good morning." What is the etiquette when you're an apostate working with the mother of the man you just cheated on?

Immediately, Barbara began knocking her chair into mine. Our chairs rolled on the same rubber carpet protector, separated only by the 90-degree angle of the L-shaped desk. I faced north; she faced east. And now she insisted on pushing her rolling task chair progressively west.

"Why?" she asked. "Why did you do this to Alan? Why did you hurt my baby?"

Barbara was typing sales receipts for our salesmen, then placing them in a pile for me to sort. One pink stack. One mint-green stack. One gold stack. All facedown. White copy folded in thirds, then mailed to the customer.

"Why did you want to hurt him?" she asked again. "Don't you love Jehovah? You've made Jehovah very sad."

"Of course I love Jehovah," I slurred, sighing into a warm vodka buzz.

"You don't act like you do! You want to leave Jehovah."

"I don't want to leave Jehovah, Barbara."

"My Alan can't even eat anymore. Why did you have to hurt him like this? You're killing him, you're *killing* him!"

Working next to Barbara was like hearing malicious voices telling you to kill yourself, only instead of coming from inside your head, they were coming from a task chair located two feet away.

289

Anyway, I was drunk. So I sat at the desk next to her and sorted gold and pink and mint green and white and listened to a woman with a Southern drawl ask me why I wanted to make God sad.

My father still wasn't singing. Like a dog that won't eat, his behavior was starting to worry me. There were no more stellar Roy Orbison impressions. No more "Take This Job and Shove It," "Manic Monday," "Ruby Tuesday," or "Saturday Night's Alright for Fighting!" There were only accounts-payable phone calls and sandwiches from the deli.

"I'll pick up lunch today," I offered. I offered *every* day.

"Actually, Barbara needs to go to the post office, so she can pick up lunch on her way back," Dad told me.

Barbara smirked at me because this meant she got to go outside for 20 minutes. I was left inside, to languish in metal shavings and ponder why I hated Jehovah. I spun around in my broken task chair, spun until I rolled right off the rubber carpet protector. Then I walked to the back to the garage door, put my head against the Plexiglas window, and watched Leo saw hot, sparking metal rods in half. All those orange sparks so close to all those dirty rags and chemicals. Still, nothing ever ignited.

CHAPTER 24

Working Together to Thwart Those

Who Work Separately

"Maybe you should find a new job," Penn said when I told him that Barbara, with whom I still shared a desk, had stopped her nonstop crying in favor of calling down the wrath of the Lord upon me. What had started as "Why did you break my baby's heart?" was now an hour-long rock-block of all your favorite fundamentalist hits (with tunes like "You're Going to Die at Armageddon," "Girl, Jehovah Will Punish Adulterers," and many, many more).

"I *have* been looking for a new job," I told Penn. And I really would have been, if I'd ever been on a job interview or had any idea how to write a résumé. Couldn't I just staple a *Watchtower* to an application at the Dress Barn and hope someone would take pity on me?

> **Objective:** Recently disfellowshipped, naive ex–Jehovah's Witness seeks position that isn't too hard or too scary in order to pay rent for the first time in her life.

Skills: Reading the Bible, drinking, cutting, playing ragtime piano, meeting strangers on the Internet, dropping out of high school, waiting for Armageddon.

Prior Work Experience: Helping Daddy at the place Daddy works.

Reason for Leaving: Shunned as apostate.

At the Kingdom Hall, we spent most of our time discussing what happened to people who weren't Jehovah's Witnesses and why their religions were all complete crap. Like fundamentalist rappers, our sermons bragged about how Jehovah's Witnesses were the dopest emcees. By following God's laws, we had built-in protection. This could be proven at any given time by watching the local news and noting how many Jehovah's Witnesses had been killed walking home late at night from a strip club. Inevitably, they were Catholic.

For example, Jehovah's Witnesses would never get AIDS, because we were heterosexuals who refused blood transfusions. We eschewed turning gay and the marijuana injecting. Our wives didn't get cervical cancer because we knew it was wrong to have sex while you're menstruating. And if anyone ever tried to rape you, well, all you had to do was call on the name of Jehovah and he would send angels to scare the attacker away.

I spent my childhood learning that when you were outside the Truth, you were miserable. Those who left the fold became AIDS-ridden, cancerous rape victims, who spent all their money on cigarettes and gay clubs, and never, ever would be truly happy again. Now I was one of them. I was outside the Truth. Emily wouldn't speak to me; neither would Lisa. The congregation was done with me. Even Sister Bailey, had I run into her on the street, would have pulled her surgical gauze down over her one good eye and kept her mouth shut.

Where was my life going? I had a pot addict boyfriend and was living in the home of strangers who were living in Michigan. I worked with my ex-mother-in-law and had no idea how to get a job or invest money in the future because there wasn't supposed to *be* a future. I hadn't prepared for any of this, and on top of it all, I'd never seen *A Christmas Story*. I wasn't going to live forever anymore, so what was there to live for?

The Jehovah's Witnesses had been right. There was nothing out here for me.

I could kill myself now or wait until God had me beheaded at a birthday celebration, but I decided to let condemnation run its course. I'd only been an apostate for two months, and despite the culture shock, it was still kind of an adventure. It also didn't hurt that I had been drunk for about six weeks straight.

As my main diversion, my free time was spent preparing for the National Poetry Slam. I was too busy longing to become a world-famous poetry slammer to think about having been abandoned by everyone I'd ever trusted.

The National Poetry Slam took place in a different city every year, like a Super Bowl for pretentious, attention-starved book-store employees. In 1997, that prestigious hosting spot was won by Middletown, Connecticut, even though the only available performance venues were a fluorescent-lit bagel shop, a sports bar, and a gymnasium. They must have had a stellar proposal.

The only requirements for sending a team to the nationals were that your community held a long-standing poetry reading and you sent them a check for the entry fee. Teams could not be chosen arbitrarily or via pick-up sticks; they needed to be chosen by random, unbiased audience members during a series of pre-liminary bouts.

At Penn's urging, I began to compete for a spot on the Worces-ter team. Under Penn's coaching, I won one! So did Penn, punk-rock Stacey, and a six-foot-tall redhead in leather pants named Jodi.

Being on a slam team meant that I got to represent our can-do local arts scene. Little Worcester would be competing with big guns like Chicago, Boston, and New York. These city folk already acted like they were the real winners simply by virtue of having extensive public transportation. They thought everyone else was just there to be the Washington Generals. But Worcester, Massachusetts—home of the birth control pill, deadly factory fires, and a bronze fountain in the center of town that looks like some kid is seriously *getting it on* with a frightened sea turtle— aimed to prove them all wrong.

Boston had distinguished, published writers and New York had wild style and knew how to break-dance. But Worcester had something they didn't have: We weren't too cool to act like we cared.

Aidan and Stacey held slam practice in the kitchen of their apartment, on the first floor of a three-story building. We practiced constantly; our team was more disciplined than a ten-year-old Soviet gymnast. We'd perform our poems next to the spice rack and make notes on vocal inflections and gestures. Comedy pieces received the correct, canned laughter. Dramatic pieces made us cry or clutch the stove. We were the best audience you could ever hope to have *and* we had access to a coffeemaker. "Do it exactly like that tomorrow night," we'd say, "*and we'll have this slam in the bag.*"

Eventually it was time to leave the safety of our kitchen stools and road-test our pieces at big-name slams like Bar None, home of the most well-respected open mike in Boston. To foster a little friendly competition, Boston held a yearly scrimmage against the teams from Providence and Worcester. It was meant as practice for the main event, but over the years, it had come to symbolize more. The national slam, people said, was mostly a cult of personality, whereas the Bar None slam was about the cult of personality's *poetry*.

Team Worcester descended the steps into the imposing basement bar, with tattered notebooks under our arms like poetic debutantes presenting ourselves. Suddenly a *buzz* was coming out of Worcester, buoyed by the fact that both Aidan and Penn had been featured in *Slam and Deliver*. Providence and Cambridge stood in the back of the room with their arms folded, bemused by the little slam team that thought they could win it all.

Since we were the underdog, we felt the judges occasionally turned on us. Penn might score a 7.6 when he should have scored a 9.0. At that, we'd huddle, regroup, and come up with a new strategy. "It all went so perfectly in the kitchen," we'd say. Was it because he'd chosen a funny poem about vitamins right after that 14-year-old girl read a poem about orphans in Yugoslavia? Were the judges too young and naive or too old and stodgy? It all came down to one thing: What could we do to ensure this wouldn't happen when we got to the nationals?

Also featured in *Slam and Deliver* was a poet and English teacher named Trevor Bali. Blessed with blue eyes and Connecticut money, he played the part of the evil slammer, determined to win at any cost. Now he was back for more controversy, on the very first corporate-sponsored team named after a fledgling independent poetic record label called Big Mouth. Spurred on by radical indignation over such obnoxious product placement, Worcester was even more determined to bring the pain.

One day during practice, Penn and I left the kitchen and went out for some air. This seemed as good a time as any to propose, so I did.

"Penn, we should get married," I said.

"You think so?" he asked.

"Absolutely! I'm almost divorced now. I love you!"

"I don't know, Kyria, I mean—"

"Oh, Penn, don't be like that. You know you love me! You love me, don't you?"

"Uh, I mean, yeah, of course."

In the distance, the MTA commuter train bellowed a deep, habitual horn. Everyone would end up moving forward, even if they were sitting backward in their seat. We walked back to Stacey's kitchen and stood next to the spice rack.

"Penn and I are getting married," I announced. No one said anything.

"Penn, can I talk to you for a minute?" Stacey asked suddenly. "In private?"

Penn shuffled away, then shuffled back with his hands still in his pockets. When he returned, I asked what they'd talked about.

"Ah, nothing," Penn said. "You know, poetry."

"Oh! What about an engagement ring?" I asked. "I need a ring!"

I grabbed a twist-tie from a loaf of bread, and Penn tied it around my finger.

"Look, everybody!" I swooned. The kitchen collectively coughed and looked at its lap.

I saw Big Bill at the next Words Out Loud reading. I hadn't seen him since I'd left Alan and wasn't even sure whose side he was on these days. He'd stopped coming to the readings after I stopped driving him. Now he was there with his wife, ostensibly "checking in on me."

"We just wanted to know if you're okay," his wife said. "Where are you living?"

"I'm fine," I told them. "I'm crashing with my fiancé."

Bill rudely ignored that fact that I was now engaged. "We were very worried about you," he said. "No one knows where you are."

"You should both come to our wedding! It's going to be on an old train car because when Penn proposed to me, there was a train whistle in the background. Do you know where I can rent an old train car?"

"No, I'm afraid I don't. So where exactly *are* you living, then?"

I was having trouble following the conversation. Both Bill and his wife looked like they were about to cry, and, as usual, Penn and I had gotten high before we'd come. I'd also shaved the back of my head with the number two razor setting and had stopped sleeping. Now I was asking about Pullman rentals.

"Do you know him?" I asked, pointing at Penn. "He was in the documentary *Slam and Deliver*. It's *so* good. You should watch it!"

"We'll do that."

"I smoked pot before I came," I said. "So, you know, sorry if I'm like, totally high or something."

"Okay," was all Bill said.

This was annoying. They would only respond to me in short, soft sentences, like they thought they were trying to talk somebody off a ledge or something. I didn't understand what their problem was. Weren't they impressed by how worldly I'd become?

"I was disfellowshipped," I said. "No one will talk to me. They kicked me out."

"I heard," Bill said.

"Well, I think the Jehovah's Witnesses are a cult," I said. I heard these words as if someone else had said them. I wasn't even sure if I believed it. Mainly, it was something I'd heard other people say and I was repeating it. If I couldn't impress Bill and his wife with my punk-rock shaved head and drug use, I'd impress them by acknowledging I'd been in a cult. I was no rube, I was saying. No one had tricked *me*.

However, there were a lot of implications in the word "cult." Couldn't Catholics technically be considered a cult? What about Orthodox Jews? I'd never lived in communal housing, worshipped a central guru, or had a man with a gun shoot my children because they weren't drinking Kool-Aid.

Sure, I was going to be shunned by everyone I'd ever known and loved, but wasn't it *my own choice* to get baptized? My brain was foggy and this was very confusing. When *was* the last time I'd slept?

"Yes, I knew that," Bill said. He looked at me, not like I was stupid, but like he was very sad.

"You *knew*? So why didn't you tell me?" I was suddenly incredibly pissed off.

Bill had no answer. I was abjectly horrified that he had kept this information from me.

"You knew they were lying to me," I yelled. "You should have told me!"

"I—"

"I mean, they lied to me! Did you know that? Did you know they lied to me?"

Big Bill said nothing, and his wife grabbed very tightly on to his hand. How long had people been thinking these things but not said anything? Sarah had her book, but that was so long ago. Of course I yelled at her! Why didn't she try again? This was all Sarah's fault for not trying a second time.

Bill knew I was in a cult? How many other people had been talking about me behind my back, snickering at the decades of toilet paper trailing off my shoe?

I had no phone at Penn's place, no way to be reached. So I wasn't surprised when one day I looked up from my desk, across my angry, pre-seizuring mother-in-law and saw Lisa. She was wearing her dress clothes and holding her Field Service bag with the latest *Watchtower* peeking out.

"Anyplace around here to get a cup of coffee?" she asked, snagging her heel in the ripped industrial carpeting. My disfellowshipping was imminent, but hadn't been officially announced yet, so it was technically safe for her to talk to me.

"There's a Dunkin' Donuts up the road," I said.

Lisa and I walked to the car in silence. I saw her at the Kingdom Hall, but we didn't hang out like we used to. I pointed in the direction of Dunkin' Donuts and the Colt propelled forward into the drive-through, like a very sad amusement park ride.

"Just because we don't talk, doesn't mean I'm not your friend," Lisa said. "Do you want a corn muffin?"

"Toasted with butter. I never thought you weren't my friend."

"I know you made some mistakes, but what's important is that you want to set them right. I know you. I know the things I've heard about you. I know they can't be true."

"They're totally not true," I protested. I was a little drunk from being at work. I needed that muffin.

"I didn't think they could be true. I mean, I heard that you . . . committed adultery!"

"What? Absolutely not true!"

"Of course I knew it wasn't! But look, I have to ask this. You're not going to leave Jehovah, are you?"

I was aware that Lisa would later mark me down on her Field Service slip as time spent witnessing, but I didn't mind. Counting an "upbuilding conversation" with a friend in order to make your monthly quota was as common as selling your kid's Girl Scout cookies at the office. I considered this conversation worth a box of Thin Mints.

"No, of course not! I . . . I love Jehovah and I want to make him happy. I could *never* leave the Jehovah's Witnesses," I lied. There was no reason to get involved in a religious debate with Lisa, and besides, I might change my mind and decide to repent.

"Well, good. I'm so glad. And you want to turn things around, right? You want to come back to the meetings?"

"Oh, absolutely! I am going to start coming back to the meetings really, really soon." Lisa was so happy to hear me say all this, it made me want it to be true.

"I'm ready whenever you are, kiddo. I have some Bible studies I'd love to take you on."

"I can't wait," I said. "How about next week?"

"Wonderful! Hey, I'm sorry to come find you at your job like this, but with everything I've been hearing . . . I just needed to touch base with you and make sure that you're okay. Now that I've talked to you, I can see that gossip had gotten out of control. I'm going to set things right with people. They have no right to be spreading these lies about you."

"Absolutely. Total lies, all of them. Nothing happened. I love Jehovah. I want to be a Jehovah's Witness forever."

"Let's say a prayer together, okay?"

I slurped iced coffee, put my head down, and said, "*Amen.*"

The next week, I drove to the Kingdom Hall for my official disfellowshipping hearing.

"You don't have to go to this," Penn said. "You shouldn't let them do this to you."

That didn't make any sense to me. Of *course* I had to go to my disfellowshipping hearing. How else could I be disfellowshipped? Penn's view of the world seemed very skewed to me sometimes.

Anyway, I was no Goody Two-shoes, because I planned on getting drunk before I went. Penn didn't seem impressed.

"You don't need to get drunk before you go, because you don't need to go at *all*," he said.

"How can I not go?" I asked. "I mean, I just want this to be over with already."

The disfellowshipping hearing took place in the library of our Kingdom Hall. Every congregation elder was there. I sat at a cherry conference table, with a tasteful wingback chair in each corner. Everything in the room was coordinated. The blue country curtains matched the blue country rug, and even the elders' light blue polyester suits seemed hand-picked as if by a set designer. I wore jeans, an R.E.M. T-shirt, and the scent of whiskey. We opened with a prayer.

"Jehovah, these matters are never easy. When a sheep strays

from the fold, we try to bring them back with kindness. Please guide our proceedings this afternoon with your Holy Spirit. Amen."

"Sister Abrahams," one of the elders began. "We've known you a long time. Some of us have known you since you were born."

"Look, I've been smoking pot and having sex," I blurted out. "So you might as well disfellowship me now."

The elders made a face as if I'd just dropped my drawers and revealed testicles. A handful of white-haired men in suits stared at me with collective shock and horror. I'd insulted their very honor. I felt like I'd just told the Founding Fathers of our country that I thought taxing tea "wasn't *that* bad an idea."

"Kyria, you are asking to be disfellowshipped. I would strongly advise you to . . ."

"Listen, Kyria, this isn't something you want to do . . ."

"Kyria, maybe you'd like to discuss this first . . ."

"If you'll repent right now, we can stop this from happening, Kyria."

Gathered in this room was everyone I'd ever needed to be good for, everything I'd ever been scared of. If my skirt was too short or my attitude too brusque, these were the men who would have disciplined me with kindness. One of these men had led me to baptism; one of them had married me.

"I don't want to repent," I said.

They nodded at each other and I put my head in my hands. It was like telling your grandmother you not only like to be spanked but want to dress up like a fuzzy blue fox while it's happening. There was so much to explain. So much they didn't know about the world, let alone about my interest in it. I didn't even know where to begin.

I didn't need to wait around for the prayerfully considered verdict. I knew for a fact that I would be disfellowshipped because I'd just asked for it. At the next Sunday meeting they'd announce that I was no longer a member of the Jehovah's Witnesses, and people would gasp. This was the Abrahams family, where the father never had set a decent example and the mother was a disfellowshipped adulteress. Well, no wonder! Even the brother had disappeared, stopped attending the Kingdom Hall, and grown sideburns. After the meeting, people would gather in little groups and mutter, "Like mother, like daughter" and "I always knew something was off about her" and "You can hide your thoughts from men, but you can't hide your thoughts from Jehovah—he always knows what's truly in our hearts."

I walked out to the parking lot and got into the car I'd borrowed from my worldly boyfriend. It seemed like I should feel something more—some remorse, some epiphany, some stomach cramps. I grabbed a bottle of vodka out of the glove compartment, took a swig, and drove to Lincoln Woods. I parked sideways and walked into the middle of an appropriately artistic, dramatic field. There was some crawling, some drunken falling, all lost for posterity in the darkness and solitude of a recently mowed lawn.

"Jehovah," I said. "I'm sorry. Look, it's nothing against you or the Jehovah's Witnesses, all this disfellowshipping. I don't want to die at Armageddon and I don't want to sin against you. But I hope you'll understand that I just can't be married anymore and there's no other way out."

A pine tree might have moved. I stared into it like God had a tree house in there and was just biding his time, waiting for me to throw a handful of marbles.

"If you really exist, and if Jehovah's Witnesses are really the one, true religion, God, please give me a sign. If you'll give me a sign, I promise I'll repent, I'll stay married, I'll come back to the organization, I'll sit in the back of the Kingdom Hall, I'll be a Jehovah's Witness forever. I promise, God. I'm not trying to be a bad person. I just don't know what to do. Please, Jehovah, just tell me what to do."

The pine tree did what pine trees do. It stood in one place.

CHAPTER 25

Lovingly Withdrawing Godly Support

No one seemed as happy as they should have been. Penn and I were getting married, but when I showed them my ironic twist-tie engagement ring, they curled their lips and turned away. Even poets in kitschy bowling shirts didn't seem amused.

"You're a little too good for Penn, don't you think?" some performance artist in mechanics overalls and Buddy Holly glasses would say. "We're really surprised that someone like you is with someone like him."

Someone like him? Penn was kinda greasy, sure, but he was a superstar poet, a talented electronic musician, and a way-cool raver. He'd even been in a real movie and was therefore a real movie star! He was miles more famous than anyone I'd ever known. Someone like him? I was surprised that *someone like him* would even consider having sex with me!

I told everyone how we planned to get married in an old train car, because of the commuter rail whistle we'd heard when we proposed to each other. This would be so romantic and poetic. God, we were totally soul mates! I wondered if his parents would pay for the wedding. How much could it possibly cost? Maybe $2,000? All my new friends would be there, and all my old friends would see the announcement in the paper.

I asked Penn if he'd told his mother we were getting married. "Not yet," he said. "They're very busy."

Penn's parents were flying back and forth from Michigan, trying to sell their Rhode Island home—our home—the home Penn and I were staying in rent-free. The family hadn't yet surprised us by announcing they were going to wrap the two-story bungalow in a red, yacht-christening bow and give it to us as a wedding present. Still, it was only a matter of time. Their only son was getting married. Penn called me at work to announce the good news.

"I have some bad news," he said. "My parents sold their house today. We've got about a month to find a place."

I took a long, slow shower in the master bedroom, making full use of the lavender body wash and heart-shaped pumice. If Penn's parents didn't come to their senses soon, my fiancé and I might actually have to buy our own bungalow and install our own master bathroom. How much could it be? $20,000?

Penn's best friend was Ernie. He was beautiful, with sad, distant eyes hidden beneath a Red Sox baseball cap. His Ween concert T-shirt rippled with the extra fabric gathered around his flat, 20-something stomach. I wrote him love poems and pretended they were for Penn. I wished I were engaged to Ernie instead.

Penn was nostalgic about the great times he and Ernie had had together, or at least the great times they'd *meant* to have. Their self-congratulatory road stories involved a lot of intricate planning but never any actual execution.

"Ernie and I, we're big fans of *The Grifters*," Penn said, with an admiration he usually reserved for blotter acid and jungle music. "Do you know what a grifter is?"

"No, what's that?"

"You never saw *The Grifters*? That movie is like our *Bible*. We *have* to rent it now. You'll understand a lot more about me and Ernie when you do."

Unfortunately for Penn, his John Cusack was currently living in his grandmother's unfinished basement in order to afford his monthly child support payments. He worked behind the counter of a gourmet sandwich shop called Swan Point Creperie, making him the only one of Penn's friends who held down a job. If Ernie had to work on a Sunday afternoon, Penn and I would spend our day there as well—our fingerprints smudged black from reading the free alternative newspaper as we waited impatiently for the manager to leave.

"They've got some really good sandwiches," Penn told me. "Ernie'll make you one with avocado and won't charge you. Just act natural."

Ernie impressed me because he had borrowed money from his boss at a frame store and didn't repay it. He told me he had asked the owner if he could get an advance on his next paycheck; then he moved to Providence and disappeared. Ernie thought ahead and never gave him his real information. This was why I was in love with Ernie. He had it all figured out. He had decorated his bathroom with action figures and funny underwear ads. I didn't even mind that you had to push past all the stored winter coats to get there.

Sometimes Ernie looked off into the distance, and not just because he was high. It was as if he were disappointed to be associating with us. His best friend had moved to Seattle the previous summer to start a business selling homemade mustard on the Internet, but Ernie couldn't go with him. So he was left with our crew—an ex–cult member, an obese performance poet, and a bearded pothead named Dave who wore a lot of rainbow burlap pullovers. Ernie was like Brando in *The Wild One*, leading a group of outcasts and misfits to wreak havoc on small-town sody-pop machines.

Ernie promised his grandmother that he wouldn't do drugs

in her home. Instead, we smoked our pot in her old RV in the driveway, while sitting on moldy, orange-striped upholstery and listening to Portishead on a portable CD player.

"Why do, like, old people always look like they're chewing?" Dave asked, handing me the glass pipe and nodding. "It's got a carb on it."

"Oh, I know why!" I said. "Because when you're older, you lose muscle control in your face. It looks like you're chewing even when you're not."

Dave flipped his arms out from under his poncho and looked at me angrily. "I wasn't *really* asking. Why do you always do this? Come on! Why does she always do this?"

"Dave," Ernie said. "Just shut the fuck up."

"Let's *do* something!" I said, trying to drum up excitement. "Let's go bowling, you guys!"

"You always suggest bowling. We hate bowling."

Ernie said, "Hey, these cute girls I met in the café today invited me to a party tonight! They even gave me a twenty-dollar tip!"

"Nah," we said. A party with hot chicks and strangers? That sounded *real*.

Ernie half threatened to go to the party all by himself and leave us there, smoked-out in Grandma's RV and talking about elderly mandibles. But we all knew Ernie wouldn't go to a party on his own, even though he didn't really want to be seen with us. Two hours later, I convinced everyone to go duckpin bowling, a miniature version of the game featuring tiny, squat pins and little balls that fit in the palm of your hand. It's a Rhode Island phenomenon that, along with coffee-flavored syrup and the giant blue mosquito overlooking I-95, no one in the state has ever thought of as strange.

I hadn't run into a single person from my congregation since I'd been disfellowshipped. Now, at an underground bowling alley in Pawtucket, I was staring directly at the Pickerson family. Brother Pickerson had once shown me how to change a tire with the mnemonic device "Righty-tighty, lefty-loosey." His wife was an albino and a seamstress. The three daughters were dressed like Holly Hobby and had iron-straight white hair. The family kept bowling, looking straight ahead, quietly sipping soda and knocking down pins like quaint ghosts in homemade dresses.

I made a strike and yelled loudly, "Yes! All right! Whoo doggy!" I wanted the family to turn around, to know that I had new friends now. The four-year-old looked at me, but only for a second. She wasn't old enough to remember who I was.

I desperately needed a new job but didn't know how to get one. I was like an overwhelmed kid who got beat up every morning on the bus. I couldn't tell my parents. All I could do was open my notebook and write bad poetry.

At Beans and Bags, I performed a piece about working with my ex-husband and mother-in-law called "Working Apostate." After the reading, Jodi approached me, concerned. She had a job at a company called a "dot-com," which got paid $100,000 to make, like, a single Web site. The company, in downtown Boston, was called Webbers. They had free beer in the refrigerator, and she thought they might be hiring.

Stacey helped me to design a beautiful résumé on expensive paper with a retro sun graphic in the corner, and she didn't even charge me for the paper. At the bottom of the résumé, we added, "Rhode Island College: B.A., English."

With my snazzy, jazzed-up résumé and Jodi's glowing recommendation, I looked like someone who had viable skills in the arena of corporate phone-answering. I was called in for my first real job interview.

"Oh, yeah, I'm used to answering a four-line switchboard," I told Vijay, the CEO of this hot Internet start-up. "I'm really good at juggling lines."

Vijay was just out of business school and had hired all his college buddies to program in C++ and make animated GIFs. Everyone who worked there was my age or younger. There was one employee who appeared to be over 30, but he was gay. The employees wore blue button-down shirts and non-pleated khakis. They listened to techno.

"So, you were an English major?" he asked in the job interview.

"Uh-huh!" I said. "I just *love* English!"

I was offered a whopping $26K per year, as well as a set of business cards that actually had my name and title on them: "Kyria Abrahams: Administrative Assistant." Never again would I be known as a mere receptionist. I had an overblown and meaningless title, and I intended to let it go to my head.

The main obstacle to my new career was actually getting to the office to do this job. My current landlords were moving to Michigan and I didn't know how someone went about finding a place to live. Alan and I had gotten our first apartment through a Jehovah's Witness in our congregation, and the second place through his brother. My own parents had never moved, although my mother occasionally took Aaron and me to open houses for homes she couldn't afford—a maternal Holly Golightly drooling over dishwashers.

"You have to get yourself a *paper*, sweetie," Stacey explained to me as I lamented how difficult it would be commuting to Boston from homelessness. "Sack out on the living room floor with a pile of want ads and start making some phone calls."

The next time we drove to Wordplay, I grabbed a copy of the *Telegram & Gazette* and began circling every one-bedroom under $500 a month.

Penn wasn't sure if he wanted to move in with his parents or not. His parents, however, seemed quite sure that he would not be coming with them. It was hard not to get the impression that they had purposely chosen Grand Rapids as a place their "artsy" son would be sure not to follow.

"You know, I'd really like to go with them," Penn told me "but I have a record there. Some issues from high school. I don't know if I can really go back. Too many bad memories."

Penn didn't have to worry. He'd taken care of me, and now I was going to take care of him. I had a stable job with a dot-com start-up, and *that* certainly wasn't going anywhere. After a weekend of awkward phone calls in which I inappropriately explained to prospective landlords that I'd just been divorced and disfellowshipped, I signed a professional-looking lease for an apartment in Worcester, near Aidan and Stacey. Penn and I found a couch on the sidewalk and snagged a bug-infested mattress from his parents' basement. He even got a job at the local Kinko's in Shrewsbury.

"All writers have to work at Kinko's," he said with a self-satisfied chuckle. "That way, you can steal supplies. It's like, a required job for a poet!"

At night, Penn and I smoked pot and ate takeout Vietnamese food. In the morning, he drove me to the train station. Sometimes I stared at the tracks and imagined my body splattered across the front of the purple-and-silver train like a low-flying bird. Before leaving work each night, I stole beer from the techies' refrigerator and poured it into a travel mug for the ride home.

Penn could only work part-time because of his poetry and music career. Still, he had given me a place to stay when I would have otherwise been homeless, so how could I not return the favor? I paid the rent and, with the exception of gingerroot, bought all the groceries. It would all even out after we were married.

On the weekends, Penn and I went to flea markets to look for old Speak & Spell toys, from which Penn made Frankenstein musical instruments. A teacher at Brown had once told him he was brilliant. Penn hadn't actually gone to Brown, but he volunteered there. His prized possession was a vintage Moog keyboard, which he was going to get fixed very soon. He told intricate stories of how cool the homemade instruments had sounded in the past, and how the teacher had adored them. Meanwhile, he was using Kinko's dime to make poetry chapbooks that would further his career as a writer.

One night, Penn called and asked me to pick him up from work immediately. When I arrived, he was standing in the parking lot, panting and dripping in sweat. He slammed the car door and burst into tears.

"They're stealing money from me! I can't work for them anymore."

"What are you talking about?"

"This is my money. I should get what I earn! They claim they're firing me."

"I don't understand you." I didn't. This was a very intricate firing.

"Look, just drive, okay? Just drive away!"

"Did you get fired?"

"These people are crooks! All of them! I quit! I can't be a part of this!"

"Why can't you keep the job?" I was baffled and he was telling that he'd quit, but it wasn't fair, screaming something about writing an exposé for the *Telegram & Gazette.*

"They know that I know what they're doing! I'm onto them. They're pushing me out!"

"Wait, did you quit or did they fire you?"

"Look, just drive the fucking car, okay?"

After his "Kinko's period,", Penn stayed home all day to concentrate on his burgeoning artistic career. When our slam team was profiled in the local paper, Penn was photographed holding up a Speak & Read. Next to his picture was the caption "Penn O'Leary, 28, is a full-time writer."

My $26K a year wasn't lasting as long as I thought it would, especially with the cash we spent on weed each week. I was running out of money. I asked Penn to sell his prized Moog to help me pay the rent, and he magnanimously agreed. He put an ad in the free paper, but when I asked him how it was going, he told me no one responded to the ad.

"Gosh, I can't do anything right! I want to sell this to help you out, but it looks like no one wants to buy it from me!"

"Penn, did you actually publish a classified ad?"

"Of course I did! What would make you think I didn't?"

Things were getting tight. And to add insult to injury, Penn couldn't find a See 'n Say.

On the way home from the flea market, we drove through towns like Shrewsbury and Morningdale. We passed non-super supermarkets, doughnut shops with pastry-shaped signs, gas stations without mini-marts. There was nothing to do in these towns but eat potato chips and run a sad finger down your dusty high school football trophies.

Driving through a cemetery, even if it wasn't historical, was a good way to pass the time. Which is what we told the cops when they pulled us over.

"What do you think you're doing?"

"We're driving through the cemetery."

"Why?"

"We just like cemeteries."

"Sure you do. Sure. You're not here for drugs? Sure. Step out of the car, please."

Five minutes later, Penn's car was being searched and seized for outstanding parking tickets. Penn was being shoved into the back of a police car. The words "warrant for his arrest" were bandied about. Had he been trafficking Speak & Spells?

The Providence pigs, Penn said, had fucked him over again. He didn't need to pay those parking tickets, because they had been unjustified in the first place! In a similar, unjustified manner, the car was towed and I was unjustifiably driven to the station, following behind Penn and his long tail of injustice.

I made a desperate, pleading phone call, and Stacey and Aidan arrived at the station within 20 minutes. They'd helped me to move and find a job, and now they consoled me for an hour while I cried that my boyfriend was in jail because he wouldn't kowtow to society's No Parking—Fire Lane.

After about an hour, Penn flopped through the station doors, drenched in sweat and shrugging furiously, as if trying to remove an imaginary hand from his shoulder. That's when I saw him spit on the cop car. So did Aidan. And so did the cops.

Penn barely made it to the bottom step before being dragged back inside the station like Dennis the Menace.

"I should just leave him here," I said, having already posted his bail and paid the tow-truck driver.

"Yeah, you should," said Aidan, a hint of excitement in his voice. "Do you want to leave him here? Because I'll drive away right now!"

"Nah, I can't do that to him," I said. The women I knew didn't punish men, they stored up their anger and used it as ammunition in later fights.

"Why not? He's an idiot. He spit on a cop car. That's unacceptable!"

But I didn't understand what "unacceptable" meant.

If there were any hard feelings over spending a Saturday afternoon watching Penn get arrested twice, they were never made public. For the sake of poetry, we had to get over these small tragedies and bond as a team.

We drove to the National Poetry Slam in Middletown, Connecticut, as a caravan—all four team members, our coach, and several supportive local poets, all in shiny, four-door Saturns. We even had a poetry mascot along for the ride—not a poet, just a fan. I never caught his name, but he wore a bucket hat.

The slam rented out a huge block of rooms at an unsuspecting Marriott, where the other guests surely rued the day they chose to swipe their key card in Middletown. Slammers infested the hotel and the staff closed the pool on the first night, after a slew of fully clothed drunken slammers jumped in. Jodi stood knee-deep in chlorinated combat boots, holding a bottle of Boone's Farm in a paper bag. Meanwhile, one of the poets had just gotten a blow job under a bush and another was rumored to have had a small orgy in his hotel room. Someone named Catbird was handing out flyers, letting people know he had a suitcase full of "fine tea," and I was cheating on Penn with a member of the Chicago team on the concrete floor of the hotel laundry room. This was the nationals, baby—what happened in Middletown stayed in Middletown.

Performance poetry had been let loose in Connecticut, ready to awaken the bland suburbanites from their closed-minded, American slumber. We'd jump in your pool, we'd have orgies in your non-smoking suites. We were slammers and this was how we rolled. Were we, like, totally blowing your mind?

The Worcester team rammed its way through the preliminaries and into the semifinals while I rammed my way through several more slam poets. Our team performed in a poppy seed–scented bagel shop for unsuspecting coffee drinkers and in a sports bar where angry UConn fans had just discovered that their game had been replaced by a political statement on gay marriage. Meanwhile, poets grumbled over the injustice of Trevor Bali, the locked pool, and the lame Connecticut audiences who wouldn't know real poetry if it pinched their Tiffany charm bracelet.

All of our kitchen practicing and Speak & Spelling paid off, because Worcester, the little team that could, made it to the final four to compete against heavy hitters like Chicago, Cleveland, and Trevor Bali's poetry super group, Big Mouth. Suddenly I was baring my reverberating soul for an audience of 1,000 people in the echo-filled gymnasium of Wesleyan University. I performed a poem called "*I Want to Drive a Minivan*," a biting satire of today's housewives and how they, like, totally have cars and invest money and, whatever. Stacey belted out a punk-rock romance about falling in love with her husband on the freeway. Penn went to his go-to, and once again recounted the story of his best friend's fiery death in a drug-related car crash. Jodi pulled out all the stops with a no-holds-barred poem about the unborn child she never met, garnering 9.7, 9.8, and a flurry of 10s. One thousand people. A basketball hoop. Cheering. Her eyelashes wet, her voice cracking, Jodi collapsed into the arms of a competing poet, Chicago's own Professor Funk.

"I think we won!" Penn whispered. "I think Jodi pulled it out for us! I can't believe it! Come on!" While the judges tallied their final scores, Penn pulled me out the back door to smoke a celebratory joint. I put my head in my hands as he bounced on his thighs like a sugared-up six-year-old. "Two years in a row!" he crowed. "Two years on a finals team!" I took a long toke, held it in, and burst into tears. Where was I? These were not my friends. I barely knew Penn. I wanted to go camping with Emily. I wanted to be somewhere I understood.

A hand pulled me up onto the stage, where the best performance poets in the country were hugging, applauding, and doing ironic dances. Things got Woodstock blurry, and the stage seemed very high. I was dizzy and confused as they announced that Worcester came in fourth place. *Fourth-best poetry team in the country!* I kept clapping like a robot that could almost feel.

Big Mouth won the whole slam, even after Trevor broke the "no props" rule by fiddling with a belt like it was a phallus. Because of this, the team was unceremoniously booed by half the auditorium.

"Worcester should have won," someone whispered to me. "You guys are *real* poets. No props."

I looked out over the vast, disorienting gymnasium like a dazed game-show contestant goggling the camera as the host breaks for commercial. The last time I'd seen a crowd this large had been at the "Joyful Praisers" District Convention. Back then, I'd wanted nothing more than to be watched by 1,000 onlookers as I lip-synched the prerecorded drama. Now, I only wanted to disappear.

Back in our hotel room, as one of four celebrated members on the fourth-best poetry team in the country, I collapsed. I couldn't bear to go to the after party where I'd have to fake-smile my way through nonsensical conversations with poets talking about music I'd never heard and books I'd never read. I was paranoid, having a *Fear and Loathing*–style bad trip on just one toke of cheap pot. In the mental state I was in, even a Sudafed could have pushed me over the edge. "Let me stay here," I begged. Penn dragged me by my arms across the floor. "You have to go to the finals party," he insisted. "You have to go! It's what this has all been leading up to!"

The carpet burned my thighs and stomach. I had slowly begun stripping off my clothes, and was now scratching red, surface lines in my arms with ragged fingernails. I told Penn that I'd cheated on him and he could go ahead and drag me to the party like this, naked, scratching myself. I would sit at a table and cut myself—I promised this. If he made me go, I'd kill myself, and maybe worse, I'd make a scene.

"You can't embarrass the team like this, Kyria! We're on the fourth-place team! Everyone just saw us at finals. Now is our big chance!"

"You'll be sorry if you make me go," I told him, but he kept dragging me across the carpet, throwing my clothes in my face and telling me to get dressed because I was a winner.

Defeated, I pulled on a pair of vintage turquoise knit pants and followed Penn to the event room in the basement of the hotel. The disco ball threw pointless white spots on everything. The crowd danced to a song by Soul Coughing with the lyrics "and the radio man says it is a beautiful night out there." The "radio man" referred to one of the actual poets at this actual slam, once a morning drive-time DJ, now immortalized via Mike Doughty lyrics. I felt so famous by proxy that I sat down and wept.

The boy I fucked in the laundry room pulled up a metal folding chair and congratulated me on my performance during the finals. "You were great too," I said. "But I have to tell you something. I'm actually engaged. I shouldn't have fucked you. I'm engaged to Penn. We're in love and going to be married."

He immediately asked if I needed a drink, but never returned. Later I saw him dancing with a cute girl in a white dress.

A sloth's metabolism is so slow that it can remain underwater for an hour and not drown. The majority of infant sloth deaths are actually caused indirectly, because the mother simply refuses to climb down to retrieve her fallen baby. When I returned home from Connecticut, I was a sloth. It took great strength and courage to pick up a glass of water. It took hours. Each finger was an oppositely charged magnet. I was prickly and asleep, like my whole body had been slept on wrong. I fell onto the couch and watched my hunched reflection in the gray glass of the television.

"Yeah, it's kind of a letdown now," Penn said, crashing next to me. "Oh, well! Back to reality."

I felt like I'd just finished a marathon, like I should be wrapped in a foil blanket and spoon-fed electrolytes. For the past few months, my life had been lived inside the bubble of the poetry slam. I was vaguely aware that I'd had some recent, life-changing experience such as a divorce or a shunning but hadn't had a chance to look into it. I'd been preoccupied with denial.

What was my life made of? There was my morning commute, this apartment, this guy sitting next to me. There was low-end weed and nitrous oxide from whipped cream cans emptied into balloons. Alan had already sent me my divorce summons and explained that he was declaring bankruptcy. I drove to Providence to sign papers in court and I brought Penn along just to show Alan that I already had a better husband. Even if he was fatter and poorer, at least he'd done acid.

CHAPTER 26

Sit Down! For God Is About to

Smite the Sinners for You!

The Jehovah's Witnesses thought I'd be miserable and alone without them, but I'd shown them. I'd gone and found another husband before I'd even divorced the last one. I had so many great new friends like Penn and Ernie and every poet I fucked in Connecticut. I talked about my new pals to everyone.

"Do you know Penn's friend Ernie?" I'd ask. "He's so funny."

"No, I'm afraid I don't know him," people would say.

"Oh. Too bad. He's really funny!"

Since the nationals ended, my phone had been ringing off the hook. For example, Alan called to make sure I knew that he couldn't have sex anymore and it was all my fault because I'd left him. Then my father called to see how I was, and when I told him I was fine, he told me he'd speak to me "in about a year." My mother rang to tell me that she was trying to get reinstated as a Jehovah's Witness, and that Maya Fein had recently gotten disfellowshipped for having sex with her new boyfriend, who wasn't even a Jehovah's Witness.

"It would be good if you could give Maya an encouraging phone call. She's feeling very alone."

If I didn't know her, it might have struck me as odd that my mother would ask me to do for Maya what she had never done for me, but this was my mother, and this was the kind of shit she said. As always, she was completely in denial. After I got disfellowshipped, no one in my family contacted me or even mentioned it. My mother couldn't even call me without using other people's pain as an excuse.

"Sure, Mom. I'll invite her to a poetry reading."

"And did you know that Sister Blanche is in the hospital?"

"Oh, well, no, I didn't know that. I wouldn't have any way to know that."

Even though I hadn't seen my mother in about a year, she made sure I was up-to-date with the latest gossip about who was in the hospital and what they were having for dinner there. I could always count on Mom for a good Sister Blanche/lime gelatin story.

"It's no good outside the organization, Kyria," my mother said, as if she wasn't also disfellowshipped. "Did I tell you I've been going back to the Kingdom Hall? Brother Gordon gave his first public talk on Sunday, you know. It was about how demons try to mislead us by masquerading as angels of light."

"That's nice."

My mother spoke as if I were still sympathetic to the Jehovah's Witnesses, like the only thing that had changed in my life since being disfellowshipped was that I didn't actively go from door-to-door.

"You should go back to the Kingdom Hall with me, Kyria. Maya told me that she is going to try to go back too. Call her and encourage her spiritually. She's still living at home."

"Wait, Betty is letting her live at home?"

"Well, of course she can't talk to her extensively, but you know Betty! She won't kick Maya out on the street as long as she's attending the meetings. She's always been good like that, no matter what the elders say."

"Yeah, she's very loving that way," I said, knowing the sarcasm of this statement would be missed on my mother.

"You and Maya should go back to the Hall together. It won't be as hard. It's the only place we need to be. We are Jehovah's lost sheep and he wants us back in his fold."

"Sure, Mom. I'll do that right away."

I called Maya and made plans to meet her for dinner. I couldn't wait to have a disfellowshipped friend.

With Maya on my side, I would have someone who understood how *amazing* it was to watch R-rated movies and not feel guilty about it, someone who didn't take Fourth of July fireworks for granted. I wanted to sing "Happy Birthday" to her over and over again. As a plus, after dinner, she could go home and tell Emily and Betty how great I was doing. That way, I could get information back to the Jehovah's Witnesses that my life wasn't falling apart, even if it was.

Unfortunately, Maya was despondent. Despite all my attempts to make her realize that being destroyed at the end of the world wasn't really the end of the world, she still wouldn't smile.

"I feel so guilty," she kept saying. "I feel like such a bad person."

"You're not a bad person," I told her. "What have you ever done wrong? So you had sex with someone. I mean, that's love, that's natural! It's not like you murdered someone."

"God, I feel so guilty. It's like God hates me. Everyone hates me," she said. My new best disfellowshipped friend looked like a sick bunny who didn't want to play with me. Instead, she just stared into empty space, as if waiting for the hand of Jehovah to break through the ceiling and smite her personally.

"Maybe you should let me set you up with someone," I offered. "You should get a new boyfriend!"

"Do you know how hard it is to live with my mom, Kyria? I mean, I have to see her every day and she looks at me so . . . disapproving or whatever. I feel so alone. So *guilty*. Don't you feel guilty?"

I had to admit, I didn't.

"Yeah, I know what you mean," I said. "I'm really . . . guilty."

"What am I going to do? I'm going to die at Armageddon!"

"Aww, come on, I know a guy. A poet. Why don't I introduce you? He's a great writer and I think you'd really like him."

"Fine. I guess so."

"And you should meet my friend Ernie too. You'll love him. He's really funny."

Peter was a poet from down south, a dark and troubled boy with father issues, a temper, and a penchant for getting violent when drunk. He wrote soft sonnets about small things happening outside his window. I chose him for Maya, out of the limited circle of acquaintances I'd begun to amass. I handpicked him to hold her naked body and make her forget about Armageddon. They hit it off, and a week later, he called to tell her that he was drunk and lying in a doorway and was going to kill himself.

I drove by Ernie's grandmother's house and knocked on the basement window like an unannounced meter reader. I couldn't hold it in anymore.

"I'm in love with you, Ernie," I said.

"Nah," he said.

"No, really. I'm in love with you. Here, take this poem. I made it for you."

"Penn's been using you," he said, waving away the poetry.

"Bullshit. I'd know if I was being used."

"I'm telling you the truth, here. He was bragging to me that he's conned you into paying all the rent. He didn't quit Kinko's—

he was fired for stealing. And he's been taking money from your bank account to buy pot."

"No, well, I smoke that pot too. So that's why. It's *our* pot. That's okay."

"No, Kyria. He's been taking money from your bank account without asking you."

"Oh, Ernie! That's not true. Come on, I want to have sex with you."

"No, Kyria. Just . . . no."

I remembered Penn telling me that there was another girl Ernie was in love with because, quote, "She let him stick it in her ass, Kyria. In her *ass*. Who else would do that?"

I'd only just learned that a man could lick a woman between the legs and not get sick. Could I compete with anal?

"Go home," Ernie said. "And don't tell Penn that I told you about the bank account. It's just between you and me. You can do whatever you want with that information."

I felt like Penn had cockblocked me. His stealing money from me was the reason Ernie wouldn't fuck me, I was sure of it. To Ernie, the seasoned grifter, I looked like a rube!

I drove home in Penn's car and immediately confronted him about stealing money from my bank account. I never told him how I knew.

"Hey, if you didn't want me to take money, you shouldn't have given me the PIN," he said.

"Pay rent or get out," I told him.

"I am going to be paying rent as soon as I land some paid music gigs. I plan on doing a cross-country tour and then I'll—"

"Get out."

"You can't kick me out! Come on!"

"I pay the rent, this is my apartment, and my name is on the lease. Get the *fuck* out."

"No," he said. He sat on the floor, blocking the door. "I'm not leaving." He would have looked quite at home on the porch with a shotgun, chewing on a stalk of wheat and yelling about his pappy's land. Only this wasn't his apartment, it was mine, and he was a guest there.

"You stole money from me, you conned me into paying the rent, and I want you *out!*"

"What? That's not true," he said, his face reddening. "I can't believe you would accuse me of this!"

I tried to pull the door open, but he was six feet tall, overweight, and sitting in the lotus position. He was zazen, an immovable tree. So I kicked him.

"Ouch! You just kicked me! I can't *believe* you just kicked me!"

"Well, get the fuck away from the door! I want your con-artist ass out of my fucking apartment! And you owe me eight hundred dollars."

"No," he said, standing up.

"Excuse me?"

"No. I'm sorry, but no."

I couldn't believe this. Could someone just refuse to leave your house when you were asking them to leave your house? Would I need to get a restraining order?

I punched him. It was more symbolic than anything, but he immediately doubled over. He grabbed my wrists and squeezed them together; I felt them bruising, bending, melting.

"You've abused me! This is abuse," he cried. "Physical abuse!"

I walked into the bedroom, Stacey's number in one hand and the phone cord trailing from the other.

"Stacey," I said, "I need to stay with you. Penn won't leave the apartment. He's getting *violent.*"

Penn had no job, no way to find another apartment, and his best friend lived in his grandmother's basement. His only belongings were a closet full of poet tie-died vests, a handful of ponytail elastics, and 700 broken Speak & Spells. This could have explained his initial reluctance to be kicked out into the lonely and temperate Worcester night, but one week later, he still adamantly refused to leave. I could have stood in the living room with an air horn and a fire hose, but Penn wasn't going anywhere. Arms folded, he was determined to ride out the storm in this old house. So I hid under an afghan on Stacey's couch while Penn hunkered down in my apartment, dipping into my bank account here and there to buy pot or Vietnamese food and spell-check his manifesto. Short of getting a restraining order, there was nothing else for me to do but admit defeat and leave him to enjoy the apartment alone, like a giant, solitary bedbug.

"Sweetie," Stacey said. "You gotta get yourself another stack of papers and start making some phone calls."

In the historic Armory District of Providence, I found the perfect replacement apartment. The streets in this area were lined with dilapidated tenements and large, watchful women who sat on the front stoops, drinking hooch in their housecoats. In the middle of all this was the mother of soulless gentrification: an enormous refurbished Queen Anne mansion with turrets and porches and stained-glass windows, currently being rented as lofts for local artists and professionals. The building was painted in bright *Architectual Digest* colors on three sides. The fourth side had been left white, and on this white wall hung three giant "crayons" proudly displaying the colors the house had been painted in: magenta, plumberry, and apricot. Someone had painted little "crayon scribbles" emanating from the tips. It was known as the Crayon House and it had even been featured in a coffee-table book called *America's Resplendent Painted Ladies*.

The building had been taken away from slumlords and put into the hands of a real estate agency known as Broadway Reconstruction. Since it was on a dubious street corner with dubious neighbors, rent was still pretty cheap. With my big-time Boston administrative assistant job, I could swing the $500 monthly rent, but I couldn't make the down payment. In the meantime, I would have to move back into my infested apartment, try to make peace with my stowaway, and wait for him to get some kind of stomach ulcer from eating ginger skin.

At the Boston reading, a poet named Evelyn approached me with a purple envelope. I didn't know her very well, but she was friends with Stacey and hated Penn. She liked my poetry and had recently been divorced. Across the front of the envelope was written, "Magenta." Inside was a card that said:

> This is what I can swing right now but I hope it's enough of a step up, step ahead, step forward into your life, one breath at a time. Pay me back by taking your place in this universe where you belong by right of birth—be strong (remember, crying is a sign of strength) be alone, be Kyria. Remember: I believe in you.

There was also a check for $500.

CHAPTER 27

Take Notice! These Godly Words Allow

Us to Believe in Eternal Life!

I was starting a life of independence and strength, but first, I needed Penn to drive me there. It was no accident that I was moving to a city named Providence. I needed divine intervention to put my clothes into his station wagon. I needed the body of my ex-boyfriend to sleep next to me, because even though we were broken up, I'd never slept in a house alone before. It was almost Halloween and I was going to dress up for the very first time in my life. I planned to go as a Jehovah's Witness. I scratched my name off the front of my Bible and pretended I'd bought it in a thrift store.

The Crayon House was far more architecturally impressive than someone who only recently stopped believing that homosexuality was a sin had the right to move into. I had hardwood floors, a disconnected dumbwaiter, and a loft ceiling. My bathroom had an original claw-foot tub, black-and-white porcelain tile, and a toilet that flushed with a chain. My bed was a futon mattress on the floor underneath a skylight, on a platform accessible only by a ladder. I fell asleep to stars. I woke up to raindrops. I passed out to vodka and a poorly rolled joint.

Despite the dangers of mixing a rickety ladder with illegal substances, I quickly became the go-to spot for smoking, drinking, and listening to Moby. Ernie had gotten his hands on some hashish from Morocco, which didn't get any of us high but still helped to burn several large holes in the carpeting.

Peter starting coming over without Maya, carrying a book of poetry by Guillaume Apollinaire. He told me that Maya wouldn't have sex with him and that she still talked about the Jehovah's Witnesses all the time. She wanted to start a Bible study with him.

He told me, "If you want to give your boyfriend a real jolt, stick your finger up his ass while he's coming. He'll love it, believe me." He read Apollinaire's "Zone" to me in a gentle drawl, pronouncing the letter *r*, which no one from Rhode Island ever did.

"Each has tormented someone," he recited. "Even the ugliest."

For the past 23 years, I'd been told that it was not possible for anyone to survive outside the safety and guidance of God's organization. Leaving the Jehovah's Witnesses would be like leaving the haunted cabin in the woods to "go check on that strange noise." Never again would a disfellowshipped person find caring friends or experience true love, as these things did not exist in Satan's world.

The day you left, you fired Jehovah as your personal bodyguard and would no longer be able to buy a cup of coffee without being accosted by a strange man with a hook for a hand who would ask you to test a new perfume, which would turn out to be chloroform. You would later awaken in a bathtub full of ice with your kidneys removed and "Call 911" or "Welcome to the World of AIDS" scrawled across the wall in blood.

Like Crazy Louie, who had stood across the street from my childhood Kingdom Hall and had caused me to grab my dad's hand for protection as we passed, apostates would never be able to move on. The message was clear: Don't leave. If you do leave, come back, or else.

After a few months of playing worldly with me, Maya decided she wanted to be reinstated. She said she couldn't handle it, being hated like this, wondering if God was going to punish her, disappointing her family, shunned by her friends. Whether it was real or not, she wanted to take her chances on the side of surviving Armageddon.

My mother called to tell me that she was getting married to Mikey, the Italian firefighter I'd met in the Dunkin' Donuts parking lot who she'd recently moved in with. Mom wanted to be reinstated into her congregation, but first she had to cease living in sin. Mom had been going through all the appropriate Jehovah sorority hazings, like sitting in the back of the Kingdom Hall without speaking and running through the quad naked with a Bible strapped to a goat. Now she had to get married. I attended the wedding, in the gazebo of the apartment complex where my great-aunt lived. Mom said Mikey had been reading the literature and now realized that Jehovah has a plan for this world, that all things happen for a reason.

After Peter left, I put the condom on the top of the wastebasket. As a newlywed, Alan had overflowed the septic system, which resulted in an embarrassing phone call to the landlord. I'd learned the hard way not to flush them.

It didn't feel wrong to have sex with my friend's boyfriend because I couldn't fathom *anything* being wrong anymore. I'd been told that murder was as wrong as eating birthday cake was as wrong as smoking, as wrong as reading books, as wrong as having sex with your friend's boyfriend. I needed time to grade each of these things on its own merit, to make sense out of the world, one ruined septic system at a time.

I had no feelings for or against the Jehovah's Witnesses. I'd done what we'd so often been warned of in the *Watchtower*—let my guard down. I had taken up with bad associations, let negative thoughts enter my mind, and had simply *fallen away*.

I'd spent my childhood being assured that I would never grow old, never get sick, never die. Only a year earlier, I still believed that my destiny was to live forever in God's perfect paradise on earth. This present world was temporary, nothing more than a hotel room in a foreign country. I had not committed the sin of being practical; I had not planned for adulthood. I had no education, no savings, no college buddies to network with. There was the money I made at my job, and at the end of the week, that money was gone.

Life in the Jehovah's Witness was a calming portrait of multicultural picnics on the edge of a crystal-blue lake, with everyone smiling and selfless and seemingly engaged in some fulfilling physical chore. The world outside was full of loud, jarring noises and Vegas lights. I felt like I'd been thrown onto an amusement park ride and then asked to fix it while still spinning.

I could, of course, have it all back. I could have eternal life and perfect eyesight and giant vegetables and a friendly panda as a household pet. I could move into any house I wanted to after Armageddon. If I called the elders right this very minute, I could stop worrying about money and start my countdown to a life of idyllic mountain streams and resurrected grandparents. I could have corn muffins with Lisa and thimbles of Jack Daniel's with Emily and a non-festive dinner with my family on Gift Giving Day. I could return, unshaken, to the religion we called the Truth, where everything could be answered in a single paragraph with a quoted scripture. All I had to do was sit quietly in the back of the Kingdom Hall and wait. I could still live forever.

My mother always said I made things harder than they needed to be.

It was Tuesday night. At 7:30, my congregation would be assembling for the Book Study, meeting in pockets in individual homes, politely raising their hand to read Bible verses from the rocking chair of a very spiritual family. At 8:00, I would be sitting at a small café table under paintings of knives and handprints, drinking chai and listening to the poetry of an obese gay goth named Spyder. He would be followed by a boy who never spoke except from the stage, a black kid adopted by white parents, a Wiccan, a Jew, a hippie, and a 14-year-old runaway.

These worldly, godless poets had loaned me money when I hadn't asked for it and had given me a place to stay. When the people I'd known for 23 years stopped talking to me, the people I'd known for 23 days helped me move.

I pulled on a pair of fishnet stockings, took a hit from my bong, and grabbed my poem for the open mike. So maybe I wasn't going to survive Armageddon and live for all eternity in God's future paradise. Maybe, just maybe, I was not actually immune from death, wouldn't live forever like a Bible-toting Highlander. Maybe, in that case, I should try to get a better job.

No longer holding back and waiting for a perfect earth, I now needed to teach myself how to survive on the actual, existing one. I had a whole backlog of learning experiences to get through, most of which would take years to be expunged from my credit report. I needed to fuck up and I needed to start fucking up soon. What else could I do but keep moving forward? After all, this life is the only one we've got.

Glossary

144,000 (Anointed Class, The Little Flock)—While the majority of Jehovah's Witnesses will live forever in an earthly paradise, 144,000 have been specifically selected to ascend to heaven in order to sit at God's "right hand" and rule with Christ. They will sit by his right hand because his left hand is presumably busy giving AIDS to gay people.

Armageddon (Jehovah's Day, The Apocalypse)—The day of salvation when Jehovah's people will be delivered from Satan's wicked world. On this day, Jews, Buddhists, and all the other morons who are undeserving of life will be clobbered by hailstones and then fall into fiery pits—clearing the path for true lovers of righteousness to live in a peaceful paradise. Afterward, Jehovah's Witnesses will try to figure out what to do with their time now that they live in a world inhabited solely by Jehovah's Witnesses.

Assembly—Multiple-day religious meetings during which the local civic center is transformed from a pagan altar for the

Ice Capades into a giant, makeshift Kingdom Hall decorated with basketball pendants and deflated helium balloons. Unlike a normal meeting, the assemblies offer the opportunity to dedicate your life to Jehovah through baptism and to stand in line for 20 minutes to purchase a saran-wrapped roast beef sandwich. Program highlights include cloying interviews with teenagers who gave up their college scholarships in order to Pioneer, as well as costumed biblical theater known as "the drama." For this highly anticipated drama, brothers and sisters who are more spiritual than you are granted the privilege of dressing up in fake beards and lip-synching to prerecorded lines like "But Moses, surely you still trust in the powerful name of *Jehovah*?" as they boom over the PA system. Mostly, the assemblies feature horny teenagers trolling the hallways in hopes of finding a hot piece of "another congregation."

Baptism—The act of dedicating your life to Jehovah through watery immersion, usually in a hotel pool. Note that the immersion has to be on purpose, and being kicked in the head by your cousin Jesús while playing Marco Polo doesn't count.

Bethel—Watchtower Society headquarters and publishing factory in Brooklyn, New York. Bethel is staffed entirely by volunteers called "Bethelites." The workers are fed, sheltered, and given a very small stipend in exchange for printing Jehovah's Witness literature and further suppressing the already suppressed sexual desires of ordinary Jehovah's Witnesses. It is the highest honor to be allowed to go to Bethel and make books for free.

Bible study—A weekly time slot for Jehovah's Witnesses to visit you at home and teach you about Jehovah's Witness literature using the questions provided at the bottom of each page of the *Watchtower*. The seed for a Bible study is "planted" when someone who is at home during the middle of the afternoon answers their door and invites a set of complete strangers into their living room to discuss why humans should never have to die. Such a person will probably be very eager for someone to come back every single week and talk to them.

Charity—A display of hubris and a lack of faith. Jehovah will take care of everything after Armageddon, so who cares? Donating money to save the whales means you don't believe God loves whales as much as you do.

Christians—Jehovah's Witnesses.

Church (Cathedral)—A disgusting, ostentatious, hypocritical den of false religion. Also, the point in any European vacation where Jehovah's Witnesses may choose to remain seated on the tour bus, eat a ham-and-butter sandwich, and feel superior to everyone. Churches are for Bingo callers, pedophiles, and stained-glass enthusiasts, not for true Christians. Churches neglectfully leave their children to be babysat at Sunday school, instead of allowing them to learn about God alongside the adults, then taking them into the bathroom and beating them for acting up during the prayer. Churches host AA meetings, fund-raising bazaars, and worst of all, even feed the homeless, which shows a complete lack of trust in Jehovah's ability to take care of people.

Congregation—The group of brothers and sisters who attend your local Kingdom Hall. Unlike hypocritical churchgoers, congregation members practice the kind of real, Christian love seen only in God's chosen people. The congregation cares for you and always will, no matter what—unless you're disfellowshipped, in which case, you are totally dead to them.

Cult—The Jehovah's Witnesses are unlike false apocalyptic cults, because they are right.

Death—Contrary to popular belief, death is not the end of life. God's original purpose was for Adam and Eve to live forever. Indeed, several men of science have vocally admitted that with the exception of death, they can find no reason why people should not live forever! After Adam sinned, mankind lost eternal life and was cursed to grow old and crotchety and demand disproportionately special treatment in restaurants. This was not God's plan.

Disfellowshipped (apostate)—An unrepentant sinner who must now be cast out of the congregation for his own good and the good of the congregation. An apostate is worse than a plain old worldly person, because the apostate once had the Truth and should really know better. Associating with a disfellowshipped person is a disfellowshipping offense in and of itself, as is reading anything that criticizes the Watchtower Society. The book you're holding is considered "apostate literature." Any Jehovah's Witness who is reading it should immediately hide it in a ventilation shaft.

Field Service (going door-to-door, preaching)—Possessing a quiet reverence for creation and a personal sense of the divine, only without the quiet or personal part.

The Good News—The joyful knowledge that soon, Jehovah is going to destroy the world!

Jews—Almost got it right.

Kingdom Hall—Absolutely, positively, *not* a "church."

Literature—The various books and magazines that are printed at Bethel, such as *You Can Live Forever in Paradise on Earth* and *The Truth Book*. The plentiful illustrations in Jehovah's Witness literature portray either idyllic scenes of the coming paradise or soul-curdling, nightmarish depictions of regretful families grabbing their hair as flaming church steeples and station wagons fly through the air. In paradise, children hug friendly tigers by a koi pond while a geisha and a sheik trade grapes in front of a pygmy with a basket full of parrots. You should give your children a stack of these books to take to bed at night so they won't be corrupted by Harry Potter.

The Memorial—The annual commemoration of Jesus' death, during which members of the 144,000 partake in emblems of wine and unleavened bread. Only the anointed may eat and drink of these emblems, so you should have a little snack before you come. A sermon is given about how Christ sacrificed his perfect life in exchange for Adam's sinful one, and because of this we no longer need to follow the Ten Commandments. Eventually, this all ties in to how much Jews suck.

No Blood Card—A wallet-size, legal document that Jehovah's Witnesses carry with them at all times. This card ensures that, in the case of an accident, no "well-meaning" doctor can try to "save your life" by offering you a sinful, AIDS-tainted blood transfusion. If you die, they might print your story in the *Watchtower* and talk about how courageous you were and how you will be resurrected in paradise. That would make you a zombie celebrity! Who's sorry they never got hit by a van *now*?

Pagan—The bisexual girl in your computer science class who wears Tevas with a velvet cape and keeps trying to invite you to her winter solstice cookout and drum circle. I think she owns ferrets.

Paradise (The New System of Things)—What the whole world will be turned into after Armageddon. In paradise, there will be no war, sorrow, or death, and no FedEx deliveries will ever be made while you are at work. Mankind will live in peace with nature and be made steward over all the animals, as in: "I'm going to own nine panda bears and an ocean in the New System of Things!" Also, the dead will walk the earth, but I think they'll be nice.

Prayer—Your prayers will always be heard and answered, unless you forget to end with the phrase "in Jesus Christ's name, Amen," in which case, *denied*!

Privileges—If you're a spiritual young brother, you will be afforded "privileges" at the Kingdom Hall by the congregation elders. You will be allowed to stack chairs, mow the lawn, or work at the literature counter. This is also what the elders will take away from you if you sin, so maybe you'll be lucky enough to turn gay and get out of vacuuming.

Publisher—Someone who goes door-to-door for ten hours every month. A Pioneer goes in service for ninety hours per month. Kids on summer vacation are encouraged to use their time wisely and Auxiliary Pioneer for 60 hours a month. And for just 120 hours more, you can be a Special Pioneer and get this complimentary WNYC canvas tote bag! Donations from publishers like you will help us reach our goal of "contacting every person on earth" so that we can continue to bring you the unique apocalyptic rhetoric you just can't find anywhere else! *The preceding paragraph was made possible by a generous grant from the Geraldine R. Dodge Foundation.*

Resurrection—After Armageddon, the "tombs will cry out" as the dead rise from their graves and are reunited with their loved ones. The work of Sam Raimi will suddenly be seen as on par with Ben Franklin's. Unbelievers who died before having a chance to hear Jehovah's message will also be resurrected into paradise and given one last chance to become Jehovah's Witnesses. Oddly, some of these people will still say no.

Salvation—Those who are righteous have God's salvation and will be spared at Armageddon. If you are not sure if you will be spared, ask yourself: *Am I a Jehovah's Witness?* If the answer is no, then you will be killed. Everyone will be killed. Yes, even her. And that guy too. Yes, they will all be killed, please stop asking—Yes, Maya Angelou will also be destroyed by fire. No, not because she's black! Okay, Big Bird is a puppet. Now you're just getting smart with me.

Spiritual—Instead of focusing on immediate, worldly goals like a career in advertising or a modern condo, you focus on the future. Because you have devoted your life to the preaching work, you're 45 and have never had a girlfriend. You believe that homosexuality is a sin and God will have his vengeance. You don't engage in immoral thoughts such as inappropriate sexual yearnings for your roommate, Brad. You don't associate with unbelievers, many of whom wear tight, pegged dress pants. You consider cigarettes and marijuana to be just as harmful as the sorts of drugs homosexuals take at the gay dance clubs where they serve mojitos and play that Christina Aguilera song you like so much. You attend every meeting at the Kingdom Hall and engage in the preaching work, often partnered with Brad. Look, you're just waiting for the right girl!

Stumble—Being so corrupted by the thought of someone else's sin that you begin to have doubts about your own beliefs. You should take great care not to stumble others by discussing violent movies or your organ transplant.

The Truth—The beliefs of Jehovah's Witnesses. You are either "in the Truth" or "outside of the Truth." However, occasionally the Watchtower Society receives "the proper food at the proper time" and "new light" is received from Jehovah. The infallible stewards of Jehovah then report this new information to Christ's followers, who simply adjust their beliefs moving forward. For example, it is no longer a sin to accept organ transplants. So if you died from renal failure in the past, feel free to have a guilt-free, new kidney transplant today!

Worldly—You.

Acknowledgments

To put all this on paper was the most daunting project I've ever undertaken, and I in no way did it alone. Thank you to my amazing agent, Laurie Abkemeier, and to my editor, Amanda Patten—you made me feel like a real writer and everything! Amanda, you helped shape this book into what it is; thank you!

This book itself would not even exist were it not for the time and encouragement of Janice Erlbaum. Platinum-club thanks to Wendy Spero, Erik Seims, and Jennifer Glick. Thank you, Todd Serencha, for bringing art back into my life. Thank you, Tim Ledwith, Rachel Bonham-Carter, Chris Niles, Richard Zimmerman at redapes.org, Stephen Cassidy, and all my friends at UNICEF. Shout-outs to Rachel Alberg, Mike Birbiglia, Ritch Duncan, Sage Francis, Dawn Gabriel, Dave Inkpen, Gina Larson, Ross Garmil, Bill and Sou MacMillan, Sam Seder, Eve Stern, Dan Newbower, Bob Powers, and all my pals on LJ. I know there are more, but my thanks is no less heartfelt.